☞ **W9-ACW-529**

Mafia

MAFIA

Inside the Dark Heart

THE RISE AND FALL
OF THE SICILIAN MAFIA

A. G. D. Maran

Thomas Dunne Books
St. Martin's Press
New York

'The Mafia is a human phenomenon. And like all human phenomena,
it has a beginning, a zenith and it has an end.'

Giovanni Falcone, the magistrate
who started the break-up of the Mafia

THOMAS DUNNE BOOKS.
An imprint of St. Martin's Press.

MAFIA: INSIDE THE DARK HEART. Copyright © 2008 by A. G. D. Maran.
All rights reserved. Printed in the United States of America. For information,
address St. Martin's Press, 175 Fifth Avenue, New York, N.Y. 10010.

www.thomasdunnebooks.com
www.stmartins.com

Library of Congress Cataloging-in-Publication Data

Maran, A. G. D. (Arnold George D.)
    Mafia : inside the dark heart : the rise and fall of the Sicilian Mafia / A.G.D.
Maran.—1st U.S. ed.
        p. cm
    Includes bibliographical references and index.
    ISBN 978-0-312-64658-5
    1. Mafia—Italy—Sicily—History.   2. Mafia—Political aspects—Italy—Sicily—
History.   I. Title.

HV6453.I83M358355 2010
364.1'0609458—dc22

2010034782

First published in Great Britain by Mainstream Publishing Company

First U.S. Edition: December 2010

10 9 8 7 6 5 4 3 2 1

ACKNOWLEDGEMENTS

Many people have tried to help me understand the Mafia and much of my learning has been by osmosis over cups of coffee in various piazzas. Writing about secret societies presents certain obvious difficulties because the primary sources are secret and the nearest one can get to finding out the truth comes from court proceedings, confessions or police statements, but even then, in the convoluted environment that is Italian politics, perhaps not even these documents illustrate the truth.

I owe a great debt to the friends who have been willing to share their opinions with me, especially those whose position in politics made it potentially damaging for them to talk freely. The people I was introduced to in Sicily by my medical colleagues seemed to know more than the average citizen, and while I could thank them publicly they would not thank me for doing so.

I am grateful for the help I received from the Miraglia family. Accursio Miraglia was one of the eight elected Communist mayors murdered by the Mafia in January 1947.

I was particularly fortunate in having a relative who was a high-ranking official in the Communist Party for over 30 years. I must mention and thank Professor Carlo Corradini, who first gave me the concept of the differing character the Mafia has taken.

The Italian language comes in various sizes – colloquial, dialect, 'proper' and legalese. I can do 'proper', but when I needed help with the other varieties I was aided by Anna and Maurizio Meoni, Paola Antonini and Elio Marcantonio.

I am grateful to the Grand Lodge of Scotland, which introduced me to the Masonic historian Yasha Beresiner, who has been Master of Lodges both in Israel and Italy, and his research helped me greatly in the chapter on the infamous P2 Lodge.

Writers need help from libraries and librarians, and I must single out Marianne Smith, Librarian of the Royal College of Surgeons of Edinburgh, both as a source of help and a shoulder to cry on. Chris Flexen of the college's publications department did the maps during a period when he was moving house and he knows how much I appreciated that. I am also grateful to Ian Milne, librarian of the Royal College of Physicians of Edinburgh, for helping with some research.

Coming from the world of surgery rather than letters, I do not have rafts of literary friends who are able to give constructive criticism, but I must thank John Loudon and Stewart Russell for reading early drafts, and Stan Robertson for educating me in some aspects of banking and money laundering.

I had great help on the subject of psychopathy from the forensic psychologist Dr Keith Ashcroft, and for the conditions surrounding the death of the Pope John Paul I, I must thank the forensic pathologist, Professor Tony Busuttil. I was also helped in cardiac matters by Professor Sandy Muir, once the Queen's physician in Scotland.

My editor Deborah Warner has painstakingly gone through the manuscript and filled cyberspace with hundreds of emails concerning queries and corrections. No one could have done more and, had I been her, I would have broken off midway in order to arrange a 'hit' on me.

What remains incorrect is entirely mea culpa.

Thank you all.

CONTENTS

TURIN
Camille Cavour

MILAN
Bettino Craxi,
Silvio Berlusconi

GENOA

FLORENCE

AREZZO
Licio Gelli

ROME

NAPLES
The Camorra,
Charles 'Lucky' Luciano

GIOIA TAURO

SAN LUCA
Ndrangheta

REGGIO CALABRIA

PALERMO

SICILY

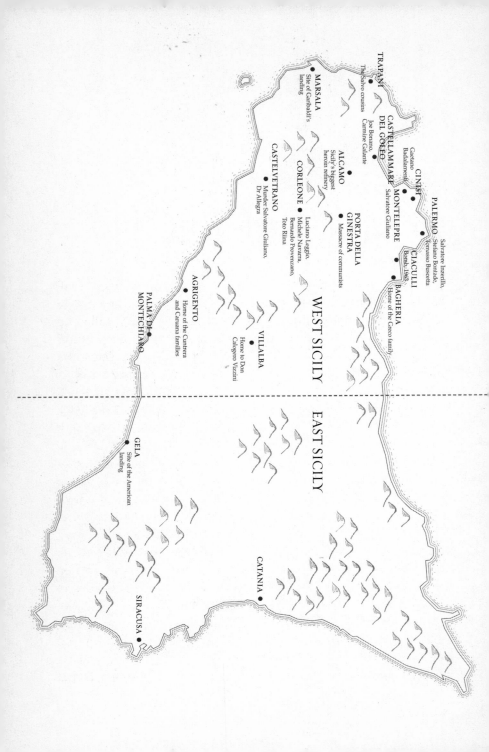

TRAPANI
The Salvo cousins

MARSALA
Site of Garibaldi's
landing

CASTELLAMMARE
DEL GOLFO
Joe Bonano,
Carmine Galante

CINISI

Gaetano
Badalamenti

MONTELEPRE
Salvatore Giuliano

PALERMO
Salvatore Inzerillo,
Stefano Bontade,
Tomasso Buscetta

ALCAMO
Sicily's biggest
heroin refinery

CIACULLI
Bomb, 1963

CASTELVETRANO

CORLEONE
Luciano Leggio,
Michele Navarra,
Bernardo Provenzano,
Toto Riina

PORTA DELLA
GINESTRA
Massacre of communists

BAGHERIA
Home of the Greco family

Murder Salvatore Giuliano,
Dr Allegra

AGRIGENTO
Home of the Cuntrera
and Caruana families

VILLALBA
Home to Don
Calogero Vizzini

WEST SICILY

PALMA DI
MONTECHIARO

EAST SICILY

GELA
Site of the American
landing

CATANIA

SIRACUSA

PREFACE

For any family in Great Britain, 1941 was not a good year, but for mine it was an *annus horribilis*. The Second World War was in its infancy, but my father had already been called up to serve in the British Army and so my mother, like many others her age, had to go out to work. But she went with problems that did not affect her peer group, namely the ever-present risk of arrest and imprisonment. My mother was Italian and so when Mussolini entered the war on the side of Germany in June 1940, Italians like her were among those listed for internment or jail if suspected of spying.

A few years earlier, my mother had brought her mother, brother and sister across to Scotland so that they could live near us – a typical Italian arrangement. Unfortunately, her sister, who is now 102 and lives in Rome, had a boyfriend who was an Italian fighter pilot and so she and her brother were imprisoned for a year, suspected of being spies. My aunt was later released, but my uncle was interned. We had also lost a number of relatives when the commandeered liner the *Arandora Star*, carrying internees to camps in Canada, was sunk.

Thus I spent a lot of time with my *nonna*, my Italian grandmother. She was small, probably no more than five foot, and at that time she would have been in her late 50s. Everyone is nostalgic about grandmothers, and the universal memory is that grandmas were *very* old. Nonna was very, *very* old.

She was not only a widow but was burdened with the terrible memory of burying one of her beloved sons, who had died of diabetes several years previously (insulin having not yet reached rural Italy). Although she reflected this lifelong grief by dressing in shades of grey, black and purple, which made her look even older, her demeanour was exactly right for a nonna: bouncy, smiley and cuddly. In later years, when I asked the few surviving villagers who remembered her to share their memories with me, they always used the same word: *allegra*, which encompasses all of the above, plus everlasting good humour.

Her apartment in a poor area of Edinburgh was small, sparsely furnished and, apart from the basic tools of life, contained an abundance of only two things: religious icons and the smell of Italian cooking, the latter an aroma as foreign to 1940s Scotland as curry or sandalwood. Although I loved the food, my enjoyment was always tempered by the thought that if the neighbours smelled it, they would realise (as if they didn't know already) that we were aliens and that this would bring down even more retribution on the family.

There were very few books in her house, probably because she was illiterate, but I remember quite clearly the one I enjoyed most; it was a sort of miscellany called *Wonders of the World* or some such title, which was meant to be 'good' for little boys to read. One day I came across a story about the Mafia. I recall that it was spread over two pages and was illustrated with a picture of a man holding a shotgun from which several lines were emerging and travelling in the direction of another man, who was in the process of falling over backwards.

'You lived in Italy, Nonna, tell me about the Mafia,' I recall saying to my grandmother. Instead of answering, she quickly took the book out of my hands and told me never to mention that word again. Even a five year old can tell when an adult is frightened.

I never saw the book again and neither of us mentioned it for the remaining 30 years of her life. I never forgot that day and, although I frequently tried, I could never pluck up enough courage to ask her about the Mafia.

It was only a few years ago that a chance meeting with an old man in Nonna's village brought the cause of her reaction to light. It must be remembered that she was a widowed alien in a foreign country with two of her children in jail and a few relatives in distant towns.

I discovered that she had three brothers who had emigrated to the United States at the beginning of the century. They must have done reasonably well because they either owned or rented a bar in New York. Great-uncle Antonio, unusually for a southern Italian, was a big man, but his two brothers, Giovanni and Quirino, were more typically small and squat – a second-row forward and two props.

The brothers were no different from other Italians in business in New York at that time in being approached by the mysterious Black Hand Gang. Little is actually known about the gang because there were no informers, no records, no discovered documents and no personal accounts of the background to the organisation. The group lived off extortion, sending letters to immigrant Italians with threats of retribution in the event of non-payment or calling for police aid. The letters were usually decorated with a skull and crossbones, men hanging by the neck, a black hand, or knives and bloodstains. The core group was probably Sicilian but all sorts of vagabonds aped the style, so those on the receiving end never knew how seriously to take the threat and whether or not to pay up. If the letter had come from the bona fide Sicilians, then the smart thing to do was to pay, otherwise you could be beaten or killed, or your business burnt down; however, the problem was that the message might well have come from a neighbour, someone you had slighted or a petty criminal who happened to think you had some money. It was a sort of Russian roulette. The only way to find out if the threat was real was to see what happened if you didn't pay – not a good option for young men in search of the American Dream.

This was the dilemma the brothers faced when they received their letter. They were not only told to prepare a weekly sum of money that would be collected but also to change their beer supplier. The second demand should have been a signal that the threat had come from professionals rather than amateurs, but that was not the way my great-uncles saw it. I think anger and hurt prevailed over logic.

When the courier came for the first payment, it was after midnight, the bar was shut, the brothers were alone and the only activity was washing glasses and floors. When they heard the knock at the door, they put into action what had been rehearsed and agreed. The smallest one of the three, Quirino, opened the door and let the Blackhander in. Antonio and Giovanni then emerged from the back of the saloon with baseball bats, and together the brothers gave the man what they thought was just a good beating. Unfortunately, they had hit him once too often, because he died.

This meant a sudden end to their American Dream, and also that they couldn't go back to the Naples area from which they'd come. So they went to relatives in London, got shelter and money, rented and then bought shops from which they sold ice cream and fish and chips until they died peacefully in their beds, having become relatively wealthy men.

And that was why Nonna was frightened, and why I became interested enough in the Mafia to write this book.

Arnold Maran

INTRODUCTION

I taly is not a normal country. It has been corrupted by politicians who have observed standards and ethics that would not have been tolerated in any other western European state. It is a country where the Prime Minister has been convicted of felonies but has escaped sentencing because of the statute of limitations. Another former Prime Minister received a 24-year-jail sentence for association with a murderer, but the sentence was commuted on appeal because of his age. Instead of disappearing into obscurity, he was elected a Senator for Life.

In the financial crisis that started in 2008, the exposure of Italian banks was only 130 million euros – less than 1 per cent of the world problem. This was partly due to prudence and mistrust in lending to Italian citizens but also due to the fact that the rest of the world regarded Italian banks as basket cases with whom they did not do business.

This malaise has spilled over into the life of ordinary Italians, who have come to accept a second-class existence, even though they live in the country that owns two-thirds of the world's art treasures and that is regarded very highly as a place to live by most foreigners because of the sunshine, food, natural beauty and grace of its inhabitants. But they are a people cowed down by *il sistema*, a people who accept that 'things' don't work: that the postal system may or may not deliver, that bureaucracy makes the smallest transaction a nightmare, that getting a job without patronage is virtually impossible and that even the national game of football has been shown to be corrupt. And what is their response? *'È cosi'*, meaning it's always been like this and it'll never change. It is a tired and sad response from a nation that has produced so much creativity in design, art and technology.

So what happened? Why is politics not normal and why has this abnormality filtered down into the everyday lives of its citizens? One of the causes has been the Sicilian Mafia, which in the latter half of the twentieth century polluted politics. There are many Sicilians who deny that the people of this period were Mafia, decrying them as common criminals, but the relationship existed, and the culture within which it flourished had its origins within that ancient Sicilian sect.

Sicily was accustomed to living with and under invaders; some had been constructive, such as the Greeks, Romans and Normans, while others, such as the Angevins, had been brutal. At the beginning of the nineteenth century, as the spirit of revolution was sweeping through Europe, the rulers were the Spanish Bourbons, who controlled the whole southern half of the Italian peninsula, from Rome to Sicily. It was called the Kingdom of the Two Sicilys.

When the patriot Giuseppe Mazzini and other revolutionaries had thoughts of uniting the states of the peninsula, there was very little enthusiam from ordinary citizens because most were comfortable in their own independent state. With a general such as Garibaldi, however, they found a man who had military genius and leadership, something that had been rare in Italian history and was seldom replicated in future years. His invasion and capture of Sicily in 1860 was basically a land grab by the northern independent state of Piedmont led by Camillo Cavour.

In Sicily, the Bourbons were replaced by the Piedmontese Army, who were not at all popular; what the Sicilians wanted was independence from all outsiders, but it would take them another 80 years to make a formal attempt at that. In the meantime, the island came to be run (not governed) by what was called by some 'the Sect'. This grew to become the Mafia.

From unification until the Second World War, the Mafia promoted a social system and a way of life that most people seemed to accept as being no worse than the rule of Rome, but after the war the organisation changed to become criminal. The Cavour–Garibaldi mission to free the Sicilians from the tyrannical Bourbons left a situation of civil war similar to that of the Bush–Blair mission in Iraq. One political group of masters was replaced by another, who were at first welcomed but came to be despised and distrusted. Although we have yet to see the final outcome of the invasion of Iraq, we know that the outcome of Garibaldi's invasion of Sicily was an accepted, established and respected order, which came to be called the Mafia.

There are three very definite periods in the life of this most famous organisation. The first Mafia, in the form of the Sect, had existed for at least 30–40 years before Garibaldi landed on the island and in the following years it gradually became a way of life. Although people were at first wary of the changing social scene, there were those among the aristocrats who saw it as a change for good. At one point in Giuseppe Tomasi di Lampedusa's great novel *The Leopard*, one character, Tancredi, who was going off to fight with Garibaldi, said to his aristocratic uncle, the Leopard, 'If we want things to stay as they are, things will have to change,' a sentiment that the Leopard immediately appreciated. The Sect had brought about a new social order, inserting itself between the aristocrats and the peasants.

Garibaldi was not a clever man and was certainly no politician, even though he is immortalised in every Italian town and village. Thinking that he was doing 'good' by getting rid of the Bourbons and bringing in the Piedmontese, who understood little of what was happening on the island, he breathed life into this Sect and it became an integral part of Sicilian life, being both feared and respected. It was not so much an organisation – just a way of life.

The Mafia continued in this manner until Mussolini arrived on the scene in the late 1920s. Men of Honour, as they had come to be called, either held all the top jobs or appointed their friends or relatives – in much the same way as we see in some present-day governments. There is virtually no evidence that the first Mafia was 'bad'. It seemed to be accepted by the vast majority of the population and did not upset too many people; the islanders got used to paying a percentage of their earnings to the Mafia, passing on the extra costs to the public. In return they could ask the Mafia for favours or help, which might or might not be granted. The politicians in Rome, understanding how 'things' were, did not interfere.

Mussolini, however, wanted no subversive opposition to his Fascist Party and so he banned both the Freemasons and the Mafia, underlining his determination with some brutality in Sicily. Jailed or exiled mafiosi were firmly labelled as anti-Fascist, and so when the American Army arrived in 1943, these mafiosi were rewarded with positions of power and influence, thus restoring them to their previous roles. The politicians in Washington would certainly live to rue those days, which laid the foundations for the second Mafia, whose drug dealing was to severely damage at least two generations of young Americans.

Few people are alive today who remember the Mafia before Mussolini, but those who do have nothing bad to say about what was essentially an alternative Sicilian government. In 1964, Norman Lewis, an intelligence officer in the British Army during the last years of the war, wrote a classic book entitled *The Honoured Society*. He described the very peculiar system of living on the island and admitted that he could penetrate neither the 'why' nor the 'what' of it. He was followed by Gavin Maxwell, who wrote a number of books about post-war Sicily, including *God Protect Me From My Friends*, a story of great insight about Salvatore Giuliano, the man who was used by the renascent Mafia to try to separate Sicily from Italy. Maxwell admitted that he didn't understand anything about Sicily before he went there and understood even less by the time he left.

The second Mafia was different. So different, in fact, that most of my educated Sicilian friends deny that leaders such as Charles Luciano, Stefano Bontade and Luciano Leggio had any connection to the original Mafia. These men are seen by some Sicilians as gangsters who started getting rich on government public spending and who then graduated to the drug industry. When caught, many of these men would try to obfuscate their offences by claiming that the Mafia was 'just a way of life', but the often-used argument was a cloak of convenience. They were basically a group of Sicilians who were brought up in the Mafia tradition and whose 'family' collaborated with American blood relatives to run the drug industry. What they did had little of the tradition of the Sicilian Sect but, with the help of Hollywood, the medium became the message and the phrases 'organised crime', 'the Mob', 'Murder Incorporated', 'Cosa Nostra' and 'the Mafia' became, to the public, an alphabet soup of organisational confusion.

It was the film *The Godfather* that both glamorised and gave credibility to the second Mafia by incorrectly setting it alongside the values of the first 'good' Mafia. And so a self-fulfilling prophecy came to pass, with the term 'gangster' meaning Mafia, Mafia meaning 'violence', and violence drawing audiences into cinemas. Other films followed, such as *Goodfellas* and recently *The Departed*, and on television *The Sopranos*.

The second Mafia was a criminal venture that made obscene amounts of money from the distribution of drugs to Western Europe and America for a period of 30 years. This money was laundered and now forms a large proportion of the world economy: although there are many differing estimates, it seems 30 per cent is not far from the truth. Thus, many businesses will have been funded by laundered money and may still be 'innocently' unaware of its sources.

The second Mafia would have had a much shorter life had Italian politicians and the FBI not dragged their feet in enacting legislation that could have eased the task of the investigators.

The Americans were well ahead of the Italians in bringing in the RICO (Racketeer Influenced and Corrupt Organisations) laws, which made association with organised crime punishable by long jail terms while easing the burden of proof. They were also to the fore in establishing witness-protection schemes, which made evidence from informers much more available. The reason for the tardy response of Italian governments eventually came to light: the Mafia had 'bought into' government.

What remains might be labelled the third Mafia. It could be described as having two layers. First, there is the original Mafia, which still exists in Sicily and raises money by the traditional *pizzu*, which are basically contributions from small and larger businesses for 'protection' and by controlling public-works contracts. The second group is what one might describe as the 'children of the laundered money'. Most of these people live good, law-abiding lives and some might run major corporations and businesses with no need to call on the services of hit men or thugs. They have the capital to set up legitimate businesses and professional offices and are contributors to society. As an example of the concept of the children of criminals earning respectability in society, there is a story behind the naming of O'Hare Airport in Chicago.

Edward O'Hare was Al Capone's lawyer and was ultimately the cause of his imprisonment on tax-evasion charges because he became an undercover informer and directed the police to Capone's bookkeepers, where officers found all the evidence they needed. Why he did this is unclear, but it may have been that speculation about his association with Capone would have stood in the way of his son getting into the US Naval Academy at Annapolis. In fact, Butch O'Hare graduated in 1937 and became one of the most successful US pilots of the Second World War, being posthumously awarded the Congressional Medal of Honour for his bravery. And it is in his honour that Chicago airport is named O'Hare.

◇ ◇ ◇

Italians enjoy living in one of the most beautiful countries in the world and savour their surroundings – the weather, the style and grace of those around them, and most of all the food – but working in Italy without 'connections' represents an unenviable life. Many young people live at home till they are at least 30 and have difficulty getting jobs, even with higher education, unless they have a relative or friend who is willing to help them. In a recent survey conducted by Cambridge University, Italy came 15th out of 15 European countries when national average happiness was measured.

Even the professions are not immune to this social paralysis. In my own field of medicine, although things have improved in the last decade, I used to be ashamed and angered at the lip service paid to European rules and regulations by my Italian colleagues. If they bothered to come to meetings, they had little idea of the subject matter, spoke little English and invariably left early. Surgeons used to exit from a so-called training programme with a certificate that said they were European specialists, having merely watched their professor work; some hadn't even laid a hand on a patient, never mind operated. It was grossly nepotistic. Both public and university appointments were made on the basis of who you were rather than what you knew, sometimes with disastrous results. Since 1990 the profession has tried to clean up its act and a number of Italian professors have since been tried by the various courts of corruption in public appointments.

Yet the damage the Mafia caused to society lives on, even though things have changed at the top. I remember going to see a lawyer in Rome to get advice on how to deal with property and other related subjects essential to life and the first words Avvocato Alberto said to me were: 'You have to understand *il sistema*.'

He went on: 'Let me give you an example. Last year the government passed a law that basically said public servants must serve the public. Italy is not a normal country. Corruption is now such a way of life that we've gone overboard in the other direction. Our bureaucracy is now worse than that of the United States. You must fill in forms for everything and show original documents if you want anything done, and that means that the people with the forms and the official stamp have the power. And who are these people? Voters from the South who have been placed in public-service jobs by politicians they or their families have supported. Trying to get anything done is impossible and that's why the young are all learning English in an attempt to leave – but none of them really want to go anywhere else. They really just want Italy to get better.'

I enquired of him what the alternatives were and what *il sistema* was.

'You must get an entry card to an allegorical place called *Italietta* because that's where things get done. All you do is hand your request to someone in "that" Italy and everything will be done for you and the wheels will move again.'

'So where do you get the ticket?' I asked.

'You used to get it from the local parish priest,' he joked, 'by giving a suitable donation to the St Vincent de Paul Society. But now you just have to get to know someone with an entry ticket and you won't know when you've met him or her. Someone will just appear on your radar who approves of you and will help you. If you're young and Italian, that means that you'll get a *raccomandazione*. In England you call that a reference, but here it's quite different; it's much more powerful. A competition for a job is a competition for the best *raccomandazione*. In Britain you say, "It's not *what* you know that counts, it's *who* you know", but at the top of life in Italy it would be better expressed "It's not what you've got that counts, and it's not who you know that counts, it's what you've got on who you know that counts."

I liked Avvocato Alberto. He was in the system and he saved me money because he explained that in order to avoid Italian tax, which he would have had to add to his fee, I should pay his son, who lived in London, in cash!

Italian politics are determined by their geopolitical position in the Mediterranean. The country is not an inherent part of Europe but a peninsula of the central mass looking east to Arabia and west to Spain. It is therefore imprisoned in the Mediterranean culture of what Italian historians such as Denis Mack Smith and Paul Ginsborg have described as patronage and *clientelismo*. Due to a weak state tradition of social care, the important thing has become family and clan.

Patronage is usually delivered as a 'thank you' for services rendered or as a placement to secure control of an organisation. Few countries in Western Europe have abused patronage as openly and as disgracefully as Italian governments have since the war and, as a result, patronage has become an accepted and integral part of the Italian social fabric.

I have made reference to the difficulties of getting a job in Italy without having a *raccomandazione*; for young Italians, there are two ways of getting 'help'. The first involves your direct family. The second is *raccomandazione* from friends. An Italian would expect any of his extended family (which includes third cousins with up to two removals), together with everyone who has had the good fortune to marry into this group, to come to his aid if he had a problem – and that would probably happen. Although in Britain we would expect the State to look after any person suffering misfortune, in Italy 'the State' is too distant and unapproachable – you need an intermediary from the 'family' to intercede.

This is also the reason that saints are so important in non-intellectual Catholic worship in Italy. Different saints have powers bestowed on them in the same way as the Hindu gods and goddesses have different functions and skills. As an extreme example of this, my very Catholic centenarian aunt uses her dead brother as an intermediary to God in her prayers. She *knows* that he is actually in heaven and will certainly have found some friends who will act as intermediaries to reach God's ear on behalf of his sister!

I have my own experiences of seeing how il sistema works. Although I am from an Italian background, the first time I went to Italy was in 1951 when I was 15. My aunt had married a landowner with several large farms and I spent the summers of the '50s in Umbria at a time when the contrast between post-war Britain and *la dolce vita* in Italy could not have been starker. But life changed and, after 1960, my visits lessened, though I still kept in touch.

When my mother died, I inherited her share of the old family house in a village that lay halfway between Rome and Naples, in the foothills of the Apennines. To call it an inheritance is perhaps an exaggeration. What I had become heir to was the detritus of a once grand house that had collapsed during the 1983 earthquake.

Between 1985 and 1990, I monitored, with no little amusement, the fate of the money that the government had promised for the reconstruction of the valley and particularly what was now my house. Somehow the money kept bypassing the valley and arriving in the hands of the Neopolitan Mafia, the Camorra, who had been awarded most of the big contracts. Money travelled, but workmen didn't.

For me, it was a mild irritant, but for the hundreds of people left living for years in ruins in the valley, the delays were heartbreaking. Had this happened in Britain there would have been TV programmes about the scandal of corruption, ministerial resignations might have followed and exposés by the press would have been repetitive and sensational. But that did not seem to be the way Italy worked.

What did surprise me was that none of the locals ever seemed surprised. They just got on with life as before, getting water from the fountain in the piazza, using candles at night and heating with paraffin in winter. When the rebuilding money finally arrived in 1990, the building began.

Again I watched as contracts were fixed. The way contracts for public works are awarded in Italy is by auction, when closed bids are opened in public in the *commune* (the town hall) on a stated date. No one, however, usually bothers to turn up to watch the outcome of this process, which is conducted with the utmost formality, because everyone knows the outcome days before the sealed bids are opened. In Britain there would have been uproar and scandal, but in the valley no one even let a wry smile cross their face because that's how it was in Italy in 1990. They understood *il sistema*; to a non-Italian, it was incredible but in Italy at that time it was just the way things were done. There was an Orwellian aspect to watching a people accept a system that could not function in any other Western democracy.

I did not want to retire to village life and so now live in Umbria. The region has been governed by the Communist Party since the war and it has the finest public services that I have ever seen.

I was introduced to communism during my first visit to Italy in 1951. Each afternoon, with my two cousins, I would listen to the radio commentary of the Tour de France. The two greatest cyclists in the world were then both Italian, Gino Bartali and Fausto Coppi, but they were as different as chalk and cheese. In Italy, they did not rejoice at Italians coming first and second every day. No, it was far more complex than that, especially to a boy whose only experience of politics had been mock elections at school. Bartali was a Communist and Coppi was a Christian Democrat. One cousin supported Coppi, the other, who went on to work for the Italian Communist Party, supported Bartali. Had Everton been Communist and Liverpool Conservative, it would have amounted to the same thing.

But I'd never lived in a country at war. I'd never had to choose whether to side with a Fascist dictator or with his opponents, called Partisans (whom the West praised, not realising they were Communist). One of my uncles had lived in caves for a year trying to avoid the Gestapo and so the wonder was that one of his boys was non-Communist!

Italian communism is different from what one might expect – as are most political structures in Italy. It follows a humanistic philosophy probably far nearer to what Lenin and Trotsky had in mind when they set out their dream. Here is an example.

The town of Spoleto is full of large modern sculptures that have been commissioned by the Menotti Festival of Two Worlds over the years since it began in 1958. On Feast Days and Commemorative Days, however, the local government officials ignore the statues of Garibaldi, the modern sculptures of Alexander Calder and Sol LeWit, historic landmarks such as La Rocca or Il Duomo, which houses the beautiful Fra Lippo Lippi frescos, and even the beautifully reconstructed town hall. The mayor, with his red, white and green sash, leads his council in procession behind the local brass band to lay wreaths at a much smaller, less grand but extremely beautiful sculpture that they commissioned many years ago. It commemorates 'Those who have fallen at work'.

The ceremony is deeply moving and there is not an ounce of posturing. It is a type of humanism that only supreme political confidence can bring because no one is trying to make any political points. As far as I can tell from living in the town and talking to friends, it is corruption-free, but they feel quite frustrated by the 'goings-on' in the North, the financial scandals and the movement for federalism.

As for the South, they, along with most other Italians living north of Rome, are ashamed to admit that it is part of Italy. Many, in fact, deny that Garibaldi united Italy: they claim that he divided Africa!

The Church remains enormously powerful in Italy. Catholicism is the established Church of the country, though fewer than half of the population actually observe the faith. A friend once said to me that governing Italy is more difficult than governing most other countries because down the road from the parliament sits the representative of God on earth, the pope!

I was brought up as a Catholic and actually remained within the established Church for many years, but I had no perception of the role the Church played, in the decades after the war, in the fight to prevent Italy voting Communist, falling into the Soviet empire and opting out of NATO. The CIA poured money into the Christian Democrat Party to oppose communism, but what few people realise is that in later years this was done with the connivance of the KGB. The money not only helped defeat communism in elections, but it also flowed over into all sorts of other areas that remain faultlines to this day.

Feeding off this unholy alliance of Church and government was the Mafia, which, while having its own anti-Communist agenda, benefited enormously from the lax regulations, which allowed them to function in relative impunity. The Mafia was able to launder money using, among others, the infamous banking duo of Michele Sindona and Roberto Calvi, who in turn duped the Vatican and almost bankrupted it. I have two personal stories separated by 50 years that show the power of the Church.

The first comes from the 1950s. My uncle by marriage in Umbria was a right-wing candidate at a general election but lost by a record margin to his Communist opponent. However, he was a very benevolent boss. He had four large farms that were run by four *contadini* (tenant farmer) families. One of them, Gigetto, was an active Communist Party member and was the regional 'armourer'. This meant that he kept what guns they owned in his barns. In 1953, one of the leaders of the Communist Party was killed in Ostia, the party town of Rome. Sex and drugs were involved but, to Gigetto and his pals, this was the beginning of the Italian 'revolution'. Gigetto was told to distribute the arms. He hesitated. His various environmental and behavioural influences clashed and he became unsure about what to do. Being brought up to believe that the Church was the final arbiter, he went to the priest to discuss what he should do.

In those years, the writer Giovanni Guareschi published a series of stories about these very tensions and used as his characters the opposing forces of the priest Don Camillo and the Communist mayor Peppone. He was telling real tales.

The next story illustrates the contemporary power of the Church. Among my many Italian medical and surgical friends is one who works in a hospital in Rome, where a suite is kept for any papal need. Before he finally died, Pope John Paul II was admitted to have a tracheotomy performed to aid his breathing, a process that involved making a hole in his windpipe. I asked my friend, whose field this was, whether or not he had performed the Pope's operation. He said no, that it was one of his former trainees who had performed the procedure. I expressed some astonishment that a more junior man had had the honour of operating on a Pope. My friend replied that the uncle of the surgeon was a cardinal. I then mentioned the name of a parliamentarian known to my friend and asked why this had not made a difference. 'In Italy, cardinals trump politicians!' was his reply.

PART I

THE RISE

I

WHY THE MAFIA DEVELOPED

Criminal organisations start because there is an opportunity to make money illegally. It is the creation of an organisation rather than reliance on individual effort that distinguishes the major crime boss from the petty criminal. Neither an unlocked house or motor vehicle nor a visible purse in a handbag requires an organisation to profit from someone's carelessness. But smuggle people, provide prostitutes, run protection rackets, control illegal gambling, distribute drugs or sell arms illegally and there is a need for something bigger.

The biggest criminal organisation the world has ever known, the Sicilian Mafia, was not created with criminal intent in mind. It started as an 'alternative' form of local government in the Sicilian countryside during the nineteenth century in response to the collapse of the ruling Bourbon Empire, which comprised the whole of the south of Italy, together with Sicily. Its replacement by the government and army of Piedmont, the most northerly of present-day Italian regions, which would at that time have been as cogent to Sicilians as Belgium would have been to Australians.

It is perhaps ironic that the two men whose decisions and actions caused the upheaval in the Sicilian countryside and were the catalyst for the Mafia are regarded as heroes worthy of remembrance in statuary both in Italy and Britain.

There is not a town or village in Italy that fails to honour the role of Giuseppe Garibaldi in the formation of the Italian nation with a statue or an eponymous road or piazza. More surprisingly, however, it was an action by Admiral Horatio Nelson almost 50 years before Garibaldi arrived that was the real catalyst for change in Sicily, and which indirectly spawned the Mafia.

When Nelson defeated Napoleon at the Battle of the Nile in 1798, the Sicilians, and especially the Bourbon King Ferdinand, were so grateful that they gave him a 30,000-acre estate and awarded him the Dukedom of Bronte. This gesture was so well received in England that Patrick Brunty, the father of Charlotte, Emily and Anne, changed the family name to Brontë!

Unfortunately, Nelson never had time to enjoy his estate, but it stayed in his family until it was sold back to the Sicilians in 1980. The British occupied Sicily from 1806 to 1815 under the governorship of William Bentinck. They introduced many useful changes to the island's administration, such as a bicameral system of government and a new constitution, but, like all later invaders, they did not understand that by altering the traditional way of life they were opening doors for changes other than their own to be introduced. Feudalism was an anathema to nineteenth-century Britons and while its abolition would threaten the way of life of the aristocrats and their retainers it also actually harmed the apparently downtrodden peasants whom the British were hoping to liberate. No one was realistically going to let the peasants set up their own smallholdings in the first decade of the nineteenth century. They tried to introduce the changes just 20 years after *Figaro*, the play on which Mozart's opera was based, had been banned. It dared to challenge the social hierarchy: servants were servants and masters were masters. More importantly, when the abolition of feudalism was passed into law, the peasants lost their traditional feudal rights, which for them was a disaster.

At the time, the British held the same inflated opinion of their way of life as the Americans do today, when it came to transplanting their domestic institutions onto an alien culture. What worked well in England in regard to landownership was not going to work as well in Sicily, but the English did not understand this.

But British rule gave confidence for outside investment and many English families bought into the development of sulphur mining and the wine industry in Marsala.

The Sicilian aristocrats had remained comfortable and saw it as their duty to look after their serfs, who in turn were grateful for any handouts from their lords. The now more liberal British did not approve of this, but, with so few troops and little interest in creating socio-political upheaval, change had to await the arrival of Garibaldi 50 years later, who insisted on abolishing feudalism and so again, unwittingly, changed the system to the disadvantage of the group he was trying to help.

To implement the abolition of a centuries-old system and institute change was virtually impossible for 17,000 British troops, none of whom could speak Sicilian dialect. Neither was there a 'popular' revolt since the peasants, being 100 per cent illiterate, had no means of knowing that the law had indeed changed and that there was now an opportunity to no longer work at the grace and favour of employers. So, as they do to this day with laws that are not considered 'suitable', the Sicilians ignored them and the peasants went to work as they had always done.

At that time, the huge estates were among the richest and most fertile in Europe and their unique value lay in the citrus crop. Originally developed by the Saracens when they occupied the island in the ninth century, the fruit had been enormously profitable, especially since Dr Lind had shown that it could prevent scurvy. This small discovery transformed long-distance voyages, which contributed massively in particular to the wealth of Great Britain.

As far back as 1834, the west of Sicily had exported almost half a million cases of oranges, lemons and limes a year, and by the end of the century this total had risen to three million. It was a high-investment but high-profit crop. It took about ten years before trees produced fruits large enough for export and in that period, because their water supply was critical, they became a common target for vandals who had not been satisfied by the *pizzu* payments. The word *'pizzu'* meant 'the bird's beak' and the term arose from an old Sicilian tradition allowing the baron, and subsequently his employees, his 'right' to scoop some grain from the threshings of the peasant. Decades of hard work could be undone if the water supply for the irrigation of an estate was dammed, diverted or otherwise interfered with. But what was a threat to some was also an opportunity for others to profit and so, in some ways, the landowners had become prisoners of their own possessions.

In the first half of the nineteenth century, Palermo, the capital city, was the 'party town' of Europe, mainly because of the ease of access and the gentle winter climate. The then huge number of European royals spent their winters there and this drew the increasingly affluent Sicilian aristocrats away from their estates to the centre of social activity. When the aristocrats left the countryside, the management of their estates was put in the hands of trusty employees who, in author Giuseppe Tomasi di Lampedusa's words, were the 'new men' of the early Mafia. These *gabellotti*, as they came to be known, were virtually estate managers and their primary role was to provide protection against vandalism and ensure profitability. Their primary helpers were overseers called *campieri* and protection was supplied by their own guards, called 'the boys' – *picciotti*.

The feudal system that they advanced had been in place since the Norman Conquest in the eleventh century and when the aristocratic migration to Palermo left a social vacuum, the new men became central to the community. There was little evidence of the State in the countryside, and the police, who were so poorly paid that they took what they could squeeze from the peasants, were practically powerless; they certainly were not about to upset or challenge the new Sect and so the *gabellotti* and their employees became the local rulers. Long before Britain had a middle class, Sicily had developed one.

Another important factor in the social equation was the priests, nuns and monks, who acted as a bridge between the *gabellotti* and the desperately poor peasants, doling out charity along with the new men as a glue to keep the community together.

When, by the 1860s, to the horror of the ruling classes, Garibaldi attempted to resurrect the law to abolish feudalism, the situation was slightly different. Garibaldi was a hero. He was not a 'foreigner', like the British had been. He had got rid of the Bourbons, who had used Sicily like a cash cow, and he was, at least to the Sicilians, the dawn of their independence. Italy had had very few heroes since the Romans and here was a man who seemed to defy bullets, wore a poncho and a large hat with an ostrich feather in it, and cracked a whip. He was an early-day Che Guevara: a brilliant soldier and general, who had experience of helping in South American revolutions but was a useless politician. He had come to the notice of Camillo Cavour, the real architect of Italian unification, in the early wars with Austria in the north and after a failed occupation of Rome.

After tasting power at the top table of Europe, Cavour craved a place for himself, but this was not going to come to pass unless he had a country bigger than Piedmont. He saw that opportunity in making the geographic entity that was the Italian peninsula into a political force. Originally his aim was more modest – to unite the North with Central Italy, leaving Rome to the Popes and the South to the Bourbons. He realised that if he ordered the Piedmontese Army to march towards Rome, the Austrian and French forces would interpret the move as a threat to the Vatican and would intervene to protect the Pope.

His tactics, however, changed when Garibaldi put forward the idea of invading Sicily and the South. Unknown to Cavour, this idea had been planted in Garibaldi's mind not only by Sicilians but also by fellow Freemasons and it was their cause of 'freedom' that he was supporting rather than Cavour's unification agenda. Garibaldi had been approached by the *Carbonari*, the original secret society in the Bourbon Kingdom of the Two Sicilys, which wanted independence for Sicily. Cavour, therefore, saw an opportunity in allowing an acknowledged adventurer to sail down to Sicily in an attempt to get rid of the Bourbons. If Garibaldi failed, Cavour could stand back and claim that he had not helped Garibaldi by supplying money, men, arms or transport (even though he had made it very easy for him to obtain all four). He could easily wash his hands of the whole affair and denounce Garibaldi as a loose cannon. But if Garibaldi succeeded, then Cavour was halfway towards unifying Italy without alarming the rest of Europe. It was a win-win situation, with Garibaldi as the fall guy.

Although Garibaldi was said to have arrived in Sicily with his famous 'thousand', who were supposed to have been a motley collection of largely rich European Romantics, revolutionaries, ardent Freemasons and the barking mad, this is quite wrong. He originally intended to go with only 500 men in order to lead the Sicilian population in a popular uprising, never intending to challenge the Bourbon Army directly in the battlefield. But the response from all over Europe, especially from students and Masonic lodges, was so great that after interviewing every man personally he did take a thousand. But it was the 22,000 Sicilians who joined him when he landed who made victory over a relatively competent Bourbon army possible.

There had been rumblings of discontent with Bourbon rule for at least 20 years before Garibaldi arrived and it was obvious at all levels of Sicilian society that the Bourbon rule had run its course. The Sicilians wanted independence; what went on north of the Messina Strait, and on the continent of the peninsula and the rest of Europe, was not even on their radar.

The nature of the Sicilian countryside meant that bandits had been an ever-present threat in the west, but this was exacerbated when the 1848 rebellion was brutally crushed by the Bourbons, an action which did not help their popularity. With nothing to lose and everything to gain if Sicily became independent, the survivors of that rebellion formed the bulk of the 22,000-strong force and subsequently were described as the *squadristi*. As well as bandits, the group was made up of fugitives and the private armies of the countryside, the *gabellotti*, *campieri* and *picciotti*. They were discreetly supported by the rural clergy but not by the established Church.

Garibaldi could thank the British for an immense stroke of luck that allowed a safe landing rather than a total defeat by the Bourbons. The British Navy were in the port of Marsala when he arrived and the crews were ashore either visiting the Marsala winery or sitting on the seafront eating ice cream. Since England at that time 'ruled the waves', the Bourbon ships, which were sitting offshore, could not fire towards land for fear of injuring a British sailor. So when one of his ships ran aground at the landing, instead of being blown out of the water he was able to disembark his troops safely, the shambolic landing being watched with some amusement by the British sailors.

His second piece of luck, courtesy of the British, occurred when he arrived in Palermo. He was being hotly pursued by one of the better Bourbon generals, who would certainly have expelled his group from the town, but when the Bourbon general arrived he was prevented from attacking Garibaldi by a British naval lieutenant, who informed him that peace had been arranged by the British and American Consuls because they did not want any of their nationals in Palermo injured by Bourbon shells!

There was then a hastily arranged plebiscite in which the Sicilians were asked to vote on whether or not they wished to join Piedmont. The vast majority of the voters had no idea either what or where Piedmont was, but the results were rigged with a little help from the Sect and there was a 99 per cent acceptance.

Garibaldi became a world celebrity thanks to the chronicle compiled by the most famous writer of the time, Alexandre Dumas; his later biography of Garibaldi, written with as much imagination as fact, cemented Garibaldi's status for all time. The immensely wealthy Dumas had a luxury yacht, the *Emma*, and was writing travel articles for *Le Constitutionnel* magazine, but when he arrived in Sicily at the time of the invasion he wired his employers to say that he wanted to write about what was going on on the island. They were not interested, so he sent his articles to *La Presse*, whose circulation went through the roof. His book about Garibaldi was also a bestseller, though it was more related to something like *The Three Musketeers* than what actually happened. But it made Garibaldi a legend.

The Piedmontese backing of Garibaldi was a thinly disguised land grab, devoid of both legal and moral justification. This has happened all over the world in the last 200 years and we accept that change is a part of history and revolution is a major force for that change. In the view of the Vatican, as well as the Bourbons and the Austro-Hungarians, their subjects did not have the right to rebel against their legitimate sovereigns because God had chosen monarchs to rule and only He could question their right to carry out His will. This concept had initially created tensions with liberal Piedmont, but, by the middle of the nineteenth century and in the aftermath of the French Revolution, it had run its course and its protagonists were fighting against the tide.

Once the Piedmontese were established in Sicily, they took a very tough line to suppress crime, brigandage and popular revolt, just as the Americans have in Iraq. The occupying force was the 9th Division of the Piedmontese Army; it brought in higher taxation (for their keep) together with conscription (for up to eight years) into their army in the North, which was to the young Sicilians a foreign land. So, as they set about trying to dismantle the Sicilian way of life, tensions at all levels of society grew.

The aristocrats in Palermo might have been enchanted by the fashionable, French-speaking young men from Piedmont, with their blue uniforms with smart red piping, but to most Sicilians this was just another army of occupation that they had to get on with. Were they any different from the Normans, the Angevins, the Saracens, the French, the Austrians, the English or the Bourbons? Well, they had brought the concept of a united Italy, but this did not capture the hearts and minds of any Sicilians. The rural community in particular saw absolutely no need for them and what they objected to most of all was the conscription of their sons, on whom they depended to work the land and look after them when they were old.

At least for some, life in the country had become better after the aristocrats had delegated the running of the estates to managers. Rural and small-town Sicily had settled into a pattern of life acceptable to the workers, the clergy and the *gabellotti*, who were renting and administering the estates and their surrounding community. Even the few state officials at local level were content with the way of life that had been established and did not want interference from the Piedmontese. So it was to the 'new men', the underclass who rose to become the middle class – the Mafia – that everyone turned, especially those who had mistakenly fought for independence alongside Garibaldi only to see their dreams betrayed.

Thus, building on a rural system that had taken shape in the 1830s, what became the first Mafia evolved and consolidated in the 15 to 20 years after Garibaldi's invasion.

Apart from the Piedmontese, there were two other problems that had to be solved, both created by the arrival of Garibaldi. The first was how to handle the break-up of the feudal system and the second was how to manage the break-up of the Church lands, which the first Prime Minister of the new nation, Francesco Crispi, a virulent anti-cleric, had decreed.

It was the different approach to these problems that defined the Mafia as a west Sicily phenomenon rather than a way of life for the east of the island. One of the great differences between life in east and west Sicily were the bandits, and there were a number of logical reasons why the bandits were all but confined to the west.

While bandits had long been the scourge of Sicily, declining only briefly during British rule, their number increased in the post-Garibaldi years because many young men were taking to the hills in order to evade the draft into the Piedmontese Army. Furthermore, since the population base of the island was in Palermo (west) and since this was where most crime was committed, it was logical that the main jail on the island was there. The countryside in the west is heavily wooded, with hundreds of caves and ravines, which made it easy for bandits to live in the open with little fear of capture. The countryside in the east, on the other hand, is far more open and thus unattractive for a fugitive living rough.

Another big difference was that the bandit problem made land reform very different on the two sides of the island. Very few west Sicilians lived on their own in the countryside because night attacks by bandits looking for food and shelter would have made life impossible. There are thus very few small villages in west Sicily because most people preferred to live in the safety of large villages that came to be known as agrotowns. Although it meant that they might have to walk many kilometres to and from work, carrying tools, it was better than living in fear on your own with your family in the countryside at night.

In the east, there was no system of absentee landlordism and so there was no need for private armies; for this reason, the east welcomed land reforms because the landowners realised that whatever investment was made in machinery, cattle or trees would be safe; those in the west knew that any investment they made had a high chance of either being stolen or vandalised by bandits.

As stated previously, it was virtually impossible for a peasant to buy a smallholding in the west because the gabellotti who controlled the community saw to it that peasants could not get loans for down payments and, if they somehow succeeded and had the gall to actually buy land, then their trees and machinery would be vandalised. On the other hand, land purchase in the east was encouraged because the local governments wanted to promote the transition from a feudal to a capitalistic structure. The new landowners in the east all realised that production from the land in future would entail capital investment, crop diversification and longer tenancies.

So when land reform eventually took place in the west, creating numerous small plots with multiple owners, expertise in both vandalism and protection developed. The *gabellotti*, with their private armies of *campieri* and *picciotti*, had had several decades of experience in understanding and developing the organisation of protection and so were in the right place with the right product at the right time.

And that is how the agricultural system of nineteenth-century west Sicily spawned an organisation that had another hundred years to perfect the industry of protection before moving on to the far more lucrative drug trade.

2

WHAT THE MAFIA
HAD TO OFFER

The Mafia came into being because of the lawlessness in the Sicilian countryside and the expertise that some people developed in the product of protection. But it was not only protection of property for a baron or a *gabellotto*, it was also the protection of the less fortunate in that society. At least according to Sal Contorno, one of the more credible of the informers at the major Mafia trials of the 1980s. He claimed: 'The Mafia was born to help the poor and the helpless. If something happened to these people, they would go to the local "family" and not the local *carabinieri* and say "something got stolen".'

I think anyone who has studied Mafia life and methods might reply, 'Well, maybe, Sal, but that was a long time ago.' The honourable 'way of life' of the Mafia was a myth by the time Contorno testified and the American Cosa Nostra were acting out a fantasy as seen in the *Godfather* movies, where the criminality of drug dealing and other illegal activities played alongside so-called 'tradition'.

Having the Mafia around was better than having a countryside devoid of law and policing: some order was maintained, violence might occasionally appear as an outcome of protection, but a man was much better off being a mafioso than a peasant. When the development of the American West is compared with the settlement of the British Empire, the clear difference was the rule of law. In America, new settlers were encouraged to go west and settle, but in places where there was no structure of law enforcement, only an army to protect them against the Native Americans. In the development of the British Empire, settlers went to places that had been tamed and were controlled by the army, together with surveyors, engineers and police. They did not need their own protection because there were others to sort out quarrels in society.

In Chapter 1, I alluded to the rather jaundiced view of many Italians living north of Rome that Garibaldi did not unite Italy but divided Africa. Sicily in the nineteenth century was more akin to a modern African nation or the American West than it was to the rest of the peninsula. As there was no effective State policing, the use of private violence in settling disputes was tolerated and accepted, because people understood that there was no other effective body to intervene.

It might be argued that since the Mafia was, at the end of the nineteenth and beginning of the twentieth centuries, a Sicilian tradition, it did not need an independent income. But this is not correct: their particular way of life involved violence, which in turn required pay-offs to court judges, police and lawyers for acquittals.

In the unlikely event of one of the 'family' being sent to jail, their blood family had to be taken care of and their wages paid. This was part of the deal when mafiosi were initiated. Their new family, the Mafia, guaranteed at the initiation when the man was 'made' that it would look after both him and his family in times of trouble; for his part, the initiate swore that he would be willing to die or lose his freedom for the Mafia.

Going to jail as a mafioso was not the equivalent to incarceration for a non-mafioso. Special treatment was arranged, as was a comfortable cell. They would wear their own clothes and have meals brought in from outside; indeed, they were as important as the governor of the prison. But all this needed to be paid for.

The traditional Sicilian way of getting quick money was to kidnap for ransom, the victims inevitably being the rich or their children. Hiding them was easy because the bandits were the masters of the interior of the island; if the rescuers or relatives went to find the victim themselves, the task would have been impossible. Apart from those with a social conscience or the clear realisation that things were changing, the real reason why the aristocrats and the rich chose to side with the Mafia and the 'new' way of life was fear of kidnap. This was a real fear for two reasons.

Apart from the anticipated discomfort of being confined to a cave or grotto for months, it was dangerous not only to one's wealth but also to one's health. The old might die in captivity or the victim might be killed if negotiations went wrong. Furthermore, almost everyone would know, or know of, a family who had had one of its number kidnapped: the experience would be talked about and replication would be dreaded. So a market opportunity developed for security services – and the product known as protection. Even today we have become used to seeing celebrities accompanied by their own personal security service. Some years ago when a plot to kidnap a Beckham child was foiled, the news remained on the front pages for days.

Protection is a product like anything else and is subject to market forces so that the more unique the product, the more expensive it becomes. For example, if only one landlord is protected in a neighbourhood then that service is far more valuable because he is unique; not only is the likelihood of his estate being attacked reduced but the attendant risk to his neighbours is also greater. There is an analogy to home alarms. If your home is the only one in a street to have an alarm, then it will reduce the chances of your house being burgled, because if an alarm went off everyone would know from which house it had come. But if every house is alarmed, then today's situation applies – everyone ignores the noise and the value of the protection is reduced.

Earlier, we saw how the west and east of the island differed in their methods of land reform. While the east went for the large estate, the west had the land divided up into numerous smaller estates, thus making the need for protection greater, and so with more owners there was more business.

There is also the variant of personal and property protection, namely extortion. Although 'protection' became available as a product, there was also the traditional *pizzu*. This was understood by everyone at all levels of society; for example, at the time the police received little or no pay, so they were expected to get enough in the way of *pizzu* from their contacts to make a living.

If the gathering of *pizzu* increases to become universal and is applied to things other than grain, such as a shopkeeper's weekly take, then it becomes protection money. This has been tolerated for centuries in Sicily and is an integral part of the economy. The sums involved need not be large, but if an uneducated man moves from the country into the town he would see nothing very abnormal about an offer to 'protect' his property for a weekly sum. Park your car in many places in the world, even Britain, and a child may ask you for a small sum to 'look after' your car. A peculiar aspect to this tradition, at least until recent years, was that professional classes were always exempt from *pizzu*, but we shall see later in the book that when times became hard even professionals were caught up in the net.

This was also the product that the original Black Hand gangs brought to America. If they had applied it only to Sicilian immigrants, it would have been accepted as a normal part of life, but when it was applied to 'foreigners' the response was hurt astonishment.

In order to make protection a credible product, there has to be not only the threat of violence but also the certainty of it. To make the violence effective, it must not be used wantonly: it must be applied specifically for a reason and its use has to maintain, or possibly even augment, the terror factor.

Every major business has a logo by which they hope to be recognised and the Mafia was no different. Violence and the certainty of its delivery was their trademark and symbolism both reinforced and enhanced the reputation of the organisation. The violence would always be accompanied by a sign, so that there was no ambiguity as to the source; this also had the effect of getting tongues wagging, thus enhancing the reputation of the organisation. The association between violence and symbolism acted as a clear message to the victim as well as his family, friends and associates.

Symbolism continues to play a part in Mafia life. The image that remains with all who watch the *Godfather* films is the horse's head in the bed. The last time this was used in real life was in May 1991, when three building contractors found horses' heads in their company cars. On a smaller scale, the Mafia would also use the severed head of a chicken or a cat. A metal devotional heart, a simple symbol carried by many Catholics in Italy, might also be sent, though for the Mafia it is slightly modified, having two holes in it. They may leave a coffin outside someone's door; and a dead bird placed on the seat of a locked car indicates that they can reach their victim at any time in any place.

These threats often precede violence and will usually persuade the victim to do whatever it is that he is being asked, be it increasing protection money, altering documents, giving evidence in court or changing supplier. Once the symbolism is understood it saves the trouble and expense of actually perpetrating an act of violence.

In order to supply effective protection and to apply violence as required, there has to be accurate intelligence. The capacity for gathering information forms part of a mafioso's reputation. His renown relies on his knowledge, his ability to obtain and use data from every sphere – economic, personal and political – to ask productive questions quickly and pose them tactfully with both social grace and unobtrusive loitering. He must also have a good memory.

The reason that Sicily has always been the base of the Mafia is that the island is relatively closed and the best area about which to be informed is where you were born and brought up: if you know who's who and who does what, strangers are easily identified. To become well informed, keeping a low profile is necessary, as if others feel that they, or their business, are under observation there will be little activity and thus little information will be forthcoming. Keeping a low profile means having a private life that is discreet and sober and, on the surface at least, without a blemish.

Information will come from many sources, ranging from government ministers, mayors and deputies to taxi drivers, porters and road labourers. The latter three are particularly useful because their jobs keep them on the streets, where they can watch a person's movements, his contacts and habits.

The Mafia also supply a service as intermediaries. This is a very respectable job, through which houses can be sold and financial packages or holidays arranged. In some countries intermediaries arrange marriages, while in others they help to arm terrorists. They still exist in nearly all Italian villages, where they are called *sensali* – men who are respected and who are called in to referee disputes about land boundaries or agricultural prices.

In Italy, and especially in Sicily, life is a balance between *furbo* and *fesso*. *Furbo* is savvy, smart and astute. In any deal, someone who is *furbo* will always out-think his opponent. *Fesso*, on the other hand, means that you are never quite smart enough to see the pitfalls awaiting you in any deal and you're easily tricked.

If Nino wants to sell something to Carlo, Carlo will strongly suspect that Nino will give him a faulty object under the guise of its being perfect. Nino on the other hand 'knows' that Carlo will fiddle the payment and there will be complications and somehow the whole amount will not be paid. But if an intermediary with 'respect' brokers the deal, then it's likely that both parties will end up happy. Even if each must give the intermediary 10 per cent, it's worth it because no one loses face.

The role of intermediaries arose out of an old Sicilian tradition that involved reporting stolen property to the Mafia rather than to the police, as they were more certain of 'recovering' the stolen property – most likely because they had probably stolen it in the first place. The Mafia began by collecting debts or recovering stolen property and people realised it was worth a small payment to avoid any hassle with the police.

As important as money was influence because the key to avoiding problems resulting from illegal activity is to have 'friends' in the judiciary and legislature. This means getting the politicians elected who will make the 'right' appointments so that if the appointee is not one of your family he will at least be known and beholden in some way. The most effective way of making someone indebted to the 'system' is to be in control of his electoral process and thus election rigging is an essential part of Mafia activity to this day. One of the earliest examples of this is the story of the voters of Villalba (a town that we will visit in Chapter 4) being locked in the local granary and allowed out to vote, six at a time, to make certain that the correct candidate was elected.

Attempts to rig elections have probably been going on since the electoral process was invented. It is also prevalent in Britain – in Birmingham in 2005, six local councillors were expelled from office for postal ballot fraud, the judge likening the city to a banana republic.

In 1861 in Sicily, vote rigging was easy because the electorate were mainly the aristocrats and were well disposed to the Mafia. Even though the aristocrats made up only 1.6 per cent of the population, they accounted for 23 per cent of those elected to office. At that time only 3 per cent of the population had the vote; however, as the electorate expanded, it became more important to actually influence the voting pattern, legally or illegally. By 1882, 5 per cent of the male adult population had a vote, and by 1890, when it had reached 30 per cent, the Mafia had learned how to control the ballot boxes.

The commonest method was to stand outside the polling booths with a ballot paper already filled in. This would be given to the voters as they went in and they would be told to bring out a blank voting form, which in turn would be completed and handed to the next voter.

By the end of the nineteenth century, the Mafia was able to deliver all the votes in Sicily to the party that favoured them. And with that huge block of votes it virtually ensured power in Rome to whichever party had their ear. This, therefore, created a political hierarchy. Those in power had a duty to 'look after' those who voted for them and that meant that they had to find jobs, write *raccomandazioni*, deal with bureaucracy, guide documents through the correct and most favourable channels, obtain licences for guns, vehicles and construction, and also arrange loans when required. The principle on which this worked was that whoever voted for the elected candidate and his party was owed whatever he was petitioning for.

The Mafia's electoral power was best displayed in 1983 when not a single politician but an entire party fell from grace because it hadn't obeyed 'orders'. At the time, Mafia bosses were putting pressure on the Christian Democrat Party to pass legislation to rule that evidence from informers became inadmissible. When the law was rejected, hundreds of bosses faced long sentences. It is said that an order came from within the Ucciardone prison in Palermo that all Men of Honour should see to it that the Christian Democrats were defeated.

To make a point, the small Radical Party received 10,000 new subscriptions, which gave it the potential to damage the Christian Democrats. The Radical Party and the Socialists won the election, but still the laws were not passed.

So many advantages came your way if you were part of 'the club' that invitations were frequently sought, but to gain access you had first to be made an offer, which of course you could not refuse.

3

AN OFFER NOT TO
BE REFUSED

One did not apply to join the Mafia, one was invited. And once invited you didn't refuse because it brought you to the very top level of Sicilian society. The word *mafia* is Sicilian dialect for someone who stands out in the community and who is admired for his wisdom, success and presence – in other words, someone who is 'respected'. It has frequently been translated as meaning 'flashy' but, although that might sum up the post-war organisation, it certainly could not be applied to its first incarnation. In fact, the first Mafia was the very opposite.

The old-fashioned don would have a high degree of visibility and legitimacy within his local community because he carried out functions that the State authorities either would not or could not do. The dons were regarded as the 'ruling class' and people would go and ask favours from them at a local bar, where they might hold court, deciding who and who not to help. The first Mafia adhered to the value system of their community and so respect was valued above wealth.

Respect is a concept that lived through to the violent days of the second Mafia. When Vincent Cafaro, a member of the Genovese family in New York, was asked at a Senate hearing in 1980 to explain what he had gained from joining the Mafia, he said, 'You gain honour, that's what you gain. Honour and respect . . . all over the city.'

When asked if he considered murder respectable and honourable, he replied, 'Well, in our way of thinking and our way of life, that is what it is to us. That is the way we were brought up. That is the way you are born and raised in these big Italian neighbourhoods.'

Although he was talking about early twentieth-century New York, it was a system and a way of life that his ancestors had transplanted into America from Sicily.

We have, of course, no written records detailing the way a young man would be identified as a possible future member of the Mafia, but through the Maxi Trials, which to all intents and purposes destroyed the second Mafia, and the problems faced by informers, we have some idea of how people were groomed and chosen in the post-war years. The 1980s war by and on the Mafia created characters that had never existed before – the *pentiti* (informers) who broke the code of silence, *omerta*. Many informers came forward not out of any altruistic motives but quite simply because they were seeking police protection from assassination.

The emotional turmoil they then suffered as a result of leaving a group that was to them far more important than blood family led many to seek psychiatric help. One of the doctors most involved with them, and who published widely in the professional journals, was Dr Girolamo Lo Verso, a psychiatrist in Sicily, who learned much from his hours of discussion with these people.

Dr Lo Verso describes most mafiosi as coming from and belonging to a blood family with a Mafia tradition. The boy (no women were initiated) would grow up in an emotional environment in which he had to demonstrate the male characteristics of strength, manliness, silence and contempt for the police. The members of the extended family who were 'made' men would teach the traditional Sicilian values of honour, respect, faithfulness and silence. He would learn that the relatives who had been imprisoned were victims and he would have been visiting jails from an early age to see uncles and cousins who would be represented within the family as heroes.

It would be made clear to him that he ought to be fearless, violent and good with his fists, and as he grew up he would be encouraged to sleep with as many girls as possible, if for no other reason than to prove that he was not gay. If he showed any sign of being showy or loud, he would not be chosen. The type of person the organisation sought to recruit was the strong silent type: a man who asked few questions and never gave any answers. He might be advised to avoid buying a newspaper in public so that no one could see what he was reading and what interested him. It also went without saying that if he drank alcohol he should never ever get drunk or even uninhibited, except with 'friends' – in other words, other 'made' men.

If, by the age of 18 or so, he had satisfied these requirements, he would go forward to the 'practical' classes, where he would be taught about guns and might be asked to shoot a 'cuddly' animal such as a dog or a horse. His reactions would be assessed. Then it would be a human. Could he kill without emotion?

This might seem unbelievable, but there was absolutely no fear that anyone would inform or that the police would take any action on this 'test' murder. Of course not everyone could kill in cold blood, but that in itself was not an obstacle that would debar them from membership; their role in the organisation would just be modified.

In other civilised Western European societies, the sort of mindset of people like this, who must complete the course and be initiated, seems extraordinary. On the other hand, over the last century Europe has experienced not only the industrial killing of Jews in which many 'normal' Germans took part, but also the atrocities by Serbs on Muslims in the former Yugoslavia, the Ukrainian treatment of the Poles and the Turkish slaughter of Armenians. And away from Europe, Hindus and Muslims in India, Shias and Sunnis in Iraq, Pol Pot's followers in Cambodia, and Hutus and Tutsis in Rwanda have demonstrated that ordinary people are capable of inflicting great brutality.

The difference between these people and 'normal' citizens is a psychopathic personality. Most forensic psychiatrists now hold the view that the development of a psychopath is not environmental but genetic. Research has shown that most psychopaths have lesions in parts of the frontal lobes, the area that governs thinking and reactions. A psychopath never thinks ahead, he has no concept of 'tomorrow' or the consequences of his actions. The *now* is the important thing and temporary loss of control in a challenging situation is, for them, the norm. They are the sorts of people who kill on impulse, perhaps as a result of an unimportant quarrel, or cause physical injury while they have road rage.

Interesting studies have also been performed that show unsuccessful criminal psychopaths (caught) have less prefrontal grey matter than successful (not caught) psychopaths. So even within a group, there are differences. Not all psychopaths are the same.

But why does the world so frequently see 'clusters' of psychopaths that appear from time to time, especially in wars? Just as there are clusters of conditions such as lymphomas or other cancers, which appear to be more common in one place than another, there is no reason to believe that this cannot happen with a brain abnormality that creates psychopathic behaviour. It is not inevitable that these brain patterns will lead to criminal behaviour. Many successful entrepreneurs have this sort of personality, and men such as Robert Maxwell may well have had a similar behaviour pattern and have been just as ruthless but in a different direction. He was an enormously successful man, who treated both his staff and his opponents badly. The level of his intellectual and emotional violence, if replicated in a deprived 'street' scenario, might well have resulted in murder.

When Dr Lo Verso asked selected mafiosi how many people they had killed, few were able to answer accurately. When Giovanni Brusca, a violent mafioso whom we will meet later in the book, was asked this question, his answer was 'certainly more than 100 but less than 200'. Brusca, who evaded capture until 1996, was also implicated in what became known as the 'Room of Death' in Palermo, where systematic torture and killing was carried out during the 1980s Mafia war. One of his weapons of interrogation was a chainsaw.

Men with attitudes like this are not very different from today's Islamic terrorists. Neither type has an individual mind, only a group affiliation. Life in itself has no meaning, neither their own nor their victim's – only the group has life. The reason that Islam glorifies suicide bombers is that the religion glorifies suicide in the teachings of Allah. This is not reflected in the Catholic faith; in fact, it is the opposite. Someone giving absolute obedience to the group rather than valuing his own being will live in his own world with an exalted sense of his self-image, believing that he is living in the real world and others are not. This could only happen in a male-dominated group. Mafia and Islam have this in common because women are not part of the so-called 'struggle'; they are chattels of their husbands and to kill them for a man's 'honour' is still not unusual.

Such men may well be able to hold down a perfectly ordinary job, fit into society at every level and even be reasonable next-door neighbours. This was demonstrated in London in 2005 when the July bombings were carried out by young Muslims from Yorkshire known to everyone in their communities and well thought of. In one case, even the bomber's wife was unaware of her husband's mindset. It was not secrecy: she was not part of the group struggle and therefore was not included.

Some of the occupations of the 350 people given long sentences at the Maxi Trials in Sicily in 1989 were landowners, stock breeders, contractors, guards, bricklayers, petrol-pump attendants, motor-vehicle dealers, fruit vendors, butchers, drivers, bar staff and grocers. The Mafia at this time was far more than a gang of criminals; it was a cross-section of Sicilian society. These men were victims of the history of their island and saw this method of governance as being superior to anything that Rome had to offer.

Not all initiates, however, have to demonstrate that they have the ability to kill without emotion. Every major organisation needs specialists: there have to be people such as doctors, lawyers, politicians, explosives experts, chemists, sea captains, pilots and translators. While they may be excused from violence, they have to follow all the other ordinances of Mafia life, especially silence and discretion. If we accept that the vast majority of people in these professions are not criminals, then their involvement with the Mafia must raise questions. Have they been coerced, or do they see it as a form of Freemasonry?

At a lower level, if the recruiters were to look outside blood family for members they might identify a young man who showed signs of being a good thief, pickpocket or burglar and they would arrange, provided the other aspects of his personality fitted the profile, that he was 'made'. It was as if competence at crime was the equivalent of a university degree – and the university from which people at this level graduated was often prison. If someone was confined in jail for a period of time, his behaviour when faced with hardship, stress and danger might be closely observed. If he passed the tests, then he might possibly be initiated.

Entry rituals are standard and harmless fun in many organisations – military academies, college fraternities, even curling clubs – but none of these has the binding effect of the Mafia ceremony. You can be initiated as a Freemason, change your mind and walk away from it and no harm will befall you, but you don't do that after initiation into the Mafia.

There are at least 13 reasonable descriptions of the Mafia initiation ceremony, and although some of the detail varies the common theme is a bit of minor bloodletting, the burning of a picture of a saint and the swearing of an oath. The ritual is a simplified version of that carried out by the Carbonari, who used blindfolds, knives, blood and a picture of Saint Theobald (the reason for which is obscure).

One of the first descriptions of a Mafia initiation ceremony came from Dr Melchiore Allegra, who in 1916 worked in Palermo at a military hospital where his job was to examine young men prior to call-up. It was widely believed, at least by the rural population, that the army in the north castrated Sicilians, so it was not only because they wanted to stay at home and avoid being shot at by people with whom they had no quarrel and who didn't threaten them or their families that they sought to mislead the examining doctors! One of the favourite tricks was to inject a knee with turpentine and iodine, which would cause an inflammation that would render the knee stiff and probably painful forever more – but it was better than castration. Other tricks included drinking phenolphthalein to imitate blood in the urine, or eating gunpowder to cause lung inflammation and anaemia. The doctor was very sympathetic to all the dodges, but it was not his consideration for draftees that got him into the Mafia, it was a frontline action.

Dr Allegra treated a man who had been shot and afterwards did not tell the police. He was subsequently visited by a man called Giullio D'Agate, he said, and together they talked of 'this and that'. He did some further favours for D'Agate and then one day D'Agate arrived with two other men. The doctor was invited to go with them to a fruit shop, where he was shown into the back shop, where there were several other men. D'Agate gave a eulogy about the good doctor's 'seriousness of outlook', then Dr Allegra was given a holy picture – featuring a saint, with a prayer written on the back – and his right thumb was pricked and blood smeared on the picture. He was then told to say 'I pledge my honour to be faithful to the Mafia as the Mafia is faithful to me. As this saint and a few drops of my blood were burned, so will I give all my blood for the Mafia, when my ashes and my blood will return to their original condition.'

While he was saying this, the holy picture was held in his cupped hands and set alight by a candle. One of the men cupped his hands over Dr Allegra's so that he would not drop it.

As he was a doctor, he was not asked to commit a murder; instead, money was produced so that he could buy a clinic and practise in the town of Castelvetrano and in the ensuing years he treated many men with gunshot injuries, at all times staying silent and avoiding discovery.

He did not confess these details voluntarily. It was tortured out of him by the fascists in 1937 and published in the magazine *L'Ora* in 1962.

In the first Mafia, a man would behave in a sombre manner, as would his family. He would have a well-tied cravat, a pot belly and shiny shoes, but only if it was appropriate within the village. On a Sunday he would go to church wearing a jacket and a homburg and he would sit in the pews with the women rather than stand at the back smoking with the other men. Gallantry, good manners and generosity to friends were important. The Catholic faith and its values would be followed, and so divorce or separation was out of the question. The priest would be invited to all family celebrations and the family would all go to church together not only on Sundays but also on all Holy Days of Obligation. Their children would be baptised and take instruction prior to having their confirmation and first communion. And just as it is in Italy even today, mothers would be worshipped and regarded with affection till the day they died and children would be idolised as gifts from God.

In the first Mafia, daughters would marry as virgins and the entire community would attend a wedding feast that would have up to 20 courses. The wife of a mafioso would get added respect and have a privileged place within the community, but she might well not have a deep relationship with her husband. Like many rich Saudis today, a husband could sleep with prostitutes and have mistresses provided he maintained discretion. For the wife, things were not so lax, however: if she made her husband *cornutu* by being unfaithful, she would almost certainly be killed. Wives and daughters who were given the best of everything were in turn expected to keep up appearances as members of the perfect family.

This concept did not die with the first Mafia. In 1980, a Calabrian boss ordered his daughter to be killed when she had an extramarital affair, even though she had five children. And in 1981 when the underboss of the Villagrazie family was arrested while in bed with a woman who was not his wife, he was deposed from office.

Once admitted, the new recruit would join a Mafia family consisting of anything from ten to over a hundred members, and each family would be organised in a similar way. The top three men would be the *capo* (chief), the *sottocapo* (sub-chief) and the *consiglieri* (adviser). Every group of ten *soldiers* would be led by the *capodecina* (head of ten men). Although this seems like a linear management system, the soldiers did not just work for the *capo*. Each group of ten would have their own 'patch' and they would keep the profits from extortion, skimming, loan sharking and robbery. The *capodecina* would obviously get more than the soldiers and he in turn would pass a percentage on to the *capo*. The groups would also be encouraged to make monetary tributes to the *capo* at Christmas and also on his saint's day.

A further layer was added at the suggestion of the Americans in the late '50s, namely a Commission, which would have one representative, a *capi mandamento*, for each contiguous three families. This was another failure of the American mindset of thinking that every institution in the USA should be grafted onto each of those in other countries. The Americans wanted the head of the Commission to be the *capo dei capi* (chief of chiefs), who would rule all the Mafia activity on the island. This, of course, never had a hope of functioning in Sicily because the Italian nature demands independence of thought, style and activity, a habit reflected in the fact that there are so many parliamentary parties and different types of Masonic lodges (see Chapter 23).

There would always be a clustering of small families around a big one and alliances between rural and city families, since both the city and the rural families had something to offer each other. The city offered better scope for business, while the country supplied labour, hideouts, temporary manpower and alibis.

If the *capo* of a small family vanished or was killed, the members might be reassigned to neighbouring families and their territory subsumed. Sangiorgio, a nineteenth-century commissioner of police in Palermo, described how men from a couple of families would be the kernel of what he described as a *cosca* in each town and village. *Cosca* is the word for an artichoke with overlapping segments – peel off one, you find another underneath, and so on. Each *cosca* with its *capo*, *sottocapo*, *consiglieri* and *capodecina* was arranged territorially and the stronger the *cosca* the more territory it would control.

Each *cosca* would be associated with some legitimate association where their new members might be initiated. These might be political clubs, friendly societies, religious confraternities or a Masonic lodge, but the feature common to all was that they would be connected to a political party.

At the end of the nineteenth century, it was this connection between criminals and the Establishment that puzzled the police. How could seemingly respectable people associate with known killers and kidnappers? But the association with whichever club was primarily for another reason: recruitment. Young men from non-traditional Mafia families could be assessed as to whether or not they had the qualities required for a lifetime in the Mafia. If a man was not already a professional or a businessman, his being initiated into the Mafia would be a passport of entry to the middle class. This was underscored by the fact that the clergy, the social and spiritual leaders which rural Sicily took much more seriously than did any other European country, were often mafiosi.

There were many similarities between the Mafia and Freemasonry in that all within the organisation become social equals: if a peasant or a plumber was 'made', then he and his family would get as much respect as an aristocrat or a doctor.

The difference between the Mafia and Freemasonry, however, was that behind this apparently honourable, well-behaved and integrated group lay violence. Their brutality outweighed any charitable claims and showed that they only paid lip service to their idealistic concept of 'the noble peasant' – the reason it all began.

4

PORTRAIT OF A GODFATHER

The only autobiography of a Godfather ever written was by the American gangster Joe Bonanno, more commonly known as 'Joe Bananas'. In 1983 (well after the *Godfather* films), he published a book entitled *A Man of Honour*, but instead of an exposé of Mafia life it was romantic, self-justifying nonsense. We learned nothing of Bonanno – other than the fact that he was a vain old man with false modesty – and even less about the Mafia. This is not surprising because even though Bonanno was born in Sicily, he spent his whole life in America heading one of the five famous New York families that ran organised crime. He was, however, more Sicilian than the other bosses because he spoke only the near incomprehensible Sicilian dialect and admitted only Sicilians to his family. Although by the end of his life, when he wrote the book, he was basking in enormous wealth and the enjoyment of living at home rather than in prison, he had as much resemblance to an old-school Mafia Godfather as Stalin has to Thatcher.

The term 'don' is not a word that is exclusive to the Mafia; it is a title that was formerly applied to any prominent man in any village. My grandfather was known as a don and he was a million miles away from crime. Of the old pre-war Godfathers, probably the best known was Don Calogero Vizzini. His home and seat of power wasn't Palermo, Bagheria, Trapani or Agrigento, which are the present-day urban Mafia strongholds, but a small town in the middle of western Sicily called Villalba.

Travel around Sicily and you see dozens of little towns like this – colourless, sad, empty and evocative of unpleasantness. There is no beauty. In Villalba, none of the houses is painted the vibrant colours one sees in Spain, Portugal or Greece. There are no greens, blues and yellows, or the sweep of red-tiled roofs with rust and cream facades that make Tuscany and Umbria so beautiful. Sad is the word. Villalba is set on the side of a steep hill with one main cobbled street running through it at a steep angle, bordered by small houses, which look peculiar. At first you might not notice, but then you'll realise that all the shutters are closed. While you can see no one, everyone can see you. Today there are probably no more than 2,000 people living there.

Calogero was born on 24 July 1877 to a peasant father who had married into the Scarlatta family, which owned some land, and that made him almost middle class when the only middle class were lawyers, teachers and doctors.

Calogero did not bring corruption to Villalba; he was born into it. When he was four years of age, he would have seen the 214 men on the electoral register in the village rounded up, locked in a granary and released six at a time to make sure that the Marquis was elected. To him, what we would call election rigging was not a crime or anything dishonourable, it was just the way elections were run.

His family owned a little piece of land and they were well connected to the Church. His uncle was Bishop of Muro Fucarra and his cousin was Bishop of Noto, having achieved this position by virtue of founding a monastic order. His brother also went into holy orders and became parish priest of Villalba, so it appears that Calogero was the black sheep of the family, having neither the patience nor the desire to study, and certainly not the sanctity to join the rest of the family in the Church. In fact, he remained illiterate throughout his life.

From his teens, Calogero developed into a tough guy or a

thug, depending on your scale of values. He was bigger than average, with a forceful personality, and would have been good with his fists. I, of course, never set eyes on him but, looking at old photographs, he appears to be about five foot six or seven, which is very big for a Sicilian at that time, and he must have weighed around 200 pounds.

That he was violent as a youth is probably what set him aside from other men his age and guided him to the top of the old Mafia. An example of this was his wooing of the daughter of the rich Salazzos. The family were not happy for her to become engaged to a young tough from the wrong side of the tracks, so in return Calogero forbade her from seeing anyone else. After a while she attracted an official from the magistrate's court, but after he had been to visit her he was beaten to death by person or persons unknown. Probably as a result of this, the girl never married: but nor did Calogero.

Calogero's first job was as a *cancia*, which involved transporting grain by horse and cart to a mill 50 miles away. This was a high-risk job because of the perpetual risk of hijacking and violence, and man-management of aggressors was an essential quality for the position. The tracks down which the cart had to travel were bordered by relatively high walls in many places; if you were driving the cart, you *knew* that there was likely to be someone behind that wall waiting to kill you for your load. The walls were good cover because a killer with a *lupara*, a sawn-off shotgun, would not be seen till the moment he opened fire.

No one knows how Calogero survived his journey down 'death alley' but survive he did, perhaps by making deals with the local brigands led by Paolo Varsalona, and he was never harmed.

Calogero must have had a fairly active youth because by the time he changed jobs at the age of 21 in 1898 he had twice been cleared by the courts on murder charges on account of collective memory loss by the witnesses, a pattern that was to emerge as a Mafia trademark over the next century. He and his friends then set about terrorising the owners, peasants and guards of the Suora

Marchese estate. When the owners had had enough, they put it up for auction – and there was only one bidder!

This was a frequently used tactic of mafiosi at the end of the nineteenth century: terrorise owners, kidnap relatives, burn crops, murder guards, discourage recruitment and damage machinery. Then when the estate goes up for sale, apply the same violence to any others who are misguided enough to consider bidding. Then, bingo, it's yours for a knock-down price.

The owners would have had no one to complain to because the town may have had only two policemen and they in turn owed their jobs to the mayor, who in turn owed his votes to the Mafia. There was never any proof and if some did come to light then it would disappear – but only after it had been 'secured' in the safe in the police station.

By securing a large estate, Calogero gained his place in society, his future income and local respect. Like all super-rich people, he was able to become benign and help members of the community. Although it is said that Don Calogero was made a mafioso in 1902 at the age of 25, this is almost certainly a fable because he would never have been permitted to terrorise an estate and then occupy it had he not already been initiated. Furthermore, had there been another Mafia family in the area, and had Calogero not been associated with it, the owners of the estate would have paid them for protection and Calogero would never have been able to gain control.

He settled down to oversee the running of the estate and gradually made his way up the ladder of power in the national Mafia to become the undisputed head of the organisation in the province of Caltanissetta by the beginning of the First World War.

Giuseppe Amico is tall for a Sicilian but, even in his 80s, he is erect and very fit. He owns the bar where Calogero used to hold court every day, wearing his usual collarless shirt with baggy trousers held up by braces. Ask him about Don Calogero and he will say, 'He wasn't a mafioso, he was a gentleman. He was born a gentleman, died a gentleman and lived like a gentleman. He only did good for people and was loved by everyone. He came to my bar every day and talked to everyone, sorting out all their problems. Every three weeks or so, I sent him a bill for his coffees and drinks and he always paid immediately. He was *uno vero signore*, a real gentleman.'

Amico had, of course, not known him when he was young. He bought the bar in 1948 and only knew Calogero in his golden years. He delights in telling the story of what he considered Don Calogero's greatest triumph, which was to stop Duke Francesco Thomas de Barberini from throwing peasants off land that they wanted redistributed. The peasants were led by Calogero's uncle, the priest Scarlatta, and Calogero acted as 'mediator' (which might mean that a horse's head appeared in someone's bed). As a result the peasants who were faithful to the Church got access to more land – and Don Calogero added another 290 hectares to his already large estate.

When Mussolini came to power and banned the Mafia and the Freemasons, Don Calogero tried to ingratiate himself with the leader by giving a handsome donation towards the March on Rome, but this didn't stop him suffering the fate of most of the other dons. Although he found himself in internal exile in the godforsaken village of Tricarico in Basilicata in 1928, he had stored up other favours that freed him. In 1922, he had given shelter to a young Fascist who was being sought for murder, actually hiding him in his own home, so, in 1933, by which stage that young man had risen in the Fascist Party to become an under-secretary in Mussolini's Government, Calogero was liberated.

A general practitioner I met, whose name I shall withhold, is the son of the local doctor who certified Calogero's death on 19 July 1954 from heart failure. As he was dying in the arms of his nephew, he managed to wheeze, 'How beautiful is life.' It might be easy to say this when you are a multi-millionaire, but this was not the case for Calogero. Although he was extremely rich, he was a simple man who never learned to read or write and dressed in a way that today would be described as shabby. And in this, he was typical.

5

A REPUBLIC WITHIN A KINGDOM

In any poor community in Sicily in the early nineteenth century, there were three choices for a boy. He could become a priest, he could stay with his parents and help in the fields, or he could become a bandit. After 1870, a fourth choice emerged, namely emigration to the Americas.

Between 1876 and 1924, 17 million Italians left their homeland to travel across the Atlantic and over 90 per cent were from the South. In 1900, the population of Sicily was four million; ten years later, it was halved. Between 1898 and 1914, there were never fewer than 40,000 Sicilians a year emigrating to America and some years it was five times this number.

As tales of riches were fed back home, it became the dream of every Sicilian working man to go to *L'America* and, considering the awful living conditions of the time, the wonder was that any stayed at home. Those who remained did so probably in order to look after ageing parents.

There were many reasons for this mass emigration. As a result of Roman Catholic teaching, the birth rate had always been high, but it was normally accompanied by a high perinatal mortality, meaning that the population remained static or, if it grew, it did so slowly. With the advent of slightly cleaner water, however, there was a slight fall in the perinatal mortality rate and the effect was chaotic. This small change caused a 20 per cent increase in the population and, quite simply, they ran out of food and water.

In addition, the condition of the land was fast deteriorating. The deforestation that had been going on for centuries had finally caused irretrievable soil erosion so that only the valleys and the coastal areas were fertile. An 1870 law that confirmed primogeniture meant that what land there was could no longer be run as a family cooperative and so many were left with the choice of emigrating or starving.

Even those who had successful estates felt the pinch because the market on which their riches had been built – the citrus fruit market – had now collapsed. Not only had America stopped buying Sicily's citrus crop, with Florida and California now supplying their domestic needs, but they were also now competing with Sicily for what international markets remained.

The straw that broke the camel's back, however, was Prime Minister Crispi's tariff war with France. Italy in the 1870s had been flooded with so much cheap American grain and Asiatic rice that the government imposed a tariff, primarily to protect agriculture in Piedmont. In 1887, Crispi raised the tax on imported wheat by 10 per cent. A year later, he increased it by a further 10 per cent. France replied with a discriminatory tax against all Italian goods and foods, to which Italy again responded. The result was a two-year period during which, due to excess food supplies, the price of wheat fell by 50 per cent, putting Italy effectively out of the markets. But the really big losers were the South and Sicily: wheat was the only export crop of the South and when the farmers could not sell it, the social consequences were disastrous.

As if a higher power were telling Sicily that it was doomed, there were also two major earthquakes, in 1905 and 1908, as well as a destructive viral infection of all the olive and citrus trees.

As a result of the huge exodus to America after 1880, almost every family was now split, with at least one member living in one of the Americas. This meant that people became more informed: instead of knowing little of the world apart from the town in which they lived, Sicilians were being introduced to a wider canvas. They were now being told of the life and opportunity afforded by *L'America*, as well as the new Italy and its neighbours in the north of the peninsula. The boys who had been called up to serve in the Italian Army discovered that not only were they not going to be castrated but there was also another Italy in the north where life was better.

Most of this information was by word of mouth because there was no radio or television and, although the illiteracy rate had fallen from 86 per cent in 1871 to 68 per cent in 1901, only three people out of ten could read – and the majority of them were professionals, aristocrats, politicians and priests. This compared very unfavourably with the rest of Italy, where illiteracy had fallen in those same 30 years from 42 per cent to 17 per cent.

Many Sicilian men with drive went back and forwards, making some money in America, coming home, spending a few months with the family, buying a little more land and then going back to make more money while the family worked the land. One of these men, as we will see in Chapter 11, was the father of the famous bandit Salvatore Giuliano.

Those who remained were increasingly unhappy with their lives, but the clergy were on hand to comfort them. They taught the poor to be patient and content with their lot, while the Church, assisted in many instances by the Mafia, saw to their needs. It was the Sicilian way of life.

Although the number of leaseholders increased after 1860 from around 2,000 to 20,000, Garibaldi, by trying to 'do good', had inadvertently made life worse for the peasants. Under feudalism, the superior would allow his peasants to feed their animals on his land and also to collect wood, berries and herbs. With the abolition of feudalism, the non-landowning peasants lost these rights. There would be no present of a side of pork at Carnevale, no free shoes, no wool or cheese from the shepherds. No one was available any longer to give the peasant credit facilities and there was no aid, such as medical care or commodities, in the off-season. Perhaps the biggest loss for the peasant was that he and his family were no longer part of a community. He lost his job security and there was no hope of his children being employed when they grew old enough to work. Under feudalism, if he had become ill, he would have expected to have been given lighter jobs, but now he would be laid off if he could not work. If he was conscripted, he would not get his job back when he came home.

It was not only the peasants who were in trouble. The leaseholders, and many *gabellotti* who had signed and paid for leases in the good times (and they had to pay upfront), now found themselves in difficulty. The price of their produce was falling, especially after the trade wars with France, and the labour force was also diminishing because of emigration. When this happens, the cost of labour invariably rises and so, as a result, many of the big leaseholders started renting to peasants directly. Since rents traditionally had to be paid in advance, peasants who had no credit facilities were forced to take loans from the owner, thus putting them into permanent debt because the risks of production in a depressed market had now passed on to them.

There was another clash of ideals that left the peasant class worse off and that was the outcome of the anti-clericalism espoused by the Northern 'intellectuals'. Prime Minister Crispi had decided to break up monastic estates and to either sell or redistribute their land. It was a populist move in the North that backfired in the South because the majority of Sicilians were much attached to their Church, not only because of religion but also because for many it had been a source of employment and aid. In fact, very poor families relied on monastic charity.

Another important consequence of this anti-clerical attitude in the North was that the clergy in the South and Sicily were pushed into the arms of the alternative form of government that was developing – the Mafia.

In many ways, the actions of the priests in Sicily in the late 1800s mirrored the behaviour of priests in Central and South America 100 years later. Their primary concern was for the poor of their parishes and they would side with any group that helped them look after these families. In Central and South America, it was the communist sympathisers; in Sicily, it was the Mafia. This mutual 'aid' also had the effect of totally legitimising what started as the Sect and the dons at its helm, men who were a million miles away from our present-day impression of Mafia gangsters.

Throughout the nineteenth century there were revolts in Sicily, first in 1848, then in 1860. But when there was another in 1866 it showed that all was certainly not well in the utopia that Garibaldi thought he had created. It was basically the culmination of the grumbling civil unrest against the occupying troops from the new Italy of which Sicily was now an unwilling part.

At the Commission of Inquiry set up in May 1867 to look into the reasons for the 1866 revolt, the role of the owners of the large estates – the aristocrats – became clear. The first witness, the mayor of Palermo, the Marquis di Rudinì, said that crime in Palermo was not only stronger than the law but also stronger than the government. In order to protect themselves, ordinary people were turning towards the Mafia, but in most instances the protection that the Mafia was selling was protection from themselves, as they were the embodiment of crime. It was a polite way of describing extortion.

But this extraordinary situation had another twist. There was more to it than just paying the Mafia; they also had to play along with the system, which in turn was also protecting the Mafia. In other words, there was a system that created ties of solidarity and mutual interest between the Mafia, their victims and their friends. None of the Commission had ever come across a situation like this, where a whole population, not just a few villagers, played along with a system in which the victims were protecting the victimisers. Even the police and the army were in on the system; they all knew who was who and what was what but there was never enough evidence for any criminal conviction and so arrests were rare. Most importantly, they realised that this was not a system limited to one or two villages but involved the whole country.

One of the most important witnesses was Baron Turrisi Colonna, an old aristocrat who virtually admitted to the existence of the Sect that was the Mafia. He had been brought up in the feudal tradition, where the feudal superior had a duty of care to his serfs. Turrisi Colonna could have walked away from his feudal responsibilities, as many did, to go and party in Palermo, but, with a social conscience that was not as rare as it might appear, he chose to keep his estates working as profitably as possible in order to employ the maximum number of people. This meant getting protection.

He had chosen as his chief *campiere* a man called Antonio Giammona – a 'made' man. He had worked in this position for the baron since the 1850s, which suggests that the system was in place well before Garibaldi set foot on the island. The baron's attitude was probably guided by an instinctive sympathy for the peasants; if the Mafia gave protection to his employees, then he would play along with the system for the greater good. He could afford it and everyone was happy.

He told the Commission that his concept of the Mafia was a sect that gave and received protection from anyone who lived in the countryside, from tenants to stock-herders. He himself protected people like Giammona by virtue of his position. If Giammona had a problem with the authorities, then the baron would speak to those in power and attempt (invariably successfully) to have the affair forgotten. If someone got hurt or killed, then it was probably because he had threatened the baron's estate, but the police would find no witnesses.

After Garibaldi, people like Turrisi Colonna had no reason whatsoever to side with the State against their fellow islanders. As far as the baron was concerned, being ruled from Turin in Piedmont was even worse than being ruled from Naples by the Bourbons. At least the Bourbons understood Sicily; the response of the Piedmontese to problems on the island was merely to impose higher taxes and to snatch young Sicilians away to serve in their army rather than share in family care at home.

The most curious thing about the baron's evidence is that he chose to side with what might be regarded as lower-class criminals rather than with the State. Although it would be the norm in the nineteenth century for a man in his position to side with the government, one can easily understand why he took the position that he did.

I had the opportunity to discuss this with a nonagenarian baron in the Bagheria area whose father had actually known Turrisi Colonna. He confirmed to me that his own ancestors would have thought in exactly the same way. He repeated what I had heard over and over again: that the first 'good' Mafia was merely a Sicilian way of life.

State employees were by and large poorly educated and socially of similar rank to people like Giammona, but more importantly they were doing nothing very obvious to better the situation, even though it was in their power. They had little empathy for the lives of the majority, their main aim being to skim from the tax revenue they were able to raise. Had there been a viceroy, a court or a similar kind of State presence, then men like Turrisi Colonna might have taken a different position and there might never have been a Mafia. But what he saw was one group of people, of whom he had a reasonable if not high opinion, trying to help another group of people that his ancestors would have been able to help with ease. If the 'new men' kept some wealth for themselves, then well and good – as long as they didn't flaunt it.

Turrisi Colonna confirmed to the Commission that a system such as his existed in every small town and village around Palermo. The Sect had no fear of public forces or the judicial process, and the police had come to an understanding that as long as the Sect remained well behaved they would not interfere. The baron and his like, therefore, became the bridge between the first Mafia and the State, ensuring that the wheels moved smoothly.

Another aristocrat, the Duke of Cesaro, from Agrigento, when asked about the situation said that the Sicilian aristocracy had always been united with the people. For those aristocrats who took their feudal responsibilities seriously, this certainly was the case. From the Mafia point of view, doing business so openly with an aristocrat was less profitable than other avenues because it meant that there was less to plunder or bleed with protection demands, but the big advantage was the connections that the aristocracy had with the police, the judiciary, the military and the politicians.

The central government certainly did not help the situation in Sicily. Although there had been a government of Italy since 1861, the first Prime Minister to set foot on the island was Guiseppe Zanardelli, in 1903. He was shocked by the conditions he found there, commenting that they were 'a scar on the face of modern Italy', but his attempts at reform were negated by the delaying tactics of local politicians and the Mafia, all of whom had an interest in keeping the status quo of dependency.

Three years later, someone who knew all about Sicily, since he had written a long report on the island 30 years previously, became Prime Minister. An Italian Jew with an English mother, he was the tall, slightly stooped Sidney Sonnino. He put Sicily high on his list of priorities and set out to put its economy on a par if not with the rest of Italy then certainly with the rest of the South.

It was the beginning of the twentieth century, the Boer War had ended and Queen Victoria had died. It was at this time, during a golden period for the whole of Europe, that Sonnino's proposals led to his ruin. The Mafia objected to his concept of provincial banks and extended credit arrangements and his ideas to provide state education for all with some primitive social benefits. Their opposition, voiced through their puppet politicians, was so great that there was a vote of no confidence in parliament and Sonnino's Government fell after only 100 days.

It was a landmark event for Sicily because all future governments learned from this and left Sicily alone. They understood the system of 'local governance' and also realised that they would get no support if they wanted to enforce change. What followed became the template for Italian administration of not only Sicily but the whole of the South for the next century. Society fed off patronage from central State development agencies in return for the maintenance of political office by assured electoral support. By the end of the nineteenth century, there was a social compact in Sicily whereby the Mafia controlled life with the connivance and knowledge of the aristocrats, State officials, police, Church, judiciary and probably the Italian government.

The first Mafia reached the height of its power at the beginning of the twentieth century. Between 1900 and 1922, with the system of proportional representation enshrined in the constitution, the Prime Minister continually changed, but for most of the period it was Giovanni Giolitti, who did absolutely nothing about Sicily. He did not use martial law or seek to bring in new reforms, nor did he try to suppress the Mafia, which in turn kept a very low profile, with spokesmen usually denying its existence and passing it off as just a Sicilian 'way of life'. He kept patronage flowing and confirmed the traditional dominance that Sicily held over the vital ministries of Public Instruction, Public Works and Postal Services. In exchange, he demanded that Sicilian deputies showed absolute obedience to his party.

Today, the word 'Mafia' is invariably linked to crime, but this was not the case before the Second World War. In the criminal scene in Naples or New York, there was always a sense of social hierarchy. Politicians were gentlemen and criminals were not. Politicians did white-collar crime: bribery, graft and market fixing; for criminals, it was prostitution, extortion, illegal gambling, violence and robbery. But in every country – America, Italy and even the UK – both sides need the other and sometimes collude through a Chinese wall. This was never the case in Sicily because there was no 'crime' as we understand it. There were no Chinese walls.

As the Mafia developed, it did so as a semi-autonomous, alternative form of political control to the less well-administered State government. Since illiteracy among the peasants was widespread, they could not defend themselves adequately in the face of the law and so could not react if challenged. They would depend on information from middle-class professionals, such as doctors, teachers, priests and lawyers, who themselves might well have been mafiosi.

In other words, Garibaldi had created a Republic within a Kingdom.

6

EXODUS TO L'AMERICA

C hain migration is the process used by every emigrant
group who leave one country and go to another. The
pattern consists of a group from a village, town or region locating
themselves in a new environment, becoming established and
then helping relatives and friends to join them. The new arrivals
are provided with initial accommodation and employment is
arranged for them; they subsequently do the same for their
relatives and friends. After some years, the initial location
becomes too crowded, so new immigrants are moved to a
neighbouring town and the process starts again, with those
established in the initial location holding a social superiority
over those who arrived later. There are many examples of this
in the UK, with Asian and African communities concentrated in
one town or district.

The reason that the first Sicilian community established itself
in New Orleans was that there was plenty of work. As a result
of the American Civil War, the majority of the black population
had moved north both to get away from the past and the legacy
of slavery and to exploit the greater opportunities in Northern
cities. This left a gap in the ditch-digging business.

Since Hurricane Katrina in 2005, we are all familiar with the
unique geography of New Orleans and its system of canals and
levees. The town was built on a delta and a swamp and the only

way to keep it dry was to create a system of waterways and ditches. Since the black population were leaving and the Irish immigrants were 'bettering' themselves, there was an employment vacuum, which the Sicilians filled with alacrity.

It says a lot about peasant life in Sicily at the end of the nineteenth century that so many people were willing to face the perils of swampland diseases such as black-water fever, malaria and yellow fever, which had killed so many of the original British settlers in West Africa.

Malaria did not pose as much of a threat to Sicilians as it had done to the Irish because the disease was endemic in Sicily and many immigrants would have had an immunity to it, which would lessen the severity of attacks. They would still get two or three bouts a year, which they would sweat out over a few days, but to them it was no worse than a bad bout of influenza. But yellow fever was different: it could be fatal. In fact, it almost stopped the building of the Panama Canal. Due to the dirty water supply, cholera was also as prevalent in their new homes as it had been in Sicily.

Although, in present-day terms, the death rate was enormous, on the whole, life was much better in America than it had been for many at home. The newcomers were liked by their employers and probably felt appreciated for the first time in their lives. This was because they worked more efficiently than the former slaves and were content with minimal shelter. In a relatively short time, many were able to buy some land, which, to their delight, was far more fertile than the rocky soil they had left behind. Work was easy to get and Sicilians arriving in New Orleans met others who spoke their strange dialect and so there was little need to learn a foreign language. By 1890, 10 per cent of the population of New Orleans was Sicilian.

The first immigrants moved from ditch-digging to running smallholdings, and the more successful of these went into the fruit and vegetable trade. The first settlers then rented their plots to new immigrants and so the ladder of graduation from poverty to minor prosperity was established. Soon what had been called the French Market was renamed the Italian Market. Some, like Joseph Macheca, even rose to become steamship owners, which was a pathway to real wealth because the boats not only brought in money from passengers and freight but were also floating casinos (gambling was illegal on dry land in Louisiana but not on the river when the boat was moving).

It was also easy to get tooled up for a life of crime because obtaining a gun licence and guns was as easy in nineteenth-century America as it is today. Such was the lax attitude towards arms that a new immigrant from any part of the world could get a gun licence within a week of disembarking at Ellis Island.

In New Orleans, the two major crime families were the Matrangas and the Provenzanos. The reason that the Sicilians did not follow the Irish from digging ditches to middle-class jobs was down to a young Irish policeman who got involved in the battle between these families. The particular episode also led to the Sicilians going north.

The potato blight and the resultant famine of 1845–49 meant that the Irish arrived in New Orleans and New York 50 years before the Sicilians. Like the Sicilians, they had started as ditch-diggers, road-builders and railway labourers, but, by the end of the century, they had moved upwards and onwards. When the Sicilians arrived a generation later, the children of the original Irish immigrants had graduated from labouring jobs to the public services and politics.

No white Anglo-Saxon Protestant would ever have considered joining either the police or fire services because the pay was low, the hours were long and the work dangerous, so by 1865, when the Irish formed 13 per cent of the American population, they also formed 33 per cent of the police force. It wasn't a good job, but it was more comfortable than digging ditches in a swamp, and it was available. Just as a young Sicilian village boy had the choice of being a labourer, a priest or a bandit, so those choices existed for a young Irishman in America – but for bandit read cop or fireman.

One of these young Irishmen was David Hennessy Senior, who arrived in New Orleans just after the Civil War. He had a good Yankee war record and had stayed in the South to join the New Orleans Police, where he was developing a good career and was widely popular . . . That is until he was killed in a pub brawl by an ex-Confederate soldier. At this time his son, also called David, was nine years of age. Due to his father's popularity, he was looked after by the police and when he was 11 he was given the job of police messenger.

When Hennessy was old enough, he joined the police force and quickly earned a good reputation. He was well known for beating up burglars and also became famous because he was the man who not only caught but also publicly beat up the mafioso Giuseppe Esposito in Jackson Square in the city's French Quarter. This was the sort of thing that played well for cops on the rise.

Esposito and a bandit named Antonino Leone had both kidnapped John Forester Rose, a young English entrepreneur in Sicily, almost starting a war between Italy and Great Britain. Leone was caught, but Esposito managed to get out of Sicily and make his way to New Orleans, where he changed his name to Vincenzo Rebello and started a new life of crime.

By the time Hennessy captured him, Esposito was the head of the local Sicilian Mafia. The police had Esposito deported, ignoring the pleas of Macheca, the steamship owner, who in typical Mafia-speak had asked them to 'reconsider'. Hennessy held firm and Esposito was extradited to Rome, convicted of six murders, and died in chains in jail many years later.

As a result of this triumph, Hennessy was put in charge of fighting Italian crime, but his career was interrupted by an internal dispute about promotion in the police service that resulted in his shooting his rival, for which he was tried for murder. Although acquitted on a plea of self-defence, he had to resign from the police force.

He quickly obtained other work for a private security firm and it was while working in this role that he took the side of the

Provenzanos against the Matrangas, the rumour being that the price of this support was ownership of a brothel!

Since he was due to testify against the Matrangas on 13 October 1881, he was given a bodyguard in the shape of another Irish cop, Sergeant Bill O'Connor. On the day before the trial, while going home accompanied by O'Connor, they parted at the entrance to the street where Hennessy lived with his mother. As O'Connor walked away, he heard a whistle and then some shots. He rushed back to find that Hennessy had been hit in the abdomen, chest, elbow and right leg. Bending down over his injured friend, he asked him who did it. As he slipped into unconsciousness, Hennessy whispered, 'The Dagoes got me, Bill.' He died 12 hours later.

There followed arrests of any Italian thought to be involved in crime, including Charlie Matranga and Joseph Macheca, but after a full investigation only nine men were put on trial.

When the jury gave its verdict on 13 March 1891, it cleared six men but could not come to a decision on the other three; however, as other charges lay on the books, all nine were returned to prison. Immediately after the trial in the street outside the courtroom, a young lawyer, William Parkerson, wound up a mob by telling them that before the trial more than $75,000 had been raised for the Italians' defence. The mob, which by this time had grown to almost a thousand, descended on the jail, demanding entry. When this was refused, they broke in past the helpless (and perhaps complicit) guards and lynched eight of the nine who had been tried, including Macheca. Another couple of Italians who had nothing to do with criminal activity, who were just standing in the street, were also hanged, one from a lamp post. But they missed Matranga, the 'big boss', who went on to lead a prosperous life rather like Don Calogero, dying a rich man in his bed at home in 1943.

The lynching was reported around the world and received universal approval, even in *The Times* in London. The Italian government, however, was enraged and America was forced to make reparation to the relatives to the tune of $25,000.

The streetwise Sicilians heard the message loud and clear – and went to New York. There, they discovered that they were amateurs at organising crime and corrupting politicians. Once again, the Irish had beaten them by 50 years.

The Society of St Tammany (named after a mythical Native American chief) had been established in Philadelphia in 1798 in order to protect the values of the Revolution. It was originally a social, fraternal and benevolent organisation, but by the time it was functioning from 14th Street in New York it had taken on a different hue: it was now used to influence the political process. Soon after they arrived, the Irish saw its importance and gradually infiltrated its ranks, being appointed as precinct captains, ward bosses and aldermen.

Long before the famous Gangs of New York carved their names in history, Tammany had used gangs to pull in votes in order to fix elections. A successful politician would own one or more speakeasies, saloons, dance halls, brothels or gambling houses – and would employ tough young Irishmen to guard and administer them. They therefore had virtual private armies that literally fought their election campaigns. It was in the interest of the gang members that their party won and so votes equated with survival: if your man won, you didn't go hungry, you began to get some power and you could take your first step out of the slums.

In New York at that time, the graduation process for a young man was usually from street gang to neighbourhood gang then on to one of the big gangs before being recruited by a Tammany Hall gang. One of the biggest Tammany gangs was the Whyos, two of whose leaders, Danny Lyons and Danny Driscoll, had been judicially hanged. One Whyo called Piker Ryan was arrested with his 'tariff' in his pocket, which consisted of an escalating series of violent acts, starting with $2 for 'black eyes' and $15 for a 'broken leg' through to $100 for 'the big job'.

By 1890, the Irish had begun to dominate civil service jobs, especially in the fire and police departments, and so there was no longer an imperative to be associated with a gang. The gangs therefore gradually assumed a more multi-ethnic composition, and as the Irish moved out of the slums and up the social scale their places were taken by the Italians and to a lesser extent by the newly arrived Central European Jews.

The Five Points district of New York is where five streets converge – Canal, Chatham, Pearl, Centre and the Bowery. At one time there were 1,500 members of the Five Points gangs and, although there were some Irish, German, Slavic and Jewish members, the majority were Italian – however, in this context, Italian does not equate with Sicilian. This is an error that has been constantly made in the perception of American crime throughout the twentieth century.

The Italians who formed the New York and Chicago gangs were mainly Neopolitan, with some other southern Italians, such as Pugliese and Calabrians. There has never been any love lost between the Neopolitan Camorra, the 'Ndrangheta (pronounced *indraahngita*) of Calabria and the Sicilian Mafia because their modus vivendi has always been quite different. Unlike the Sicilian Mafia, the former two were always both essentially criminal organisations with no pretext of accepting social responsibility. Very seldom has a non-Sicilian joined the Mafia, so no Sicilians were Five Pointers.

When they arrived in New York, the Italians and Sicilians lived in three adjoining streets, namely Elizabeth, Mott and Mulberry, on the Lower East Side of Manhattan. And to this day, the area is called Little Italy.

When an immigrant arrived, he would expect to be housed by a relative or someone with whom he had kinship. He would share a room with many others who would arrive and depart on a rotating basis; he might even sleep under the counter of the shop or bar in which he worked. His behaviour would be observed and if he 'passed' he would be guaranteed a bank loan and might set up a small business for himself.

The Mafia existed but did not function in any way other than claiming the usual *pizzu* from fellow Sicilians, which was to them and their kin the way of life. They did not join any of the multi-ethnic gangs because there was a language barrier: not even other Italians could understand what they said because the broad Sicilian dialect most of them spoke is virtually incomprehensible.

It was too early for them to go into major crime because there was not enough political influence to get any protection when an arrest was made. New York was not a Sicilian village where *omerta* was automatic; in America, not only would fellow Sicilians be willing witnesses if they had been harmed but there were also the Irish, Poles, Jews and especially other non-Sicilian Italians who were even more willing to inform.

The Sicilian organisation in New York was the Black Hand Gang. Their system of extortion by threatening letter was similar to that which had existed in all of southern Italy since the nineteenth century. They were known as *lettere di scrocco* – scrounging letters – and would be written in rather flowery, over-elaborate and polite Italian, a style known as *dialetico*. The letter would merely ask for a sum of money to be deposited somewhere. It would also contain a threat as to what would happen if the person failed to pay or if the police were told. The letter would be decorated with skulls, bones and daggers and smeared with blood – and always a drawing of a black hand. While it may have been Mafia or Camorra inspired, ordinary hoodlums or petty criminals found that it was often a surprisingly easy way to make money. On many occasions, a recipient who refused to pay would be murdered or his business damaged by a bomb or vandalism – but often, to confuse everyone, nothing happened. The recipient, therefore, faced a problem: failing to respond to a serious threat could be dangerous, complaining to the police was ineffectual, but paying a local 'kid on the make' would be maddening.

Someone who was certainly involved in this was one of the first Sicilian Godfathers to flee to America, Don Vito Cascio Ferro. He was an anarchist (fashionable at the time) who got involved in emigration by acting as an intermediary between the desperate peasants and the American employers. The peasants were given their fare by Cascio Ferro but then had to repay him the initial fee for services as well as massive interest. He arrived in America in 1901 from Corleone, Sicily, after being accused of 20 murders. In America, he made his fortune as the leader of a Black Hand Gang and was an expert operator of *pizzu*. He became *capo* in New York and was into everything from meat, fruit, fish and wine to sulphur, salt and organised labour, and protected everything from country houses to beggars' pitches. His appearance was what would be expected of a 'new look' mafioso: tall, aristocratic, good-looking with a groomed white beard and always well but not flashily dressed. He was depicted in *The Godfather: Part II* as the man the young Don Corleone followed by jumping from roof to roof, eventually shooting him as he was opening the door of his apartment after an Italian gala day. This, however, is pure fantasy.

In January 1908, a lady found the remains of Benedetto Madonie, his legs having been amputated and his torso stuffed into a barrel, along with his decapitated head. This story, of course, made wonderful headlines and the New York newspapers had a field day. Their glee was enhanced when the NYPD created a branch for 'Italian crime' and they made a well-known policeman, Lieutenant Joseph Petrosino, its leader.

Joe was a Calabrian, a big man and a popular figure of the time because, as was common in the police force, and as we saw with David Hennessy, he always indulged successfully in personal violence. He solved the 'body in the barrel' case by surmising that the murderer was, like Madonie himself, a counterfeiter and they had obviously quarrelled, with Madonie losing out.

Everyone in law enforcement knew that the Lupo Morello gang was involved, yet the police department made the mistake of putting them all in jail together, which gave them a chance to consolidate their alibis. Only one was put on trial, Tomas 'the Ox' Petto, and he was acquitted because of lack of evidence. The most important member of the gang, Don Cascio Ferro, managed to escape. He went back to Sicily, where he re-established himself at the head of the Palermo families and almost certainly arranged the murder of the New York cop sent to find him, Joe Petrosino.

In spite of this, Joe became a hero and people believed that he had the measure of the Italians. He started to stop suspicious Italian immigrants at the dockside and had great and public success in having others deported; his popularity at the time could be measured in column inches in the New York newspapers. Petrosino's boss, Thomas Bingham, thought that there should be collaboration with their Italian colleagues and so it was arranged, with a lot of publicity, for Joe to visit Palermo. It was not a very subtle move: on top of all the publicity as he sailed from New York, he was met by the press in Palermo, where he landed on 10 March 1909. Two days later, as he was waiting for a bus under the statue of Garibaldi in Piazza Marina in Palermo, he was shot, probably by Don Vito himself, using a .357 magnum, a weapon that produced a force that not only obliterated his face but spread his brains over the pavement.

Don Vito never admitted to the murder of Petrosino, but in 1930, when he was questioned after imprisonment by the Fascists, he said that he had only ever murdered one man by his own hand. It is likely that man was Joe Petrosino.

The officer who put him in prison, Cesare Mori, came to be known as 'the Iron Prefect' and his anti-Mafia work would disable the organisation for more than a decade.

7

MUSSOLINI AND THE MAFIA

By the 1920s, the Mafia way of life in Sicily was moving from the country to the cities. While Italy had been denied many of the benefits of the Industrial Revolution, lacking a sufficient source of coal, it did have a well-developed railway network, which helped concentrate business in the cities and allowed a reasonably successful trade programme within Europe.

As embryo industries were starting up and dependence on agriculture was lessening, the development of the cities was seen as a source of income by the Mafia in the same way that they had profited from protection in the countryside. By the 1920s, most successful businesses in Sicily were paying *pizzu* and in return were protected by those people who were also threatening them. From being a purely rural phenomenon, the Mafia was on its way to becoming an urban way of life.

As the economy grew, so did the Mafia's income: the trade-off was that some of the traditional values disappeared. The new leaders started to display their wealth, behaviour the old-school Mafia would have disapproved of. Some bought cars or built grand houses, others travelled, but all mixed in the highest social circles in the cities. For a time, mafiosi were indistinguishable from Freemasons (apart from the fact that Freemasonry was dedicated neither to profit nor violence). It was becoming more and more obvious that it was they, and not the government, who made the decisions – and not only on the large estates but also for the whole of Sicilian life. But the new leader of Italy, Benito Mussolini, wasn't having that.

Mussolini was born in Emilia Romagna in 1883, the son of a blacksmith and a teacher. He himself became first a teacher, then a labourer, then an author (writing the blasphemous book *The Cardinal's Mistress*) and then joined the Socialist Party. At the age of 29, in 1912, he became the editor of *Avanti* (*Forward*), a magazine that not only put forward the Socialist philosophy but whose title was also redolent of the name Berlusconi would use almost a century later for his new party – Forza Italia (Go Italy). Above all, Mussolini was a patriot. He had fought with the Italian Army in the First World War on the side of Britain, France and America, and although he did not achieve heroic status he was given an honourable discharge after being wounded. He disagreed with the Socialist Party's view on the war and its acceptance of the post-war reparations, and in March 1919 founded the Fasci di Combattimento (Fascist Movement) in Milan. He was well ahead of his time in realising the strength of the media because he also founded a newspaper called *Popolo d'Italia* (*The People of Italy*) and remained the editor even when he was Prime Minister (again redolent of Berlusconi's media interests).

In 1920, he formed the paramilitary *squadrismo*, who were used to break up strikes and undermine the Socialist dominance in rural areas of the North. Squads would descend on villages, destroy Socialist Party offices, purge members of that party with castor oil and beat them up – while the police watched.

Eventually, they destroyed the Socialist Party and by 1922 Mussolini's party had 300,000 members. This gave him enormous bargaining power and in early October 1922 he was able to demand four Cabinet posts in the government. Things quickly got better: within two weeks, the King invited him to become Prime Minister. This did not reflect the admiration that the King had for Mussolini; rather it was an act designed to prevent the King's cousin, the Duke of Aosta, from carrying out a coup. Mussolini became the King's insurance against a *coup d'état* and so he was kept as Prime Minister until 1924, when his power had become so encompassing that he was able to change his title to Il Duce, meaning 'leader'.

He then became the first Italian politician to re-involve the Vatican in Italian affairs. The settlement he reached with the Vatican led to the establishment of the Vatican Bank, which would come to be used to launder the drug profits of the second Mafia (see Chapter 21) and this piece of political wizardry would have far-reaching effects before, during and after the Second World War.

One of the terms of the Lateran Treaty, the name of this settlement, was that Freemasonry should be banned because it was abhorred, feared and mistrusted by the Catholic Church. Mussolini had no particular designs on the Mafia until he visited Sicily in May 1924. There he found that although the discipline and values of the Fascist Party were admired, there was neither a structure nor a power base. The party had not been permitted to open local branches because this would have compromised the old-style patronage, a cornerstone of Mafia rule. Also, to a militaristic patriot like Mussolini, Sicily's poor record of recruitment in the First World War was an anathema. While not overly sympathetic to the young men who had excused themselves for fear of castration, it was a visit he made to Piana del Greci, a village just south of Palermo, that made up his mind that the Mafia had to join the Freemasons in his plan of destruction.

This visit came about because he asked to see a typical small community on the island. The authorities chose Piana del Greci because it was close to Palermo, was easy to access and had the interesting history of being a place that had been settled not by Italians but by Greeks and Albanians hundreds of years previously. The local don, Ciccio Cuccia, was not a typical old-style Mafia don like Calogero or Cascio Ferro. He was one of the first to start flaunting power and position in society. He was boastful, showy and arrogant, demanding rather than earning that quality vital to any successful mafioso: 'respect'. On meeting Mussolini, he asked why all the police and bodyguards were with him. He insisted that there was no need for them because in Piana del Greci, Il Duce was not in Italy, not in Sicily, but in the domain of Don Cuccia and he would protect him.

It got worse. He asked Mussolini to get rid of his bodyguard and when Mussolini refused, Don Cuccia, in a fit of temper, emptied the piazza so that Mussolini spoke to a man and a dog. One of the policemen that Don Cuccia pushed aside with the insult *'sbirro'* (meaning something like 'dumb cop') was Cesare Mori.

Had it not been for this simple episode, it is unlikely that Mussolini would have interfered with Sicily. All he really wanted were some Fascist offices to be opened so that the symbolism of Fascism could flourish, and of course he would have expected some funding for his party. As it was, the insult was so gross that it necessitated a response.

It has been said that police and criminals are the same type of people operating on different sides of a line. This was certainly true of Cesare Mori. He was a 'tough guy' who always had a tendency to settle problems at a physical level, man to man, rather than use the normal legal channels. He was a Northerner, from the Milan area, and his career in the *carabinieri* was progressing well, with a record of violence against criminals, until he went a little too far by publicly beating up a local councillor in the city of Ravenna for carrying a knife. At this point, to stop further scandal, he was posted as far away from Ravenna as possible – to Sicily, to the town where Dr Allegra had had his clinic paid for by the Mafia: Castelvetrano.

While there, he was able to indulge in his usual violent methods. He applied them against all wrongdoers, but occasionally he made a mistake: he was able to identify bandits, but had never understood what the Mafia was. He presumed mafiosi were simple criminals. While beating up bandits was OK, beating up mafiosi wasn't! Yet Mori survived and was moved to Turin, from where he was promoted to Prefect of Bologna. In 1925, he would return as Prefect of Palermo to Sicily, where he was charged with the task of destroying the Mafia.

The first Mafia did not really understand the Fascists, just as 60 years later the second Mafia underestimated the investigative magistrates Giovanni Falcone and Paolo Borsellino. The mafiosi thought they were untouchable and that the Fascists were no different from any other weak Italian politicians, but they got it very wrong.

In the August 1925 elections, they supported anti-Fascist candidates with slogans declaring that the anti-Fascists were not bullies. And there was a price to be paid for their stance.

One of Mori's first moves as Prefect of Palermo was to invite the gross Don Cuccia to a cocktail party in the Ucciardone prison. Don Cuccia foolishly accepted and stayed in that prison for the rest of his life, without trial. Mori then turned his attention to the Don of Dons, Don Vito Cascio Ferro.

He was arrested and tried in 1930, accused of the murders that had caused him to flee to America decades previously. Don Vito put forward the usual defence of the time that there was no such thing as the Mafia; it was just how things worked in Sicily. However, Mori had made a rule that anyone using this defence was tacitly admitting he was associated with the Mafia and so Cascio Ferro was found guilty and sentenced to life imprisonment.

He spent the rest of his life in prison, dying in 1943, when the jail was bombed by the Americans. Ferro became a legend in prison, setting up a social security system for prisoners' families, wearing his own clothes, having meals brought in from outside and being treated with deference by the guards and governor. In this, he may well have been the model for the character Mr Bridger, memorably played by Noel Coward in the original film version of *The Italian Job*.

Mori knew the value of 'theatre' to the Italians. Anything he did was trumpeted. He knew how to use the press and after a few months there was no doubt left in the mind of any Sicilian that Mori's retribution would be greater than anything the Mafia was capable of inflicting. He persuaded landowners who had sheltered the Mafia to turn them in and, once in, there was no doubt about conviction because to use the 'rustic chivalry' defence was deemed a confession of Mafia association. He used torture during interrogation – it was during one of these sessions that Dr Allegra's 'confession' about the initiation of a mafioso was recorded – and he banned the carrying of all guns and knives, except, for some illogical reason, the traditional shepherd's tomahawk, which was classified as a tool!

Mori carried out sieges of Mafia strongholds; a number of those who surrendered were 'suicided', leaving no doubt in people's minds as to which was the stronger force. By 1928, he had arrested and convicted over 11,000 people, some of whom were not mafiosi. He invited every *gabellotto* in the Palermo area to swear allegiance to Mussolini and the Fascist Party. He made it voluntary and the response was 100 per cent – because the alternative was imprisonment.

Between 1924 and 1928 murders in Palermo dropped from 278 per year to 25, which by any standard of crime prevention is impressive. He also tried to discredit the Mafia in the schools by making compulsory teaching by the ONB (*Opera Nationale Balilla*), the Italian Fascist youth organisation, which instructed that *omerta* was not manly and was 'trumped' by the laws of the land.

As there was no available list of members of the Mafia, Mori could only guess as to whom to round up and he ended up imprisoning anyone who was denounced to him. There is no doubt that a lot of old scores were settled during this period and many non-mafiosi would have been jailed. People, such as doctors and lawyers, who were in the Mafia and had kept a low profile would keep things that way, putting 'businesses' into storage.

After shoals of complaints from an angry Palermo population, in June 1929 Mori was called back to Rome by Mussolini, with congratulatory telegrams extolling how well he had done his job. The more probable reason for his recall was an investigation he had carried out that had exposed prominent members of Palermo society and parliament – people who had the ear of Mussolini. Mori was retired, disappeared into obscurity and died in 1942.

There is no doubt that Mori damaged the Mafia severely, but he did not eliminate it. Those who were accused of Mafia association might have been put in prison but most were merely sent into internal exile on one of the Aeolian Islands, such as Ustica, or on the mainland to tiny villages in Basilicata or Calabria. Most top mafiosi were, in fact, just too smart for him and their contacts were even better. Don Calogero and his neighbour, Don Genco Russo, were among them. In Chapter 4, I explained how Don Calogero escaped long imprisonment. His neighbour and deputy, Don Genco Russo, the boss of Mussomeli, was repeatedly charged with murder, extortion and violence, but he only ever served three years because of lack of evidence and the 'disappearance' of witnesses.

There is also no doubt that many mafiosi espoused the Fascist cause because it had a sense of order that was not unattractive to them. After the Second World War, however, having been imprisoned by the Fascists was a useful thing to have on a curriculum vitae because, to the Americans, it meant you were a 'good guy'!

When the Americans arrived in Sicily in 1943, they found an organised structure of anti-Fascists waiting to be used; men who would become the nucleus of the vastly different second Mafia. Meanwhile, back in America, gangsters had become both rich and popular.

8

Prohibition and Profits

It is doubtful whether the second Mafia would have evolved as it did had it not been for organised crime in America. There, crime had nothing to do with the traditions, values and functions of the first Mafia: that is why Sicilians will correctly deny that their Mafia had any part to play in the famous Capone years.

Although you will never hear a Sicilian use the term *Cosa Nostra* – meaning 'our thing' in Italian – when referring to the first Mafia, it cannot be denied that what the emigrants brought to America was their own way of doing things. It had nothing to do with the Irish, Jews, Calabrians, Neopolitans or Corsicans, though they adopted the concept.

The term had never before been heard in public until 1953, when it was uttered on television by one of the first informers, Joe Valachi, as he was giving evidence to a hearing in Washington on organised crime in the United States. From that point on, it was wrongly applied to organised crime Italian-style, as it had little to do with what had started more than 100 years previously in Sicily.

The Sicilians despised and distrusted all other Italians. Very few non-Sicilians were ever made mafiosi in America and it would have been quite impossible for Sicilians to have allied themselves with the Jews or the Irish since no foreigners were even recognised on a Sicilian's radar – they were all potential enemies and to be avoided.

Had it not been for a Minnesota congressman called Andrew Volstead, American crime would probably never have become organised, nor would it have had the wealth to organise itself along the lines of a business. Quite simply the foundations of the second Mafia were established by Andrew Volstead's Act, which in 1919 proposed the banning of the sale and consumption of alcohol – Prohibition.

Nearly 90 years later, it seems absurd to us that this was even attempted. It turned out to be an enormous error of judgement because it not only grossed the body of criminals around $5 billion but it also earned them a degree of respectability, indeed affection, that they had never previously enjoyed. It encouraged more people to choose crime as a way of life because there was now a certainty of gain without social stigma. The risks came not from the outside bodies that should have been enforcing the law but from within the crime community and thus were more easily managed. Unlike their predecessors, who slunk around like the common criminals they were, the nouveau riche gangsters, popularised in the press and giving the public what they wanted, moved around with freedom and respectability.

The Prohibition lobby in America after the First World War was a moral crusade. It was coloured by a degree of patriotism because the major brewers were of German ancestry and had helped pro-German causes during the war. To small-town white Protestant America, drink was also associated with the black population and venereal disease. The result of Prohibition in America, therefore, was to set rural against urban, Catholic against Protestant, and Church against laity.

Prohibition also changed the drinking habits of at least two generations of Americans. Spirits were rarely imbibed outside 'joints' before the new law but thereafter became the staple drink of the middle classes, who vied for creativity in cocktail recipes.

The Volstead Act failed for three reasons: it was unpopular, it was under-policed and it was easily beaten and bypassed.

Today, health educators are successful in stopping people smoking because they have the sense not to ask that the sale of cigarettes be banned. Their campaigns also work because in general people do not like the smell of tobacco and most smokers wish they could stop. Not so with drinking. People who drink enjoy it and, unless they have an addiction problem, they do not want to give it up.

It is estimated that to have implemented the law successfully would have required 250,000 agents, but there were actually 100 times fewer deployed – 2,300.

The myth of the Untouchables, a small group of law-enforcement officers at this time known for their fearlessness and incorruptibility, promoted by the television series based on the life of its leader, Eliot Ness, bore little relation to reality. In fact, when it was first screened, a number of surviving Untouchables said that the image presented was quite false. The series was based on a book that a near-destitute Ness had written in the 1940s, but unfortunately he died shortly after the series began.

Furthermore, J. Edgar Hoover, one of the most enigmatic men of the twentieth century, backed off and did not see – or wilfully refused to see – the dangers of Prohibition. The FBI continued to stand by while criminals became rich, popular and, most of all, organised.

One of the weakest points of the Prohibition Act was that it did not include industrial or medicinal alcohol, nor did it apply outside a 12-mile coastal limit. What the legislators forgot was that the Great Lakes were bigger than 12 miles and this put their Canadian shores beyond the law, allowing Canada, which had a form of Prohibition, to be used as a base. Although Canada had cooperated with the law by banning exports of liquor specifically to America, their ban did not cover the rest of the world. Shipowners therefore would fill in forms declaring that they were bound for Cuba, but no one would display either surprise or curiosity when the same ship returned having completed the round trip within 24 hours! It took little to persuade the customs officials to turn a blind eye to what was going on.

Cuba came into the frame because it was the source for molasses. It was due to the contacts made during this business that the Americans realised the potential for Cuba as a gambling resort in later years. Networks were established that would eventually lead to the building and operating of American casinos that, in the pre-Castro days, acted as yet another cash cow for the Mob.

On the south side of Lake Michigan lies the city of Chicago, which first became a town in 1837 when the government christened it 'Gateway to the West'. This was not an idle piece of 'spin' but an essential investment to encourage the establishment of a greater America in the west. Within three years, the investment paid off and by 1840 the population had increased by a factor of three to almost 5,000. By 1928, it had reached three million, making it the third-largest city in the world. The new people were not from the east coast establishment looking for adventure, they were the new immigrants. By 1925, only 25 per cent of Chicago's population were native-born Americans, the other 75 per cent being either born overseas or the children of new immigrants. The city was also the favoured destination for newly freed slaves who wanted to escape the culture of the South following the Civil War. As the city's black population increased, so did racial tensions, but there were no open confrontations until after the First World War in 1919.

The main incomers were from Central Europe – Poles, Czechs, Hungarians, Slavs and Scandinavians. Italians formed less than 5 per cent of this multi-ethnic population and this came to be reflected in the make-up of the street gangs, which, for most youngsters, were the University of Life. Boys learnt by observation and developed an attitude of independence, indifference to law and order and an acceptance of fatalism. Those who rose to the top had organisational skills and imagination to see beyond the present and were quick and firm in making decisions. The rest admired these qualities and called them 'brains'. There were more than 500 street gangs in Chicago in the early '20s of which 45 were white American, 63 were black, 25 were mixed coloured and white, and 396 were made up of mixtures of European immigrants of different original nationalities.

At that time Chicago was no different from any other developing American city in that the political control lay in the hands of the Irish. They had been there longest and had seen how essential it was to control the political machine. The two men who ran the city's First Ward, an area that was home to 25 nationalities, were Mike 'Hinky Dink' Kenna and 'Bathhouse' John Coughlin.

One of the more successful Italian gang leaders in the area was 'Big Jim' Colosimo, who was born in 1877 in Calabria, in the toe of Italy, which was once part of the Kingdom of the Two Sicilys formerly ruled by the Bourbons. He had been brought to America as a child and worked initially as a water boy for street sweepers, eventually becoming union boss, which allowed him to pull in the votes that swung an election in Kenna's favour. As a reward, he was made a precinct captain, a position that gave him virtual immunity from police harassment and left him free to run his newly gifted brothels and saloons.

As a good, successful Italian boy, he did what his *mamma* wanted and in 1902 he married an Italian girl. Victoria Moresco was not what one might call a 'good' Italian girl, but she was a beautiful and successful Italian girl – the owner of two brothels. Most importantly, she had mastered the art of *la cucina italiana* and so Jim's mother was content that her boy would be looked after.

Colosimo strengthened the 'family' by bringing in his nephew, Johnny Torrio, who had 'brains' and who had become a successful leader of one of the Five Points gangs in New York. Young Johnny was a quick learner and rose from being Big Jim's bodyguard to running the family rackets. By then he needed a bodyguard himself and recruited one of his pals from the Five Points, Al Brown – or, as he had been christened, Alphonse Capone.

Colosimo enjoyed years of success but, as is usual for successful men, he lost his head, his heart and his judgement and left Victoria

Moresco for a glamorous American nightclub singer called Dale Winter. He got it all wrong. The Torrio gang might have emigrated from Italy, Capone might have changed his name to be regarded as American, but while you can take the boy out of Italy, you can't take Italy out of the boy: what Colosimo had done was not allowed, even in those non-Mafia circles. He had insulted his wife and the mother of his children, so, in the best Italian tradition, when he came back from honeymoon, he was shot, probably by his bodyguards, one of whom was Victoria's cousin, and the other the man who would become the biggest fish in the pond: Al Capone had the enormous good fortune of being in the right place at the right time.

While there may have been a moral reason for the murder of Colosimo, it is more probable that Torrio, like many young leaders in crime, industry and the professions, had grown impatient with the lack of eagerness of the elderly to espouse new techniques and new potential avenues of profit.

Torrio was not only ruthless but also clever and, unusually for a criminal, good at man-management. He expanded the organisation within Cook County and brought some skilful managers to the business. He developed a crude but effective system of assigning territory to each group with the application of some degree of profit sharing. He himself was teetotal and extremely careful of his behaviour. He had the sense to invest heavily in protection and never skimped on paying the police and judges. The chief of Chicago Police, Bill Fitzmorris, once acknowledged this openly, declaring that many of his force were actively involved in bootlegging. On the other hand, had Torrio not paid them well and kept them on his side, he could have been shut down to the advantage of another gang who might have been paying the police more.

The infamous mayor of Chicago, 'Big Bill' Thompson, was first elected in 1915 and promised a 'wide open town', meaning that gambling, prostitution, drinking and adventuring would all be permitted. Anyone coming to his town would be certain of a good time. One of his first gestures – dismissal of the Morals Squad – was welcomed by the many new types of people who had settled in Chicago.

Thompson continued for a second term of office during which time bootlegging, gambling, prostitution, the gangs and the police all benefited, but the open flouting of the law had become too much for the majority of citizens. As a result, he was beaten in the 1923 election by William Dever, a politician who captured the puritan vote and went on to apply the Prohibition law with some vigour and determination.

In the ensuing period of moral zealotry, the protection of criminals collapsed, which put a big strain on inter-gang relationships. Between 1923 and 1926 there were 135 gangland killings but only six men were ever brought to trial. There was no enthusiasm to spend public money on applying the law to criminals because it was clear that if things continued as they were, then the gangs were going to cull themselves.

Torrio realised that business could not go on as it had in the past, at least while Dever ruled, and so he moved his operation out of Chicago to the suburb of Cicero, which had a population of only 60,000, nearly all of whom were immigrants working in one or other of the five industrial plants that formed the town.

At that time, his gang had more than 800 people on the payroll, the majority of whom were of Italian stock; although there were also Jews, Poles and Slavs, there were no blacks. He had not migrated to Cicero because it was an Italian ghetto but because he was interested in profit, not ethnicity. The old Sicilian values of knowing who you could trust because they came from your village had long since disappeared. Johnny Torrio and his like did not live in villages and did not think like villagers. They thought like businessmen. The bottom line was profit and all that mattered was how that bottom line increased.

The important point about moving to Cicero was that Torrio would now be able to deal with a new administration, new judges and a new police force. Having achieved this, and by then having become an extremely wealthy man, he took a sabbatical and went back to Italy.

He installed Al Capone at first only as his locum at the head of the gang, fully intending to return, but then Capone got lucky. At the next election, in 1926, the Thompson campaign managers told him: 'Get us victory and Cicero is yours.' Using his control of organised labour, his background of getting votes out in New York and an in-depth knowledge of how to fix elections, he arranged for Thompson to rule Chicago at least until the end of the decade. And not only did he deliver the votes so that Thompson could be elected, he also gave the Thompson campaign $250,000.

And that is how the most colourful crime story of the twentieth century began.

Although always thought of as Italian, Capone was born in New York in 1899, the fourth son of Gabriel and Teresa Capone, who had emigrated from Naples in 1893. His father had had nothing to do with the Camorra and as a non-Sicilian he could never have become a mafioso – like most Neapolitans, he disliked and mistrusted all Sicilians. Al Capone, like many immigrant Italians of the period, was ashamed of his Italian background and did what most upwardly mobile Italians did: married an Irish girl, in his case Mae Coughlin, and changed his name to Brown.

Capone is famous not only because he won, but because he won with style. When he arrived in Chicago as part of Colosimo's gang, there were twelve other gangs involved in breaking the Prohibition law, but by the end there was only one man left standing. He had become a world figure and was not hated but admired and feared in a vicarious fashion. He had become a mythological figure and would have been more of a celebrity than many of today's icons. One of the main reasons for his success was that he wasn't greedy. In 1926, his turnover was more than $100 million a year, but he was putting 30 per cent back into paying police, politicians and judges.

Sixty years later, in the 1980s, this role reversal was also demonstrated in Italy when a whole raft of politicians were convicted of Mafia association. At one time the politicians had hired the criminals to get them elected, but as the criminals became more economically successful, the politicians became their servants.

After the Thompson election in 1926, there was no stopping Capone. He wanted to be number one and so he set about eradicating the opposition. He did this very successfully until only one target remained: the O'Bannion Gang.

Dean O'Bannion had teamed up with two Polish Catholics who had deceptively changed their names to Hymie Weiss and Bugsy Moran, and the source of their power came from the control of the Italian community's home-brewed alcohol industry, so-called 'alky cooking'. They had gained control of this by killing the clan that controlled it, the Gennas, who were the only purely Sicilian gang involved in Prohibition, all of whom were 'made' men from Sicily.

By this time Johnny Torrio had returned from his sabbatical in Italy and was acting as Professor Emeritus to his old gang. His position, though, was threatened when Bugsy Moran attempted to kill him and while Torrio escaped with non-fatal wounds, he was nothing if not a good listener. Having received and understood the message, he went back to his olives and vines in Italy for another spell.

Capone, although not a real Italian, knew an insult when he saw one and had no alternative but to get his revenge on Moran. The chosen day was 14 February 1929, when six of the Bugsy Moran gang, who had been lured to a garage at 2122 North Clark Street, were machine-gunned in what came to be known as the St Valentine's Day Massacre. The only reason Moran survived was because he was late for the meeting!

No one was ever tried for the massacre, but there is no doubt that it was ordered by Capone, who had the cast-iron alibi of being at his home in Palm Beach, Florida, and so was above suspicion.

This move left Capone totally in charge.

It was at this stage that he became a 'nice guy'. With all the money in the world, he opened soup kitchens during the

Depression, he helped many of the poor, gave money to the Church, ended the threat of the Black Hand Gang in Chicago and, like Don Calogero in Villalba, he found that when one has all the money and all the power, it's easy to be nice.

He lived showily in the Lexington Hotel, with two bodyguards sitting outside day and night with Tommy guns on their knees. He dressed extravagantly and wore his wealth in diamond tiepins and belts, showily dispensing money wherever he went and relishing the publicity he got in the newspapers, where his one-liners were always sought after by the press. He was openly flouting what little law there was in Chicago. In other words he was Neopolitan, not Sicilian – a show-off, not a plotter. And this was basically his downfall.

He was only in his early 30s when he contracted syphilis and his judgement started to fail. The disease comes in three stages. First is a sore on the penis and although this may heal, if the organism has entered the body's systems, a few months later the patient has bouts of mouth ulcers, warts and enlarged glands in the neck and groin, and the skin may be affected by acne, scabies or a rash.

After a quiet period of a few years, the final stage arrives. If the central nervous system is involved, then a patient loses feeling in the soles of his feet, suffers from leg ulcers and enlarged joints, and loses pain sensation. When the disease affects the brain, there are delusions of grandeur – the victim might think he is indestructible or untouchable, a condition that gradually progresses to complete dementia and madness. This is what happened to Capone.

As an example of his approaching madness, there is a story of a dinner he arranged with his two enforcers, the Sicilians John Scalise and Anthony Anselmi. Both had been involved in the St Valentine's Day Massacre and were walking tall, giving Capone the impression that he might be next on their list. Other gang leaders would have had them shot, but not a syphilitic Capone. He held a dinner in their honour and after finishing his eulogy on their skills he beat them both to death with a baseball bat.

Instead of enduring this deterioration in the bosom of his family, he suffered alone in prison.

In 1929, Herbert Hoover was elected President of the United States. He was a Middle American from Iowa and was incensed that what he had described as the 'Noble Experiment' of Prohibition had been beaten. He publicly committed himself to putting Capone in jail – as a new President, he could not be seen to be tolerating this sort of denial of state authority.

J. Edgar Hoover did not want his FBI to have anything to do with it, the Prohibition Bureau was too weak and so it fell to the Treasury's Special Intelligence Unit, led by Elmer Irey, to attempt to do the President's bidding. It took them two years and two trials, but eventually they proved that Capone had failed to pay over $1 million of taxes. The true figure was probably many times higher, but $1 million was enough. He was fined $50,000 and sentenced to 11 years in jail.

In 1933, he became a founder inmate of the newly built Alcatraz jail in San Francisco Bay and at the end of that year the Prohibition laws were repealed. Capone was officially diagnosed with syphilis while in jail and by the time he was released in 1939 and sent to his Florida home he was quite demented, suffering from a condition known as general paralysis of the insane. He was looked after by his family and died on 25 January 1947 at the age of 48.

Although Al Capone's name has become synonymous with Italian-American crime and thus the so-called Mafia or Cosa Nostra, he never set foot in Sicily. He was distrustful of Sicilians and helped Bugsy Moran get rid of the Genna clan, the only Sicilians operating during Prohibition.

Of the twelve gangs who started out breaking the Prohibition law, only two were predominantly Italian, plus the tiny Genna clan. Between the two world wars, the Sicilians were largely powerless in America; they were not major players in the crime business because they could not function as they had at home. There was no support system of extended family and friends, their dialect was incomprehensible to most compatriots and their isolation and exclusivity made them seem untrustworthy. They did form an association called the Unione Siciliana, but in true Sicilian tradition it did not function as a self-help group; in fact, it was the very opposite. It became a vehicle for vendetta and vengeance. And while the Mob prospered in the decade between 1925 and 1935, six presidents of the Unione Siciliana were murdered. But by the time it was all over there were a lot of very wealthy criminals in America, one of whom was to change the world of crime by getting it organised.

9

CRIME GETS ORGANISED

Apart from the Genna clan in Chicago and a minority of Sicilians who headed west, mafiosi never moved far from New York. That was where the refugees from the New Orleans lynchings had fled and where new immigrants arrived. There, they could meet fellow Sicilians who understood what they were saying; there was a meeting of minds. Although Little Italy in the lower East Side was unattractive, and was intensely uncomfortable both in winter and summer, it was a closed, manageable community, not unlike the agrotowns that the Sicilians had left behind them.

Everyone knew everyone else, a chain of respect could be established, *pizzu* could be paid and collected, and people understood the 'way of life'. The upside of this way of life was that if you kept your nose clean, there was a very good chance that the Mafia would help you if you had some problems.

Since New York was a port, Sicilian food could be imported directly and reach the local warehouses and shops within days, and when a relative arrived he could be in your house within a few hours. In fact, you could be on the quayside to meet him and take him to your home, which might be a small shared two-bedroom flat, but the smells would be familiar: prosciutto, olive oil and parmesan were always in the kitchen – and food and smells are important to all Italians.

The Sicilian Mafia in New York was never of any importance

or size until the 1930s, by which time the two main families, led by Joe Masseria from Trapani and Salvatore Maranzano from Castellammare, started to wield some power. They recruited family members from the immigrants or invited 'made' men from their home towns. These men would be recommended by contacts and when they arrived would be well looked after. The organisation used the same military-like structure as in Sicily, with *capo, sottocapo* and *consiglieri* dividing the soldiers into groups of ten, controlled by a *capodecina*.

It was the Maranzanos and the Masserias who spawned the famous five New York families that survived into the twenty-first century, and there was never any close relationship with the Chicago gangs that had become rich and powerful during Prohibition. Although similarly large profits had been made in New York from Prohibition, it was never as well known as the Chicago operation because in New York it was run by quiet, secretive Sicilians; in Chicago, the bosses were showy Neopolitans like Al Capone. The first bosses of the five New York Mafia families had at one time all been members of the Masseria or Maranzano families: Charles 'Lucky' Luciano, Vito Genovese, Joe Profaci, Joe Bonanno and Carlo Gambino.

It was at the height of the profitable Prohibition years that there was a first attempt to 'organise' crime in America. The first known meeting of the national crime cartel occurred on 6 December 1928 in Cleveland, Ohio. No one is quite sure why the police raided the peaceful meeting in the Statler Hotel: Cleveland itself was not at the centre of gangland violence and when it came to making huge profits from bootlegging it was peripheral to Chicago.

The meeting had been organised by Joe Porello, the leader of the Mayfield Road Gang, who were at the time at war with their rivals, the Lonardos. Since the Lonardos had not been invited to the meeting, it is probable that they tipped off the police in order to embarrass Porello, who had the unenviable task of bailing out the leaders of American crime from the local jail. More than twenty men were charged with possession of firearms and since they could not be freed without charge or penalty, the police fined them each $50.

To this day, no one knows why these important men were meeting at the behest of one crime family, but a second meeting six months later perhaps throws some light on what was being discussed and planned.

This gathering took place in Atlantic City in May 1929 and was attended not only by Italian-American leaders but also by mafiosi from Sicily. For three days, gangsters such as Al Capone, Charlie Luciano and Dutch Schultz negotiated and agreed on a charter in which they undertook not to attack each other, to confine their activities to their agreed territories and to cooperate against informers, police and investigators. Although dominated by Italians, it was a multi-ethnic summit, which showed that they had realised the benefits of cooperation and organisation rather than confrontation. But this was organising crime as a whole and, while the Sicilian Mafia took part, what these other men were up to had no bearing on 'our thing'. That was their birthright as Sicilians and had little to do with other Italians or Americans.

The real catalyst for the organisation of crime in America was a highly intelligent Sicilian who became the most influential man in the development of the second Mafia: Lucky Luciano.

Born in the sulphur-mining town of Lecara Friddi, near Villalba, in 1897, he was christened Salvatore Lucania. When he was ten, he was taken to the Lower East Side of New York City by his parents and brought up in Little Italy. He found the life of criminals fascinating. In the opening scene of *Goodfellas*, Ray Liotta famously says, 'As far back as I can remember, I've always wanted to be a gangster.' That could have been Charlie Luciano.

His first job was as a runner for the organisers of the local numbers game. When he was a teenager, he was arrested and charged with drug possession. Six years later he got his nickname 'Lucky' because he was found, bound and gagged, hanging from a rafter in a disused warehouse on Staten Island, with his face slashed from his right eye downwards and having suffered a severe beating as he hung. He had been left for dead, but he refused to talk to the police, saying that he would deal with it himself. The fact that he survived a brutal beating plus knife wounds gave him not only his nickname but also status within the gangs.

On 15 April 1931, Luciano invited his boss, Masseria, for lunch and to play cards at the Nuovo Villa Tammaro restaurant in Coney Island. Three hours later, the restaurant started to empty, with the diners leaving in pairs. When Luciano excused himself to go to the toilet, Masseria was left alone at the table. At that moment, four men burst in, among them Alberto Anastasia, and shot their boss.

When the police arrived, Luciano said, 'But who would want to shoot Joe?'

The answer was Charlie Luciano!

Luciano had a Jewish boyhood friend called Meyer Lansky – not the sort of friend a Sicilian boy would have been encouraged to make in the old country, but he stuck with Lansky for the rest of his life. The pair, plus Bugsy Siegel, another Jew, persuaded their criminal colleagues to behave in a businesslike manner and work under the aegis of the crime organisation formed in the '30s after Capone was jailed. When Lansky arranged for the murder of Masseria in September 1931, Luciano moved into the vacant position and became the top Cosa Nostra boss.

He was a very intelligent man and today would probably have reached the top in the City of London or on Wall Street because he had all the qualities of a successful executive. He realised that if crime were to flourish, then those perpetrating it should not only never quarrel but also never draw attention to themselves by hurting the public, the press or the police.

Luciano was as Sicilian as Capone was Neopolitan. He eschewed the flashiness of Capone and lived quietly under a pseudonym in the Waldorf Astoria in New York – all the time known within the underworld as *capo dei capi* of the Sicilian Mafia in America.

But at that time the American justice system either did not know of or recognise the word Mafia, and it certainly underestimated the cancer that was growing in its society.

One of Luciano's minor businesses was prostitution, his main income coming from loan sharking, illegal gambling and narcotics. He covered his tracks very carefully and because of a previous conviction the police had the impression that his main business was drugs, which in those days had a tiny market. They were astonished when in 1935 during a major crackdown on prostitution in New York they found that the big boss was Luciano. They also estimated that his income at the time from all sources was in the order of $10 million a year!

It was Fiorello LaGuardia who was the catalyst for the crackdown. He had been elected mayor of New York two years earlier, in 1933, and had thrown the Tammany organisation out of City Hall. There was still the rump of crooked judges and prosecutors, and the mayor had no way of knowing who was still on the take, even after carrying out a sweep of the obvious culprits. In 1935, he appointed an ambitious young lawyer, Thomas Dewey, as the youngest-ever chief prosecutor of New York.

Since 1931 Dewey had been a US district attorney to South New York and had made a name for himself prosecuting bootleggers and racketeers. The discovery that Luciano was a major criminal was not down to Dewey, however, but a young black woman called Eunice Carter. In the 1930s, she was lucky to get a job in the DA's office on account of her skin colour, but she provided the key that unlocked the door and exposed Luciano. Being female, she was naturally put on to the prostitution desk! Soon she noticed that all the prostitutes seemed to be represented by the one lawyer and always seemed to get off with a small fine. At first she could not interest Dewey in her theories, but eventually she persuaded him that prostitution was being run on a grand scale city-wide by an organised group of criminals. And she was proved correct.

On 1 February 1936, 150 police and detectives raided 70 brothels in New York and Philadelphia. Interrogation, as portrayed in the black-and-white gangster movies of the '30s, was violent and would involve unseen beatings that today would render all evidence null and void. But 1936 was another age and many of the pimps, prostitutes and madams talked. And the same name kept coming up: Charlie Lucky.

Luciano was a handsome man, with a full head of black hair, even though his features were typically southern Italian – thick and lumpy. His manner, however, was un-Italian; he was well spoken with very little accent. He was quiet and suave, apparently the soul of respectability, and even though the police had some suspicions that he might still be dealing in drugs, at that time prostitution trumped drugs.

His association with prostitution came as a complete surprise to the police. When he heard that they were looking for him on account of the testimony of prostitutes, he fled to a Mafia-owned spa in Arkansas but was traced and extradited. At his trial in New York, the evidence from the pimps, madams and hotel employees was compelling enough for the court to find him guilty on 62 counts of compulsory prostitution and in May 1936 he was jailed for 30 to 50 years. Dewey had triumphed, but he knew that the charge was manufactured and the sentence did not fit the crime; it did, however, fit his political ambitions.

Luciano should have stayed in jail until around 1980, but the Second World War was to be the catalyst for his freedom.

IO

LIBERATION, AMERICAN-STYLE

Sicily had a good war. From the time Italy entered the war on the side of Hitler in June 1940, apart from suffering some deprivation because of the Allied blockade of the Mediterranean, Sicily had not suffered much hardship. Although Germans were stationed on the island, they were there as defenders, not an occupying force. The island was self-sufficient in food and there was little in the way of hunger, especially in the countryside, where the farmers still grew tomatoes for the pasta sauce, garlic and herbs for flavouring, made sausage and prosciutto from their pigs and had a plentiful supply of eggs from their chickens, and milk and cheese from their goats or sheep. Wine and olive oil were never in short supply because the sun shone and the vines and olives flourished. The great heartache for most families was the loss of their young sons to the army, a good number of whom were sent to the Russian front never to return.

The majority of Italians had been surprised when Mussolini decided to go to war and ally Italy with their political but not ideological soulmates, the Nazis. Although he had supported the 'Nationalist' side during the Spanish Civil War, Mussolini had to balance up what would happen to Italy in the event of either a German or a British victory. He dallied and played for time until things became clearer, but when Hitler's troops cleared the British and French Expeditionary Force from European soil and Hitler's air force was 50 miles from London, Mussolini decided that Germany would win. This was a great surprise and disappointment to the British because at the time they were hoping to use Mussolini as an intermediary for peace after Germany had conquered France.

In the First World War, Italy had fought on the side of the Allies and Mussolini had been decorated, but he had felt cheated when war reparations were decided. Italy had not been very good at fighting, but it had suffered tremendous casualties and its reward was, in his opinion, negligible. Gabriele D'Annunzio set up a dissident group in the city of Fiume, near Trieste, where Mussolini visited him several times, but he never had any faith in following D'Annunzio's style of political dissent.

The reason Mussolini joined Hitler was that he reckoned if he didn't join him, then Italy would also be invaded and he would be deposed. As it was, the least he could have expected by being on the winning side was the return of Provence and Savoia, which had been taken from Italy during the Napoleonic Wars but which Piedmont saw as an integral part of their province. But by then the fervour and strategic thought that had done so much good for Italy had been replaced by vacuous self-delusion and, with his forces woefully understrength, he was hopelessly unprepared for what was to follow. As the war went on, and the Italian Army and Navy stumbled from defeat to defeat, his position with the Germans became increasingly weaker.

As far as the civilian population was concerned, government of the country went on as before, with Fascist control at local, regional and national levels. Sicilians in the south-west listened every night to the incessant bombing and bombardment of their neighbouring island, Malta, and many prayers would have been said to the Virgin, thanking her for sparing them that suffering.

Ironically the Sicilians were largely untouched by the war. They were no worse off for food than the UK and had no occupying troops until the American invasion in 1943; however, after

Italy surrendered, more German troops marched in and were billeted on the families, using their provisions; then Palermo was extensively bombed by the Allies prior to the landing on the south coast. A predominantly American force landed on Sicily in 1943, along with units from the Canadian and British armies, in order to liberate Sicily from the Germans. But this was no ordinary liberation and did not mirror the action seen in Western Europe after D-Day; it was more akin to the invasion of Iraq in 2003.

Although the Allied forces had to drive out a relatively small German force, numbering only 60,000 men, commanded by the excellent Colonel Franco Salemi, the pre-invasion plans, the supposed deals and the promises that may or may not have been made, left a murky stain on an otherwise normal military operation, the consequences of which had a huge impact on the Western world for the next 50 years.

The Americans understood the enormous power of the Mafia within Sicilian society and felt that if this power were harnessed on their behalf then the casualties would be fewer. They were not mistaken in their assumptions, but the Allies would in later years pay a huge price for this support. The freeing of Lucky Luciano from jail and his subsequent deportation to Italy allowed him to mastermind the expansion of the second Mafia into the narcotics business.

Like many momentous world events, the arrival of the Allies in Sicily is surrounded by folklore and myth. Not all the facts are known, nor will they ever be because the OSS (the predecessor of the CIA) destroyed or altered some critical documents. But first of all, here is the official version.

In the early morning of 10 July 1943, the US 7th Army landed on the south coast of Sicily in the towns of Gela and Licata. The main army cut across the island, through Caltanissetta to the north coast towards Messina, where they met up with the 8th Army, a mixture of British and Canadian units under Field Marshal Montgomery. This was the launching pad for the invasion of the Italian mainland, which lay only a mile away across the Strait of Messina.

A smaller American force turned west from Licata, arrived at Agrigento and turned north towards Palermo, whose docks had been destroyed by Allied bombing prior to the invasion. Since precision was not possible with wartime bombers, most of the beautiful villas built along the *lungamare* (promenade), many of which had been built by minor European royalty, were also destroyed.

In between the south coast and Palermo lay the Cammarata Mountains, a former hiding place for Sicilian bandits. It is a raised piece of volcanic land with many caves and steep ravines. These were used for the placement of light artillery and mortars, which would be immune even from air attack. When a mortar is placed in a ravine, the shell can fly out, but, because of the placement, it is virtually secure from destruction. Attackers would require the artillery equivalent of a golfing hole-in-one to pinpoint the mortar. The few Germans that were on the island had also blasted holes in the rocks for gun emplacements, which again made the defending troops almost immune. As well as these fortifications, all the trails through the hills were heavily mined.

These were the same conditions that the 5th Army would meet during the Battle for Monte Cassino six months later, but the conduct of the two battles could not have been more different. At Cassino, it would take 122 days, with 105,000 Allied and 80,000 German casualties, for the hill to be taken; in Sicily, it took just seven days for the Americans, accompanied by French General Juin and his Moroccan troops, to reach Palermo with almost no casualties.

On the other side of the island, however, it was a very different story. The Anglo-Canadian force, whose objective was to take the eastern part of the island and arrive at Messina to prepare for the short hop to the mainland, took much longer to travel and fight half the distance against fewer troops. They faced the poorly equipped Italian and German armies, who were not only outnumbered five to one but also massively out-gunned, with no air support. It took the Anglo-Canadians 37 days and several thousand casualties to reach Messina.

So what was the difference?

One certain difference was that a few days before the actual landing four American Naval Intelligence officers had captured the Italian naval command HQ and had discovered plans showing the deployment of the Italian fleet in the Mediterranean and also the safe paths through the mined mountain trails of the Cammarata. However something else must have happened to make the Germans between Licata and Palermo desert, thus allowing the Americans to have a comfortable, damage-free walk to Palermo.

One explanation was set out by former intelligence officer Norman Lewis in 1964. As he was serving in the invading British force, there is some credence to his story – but do not give it a run in Villalba, as any enquiries about his version of events are met with bored rejection, the local people having been questioned about it by Mafia-seekers for decades! But, for what it's worth, here it is.

On 14 July 1943, four days after the landing, a small plane with a yellow flag attached flew low over Villalba and dropped a package containing a yellow cloth with a black letter 'L' on it. It was handed to Angelo Riccioli, a lance corporal in the *carabinieri*, who gave it to the priest, Don Calogero's brother. The next day the plane returned and dropped a similar packet near Don Calogero's home. It also had a yellow piece of material with a black letter 'L' attached to it. (The yellow was the Sicilian national colour and the black letter 'L' represented the benediction of Lucky Luciano on whatever was to happen.)

A horseman is then said to have set off for Mussomeli, a neighbouring town, with a message for Don Genco Russo, requesting him to look after the Americans, while Don Calogero travelled with the main American motorised division to Palermo.

On 20 July, three American tanks arrived, one of which was flying the yellow flag. An officer got out of this tank and spoke in Sicilian dialect! Don Calogero, now aged 66, appeared in his usual collarless shirt and braces, said nothing, pulled out a yellow handkerchief for purposes of identification and got into the tank accompanied by his nephew, Damiano Lumia. His presence was evidently needed on the northern coastal plain to coordinate what was left of the Mafia.

He returned to Villalba after a week and was appointed mayor by the American officer of civil affairs. The ceremony was in the *carabinieri* barracks and while it was taking place the crowds outside were chanting, *'Viva le Allies, Viva la Mafia.'*

People in Villalba will tell you that at no time did Don Calogero leave Villalba. He remained in the village all the time and when the Americans arrived he made certain that they were welcomed and well treated. He even had the life of his predecessor as mayor spared, which was very generous, given that all town officials were Fascist Party functionaries.

But the story of messages carried by horses, yellow handkerchiefs and tank commanders speaking Sicilian dialect does not compete in terms of credibility with the story of Charles Haffenden.

The American command invaded Italy unwillingly. They wanted to go directly into France and felt that Italy was a sideshow. They could see little reason for opening another theatre of war because the victory in North Africa and the establishment of air superiority over Western Europe made a direct thrust on Germany through Europe the more logical tactic. But Churchill held sway and, true to his past (Gallipoli), felt that a sound tactic was to attack the enemy from behind. His insistence that Italy should be invaded before any landing in Western Europe was later considered to have cost a great many lives, but had it been left till later in the war the Mafia, as anti-Fascists, would still have re-emerged.

US Naval Intelligence, back in America, had already made contact with organised crime through the Longshoremen's Union led by Joe Lanza. As we have seen since 9/11, non-Americans cannot begin to appreciate the hurt felt by Americans at any real or potential invasion of their country by aliens. By the end of 1942, there was a similar feeling of fear in the USA towards a German attack as there is today towards terrorists.

The Americans had lost 71 merchant ships in the Atlantic, where the German U-boats were winning the war, and to US Naval Intelligence the possibility of German agents being landed from U-boats was real. If that happened, and if American installations were sabotaged, the public might raise questions about America's continued involvement in the war. After Pearl Harbor, President Roosevelt did not want that.

Joe Lanza was asked to supply information gleaned from all his union members regarding suspicious landings or sightings. The problem was that he held sway only in New York and its environs, and even though he was an anti-Fascist mafioso not supporting Mussolini, he had no power outside New York. He suggested that Naval Intelligence contact someone who might have greater control over the whole Eastern Seaboard and who could gather more information than he could.

That someone was Lucky Luciano, who at that time was incarcerated at an awful prison in Dannemora, Upper New York State. Dewey had seen to it that the time Luciano spent in jail was as harsh as possible and he had chosen the prison well – Dannemora was a freezing hole in winter and impossibly hot in summer. But these conditions had not broken Luciano's spirit; in fact, prison had been beneficial for him because he was diagnosed as having syphilis as well as being a heroin addict. Although treating addiction was easy in prison – leave the guy alone until he gets over the withdrawal symptoms – the treatment for syphilis was not as foolproof, but either the rather ineffective drugs worked or the disease burnt itself out because he, unlike Capone, was cured.

Luciano's attorney was dispatched to see him in prison, but Luciano told him that there could be no negotiations until he had been moved out of the 'hellhole'. When the authorities eventually transferred him to Great Meadows Penitentiary, near Albany, in Lower New York State, which brought an enormous improvement to his personal comfort, he agreed to help. Great Meadows did not represent the comforts that he could have expected as a mafioso in a Sicilian jail, and life was still very rough, but his old friend

Meyer Lansky persuaded him that some good might come from his cooperation. His advice was wise.

Luciano told Joe Lanza to contact Joe Adonis and Frank Costello, who were running his Mafia family while he was in jail. Their intervention assured Naval Intelligence of reliable information from the entire Eastern Seaboard – and as a bonus Luciano put out the message that union disputes should be stopped for the duration of the war.

As the time for the invasion of Sicily was approaching, Haffenden used his Italian contacts to collect intelligence about the Sicilian coast. That may seem over-simplistic in these days of satellites and high-altitude surveillance, but getting immigrants to provide old photographs and oral memories was the only way Naval Intelligence could build up the sort of picture of the coastline that an invasion force might meet. To his delight, the Sicilian community cooperated wholeheartedly, because the word had gone out from Luciano.

Haffenden now understood the power that a *capo* had over his community and began to expect too much. He understood how Sicily functioned, but he did not have the diplomacy to create the bridge between them and the white Anglo-Saxon Protestant population who were trying to rid America of its gangsters; this group would not take kindly to any favours shown towards an Italian.

He suggested that Luciano be released and infiltrated into Sicily to mobilise civil resistance and to supply intelligence, but this request was turned down because Naval Intelligence did not want a man like Luciano to be privy to any military secrets involving an invasion. Although there is no doubt that Luciano helped the intelligence services in their planning, it is equally certain that he never left jail during the war nor was he ever in Sicily at that time, in spite of the mythology.

The remarkable advance of the American 7th Army through Mafia-controlled west Sicily, especially compared with the problems suffered by their Anglo-Canadian comrades in the non-Mafia east, bears an uncanny resemblance to the ease with which the American forces took Baghdad in 2003. Prior to the invasion of Iraq, fierce resistance was expected around Baghdad from Saddam Hussein's elite Republican Guard. There was none. Just like Colonel Salemi's German Army 60 years previously, they 'vanished', and although there are rumours of CIA involvement with bribes, passports, new identities etc., we shall never know what occurred. Similarly, we shall never discover the influences that persuaded and then helped the German Army to melt away in west Sicily.

The Mafia, however, got the credit, and that may well have been deserved because there was no such retreat at subsequent battles in Salerno, Anzio, Cassino or in the north of Italy. Nor had the German Army 'melted away' in North Africa, a fact to which a battered British 8th Army could attest. But in the home of the Mafia, they 'disappeared'.

The reason that we will never know what happened in the invasion of Sicily is that US Naval Intelligence destroyed all records of Haffenden's involvement. They continued, even well after the war, to refute the claims that Luciano had ever been consulted and denied that his change of prison and his subsequent release had any relation to the invasion of Sicily.

When Luciano came before the parole board prior to his release, his attorney requested that Haffenden be allowed to give evidence concerning the help he might have received from Luciano during the war. Haffenden said that he could not give evidence without the prior permission of the navy and that request was refused; in fact, the navy not only kept up the wall of silence but also sought to discredit Haffenden whenever the subject was raised.

Later in the war, Haffenden fought in the Pacific and was awarded two Purple Hearts. But until the day he died in 1954 he was only insulted and denigrated by Naval Intelligence when the subjects of the Sicilian invasion and Lucky Luciano came up.

◇ ◇ ◇

In the 1940s, the American government were as ignorant about the nature of communism as their descendants have proved to be about Islam. Their dilemma was that Mussolini and Hitler represented fascism and so anyone who fought against them had to be America's friend. The Allied Military Government of Occupied Territory (AMGOT) presumed that all those who had fought or been persecuted by the Fascists were 'good guys' and all Fascists were 'bad guys'.

But the other group who did much more than the Mafia to help the Allies clear the Germans from the north of Italy were the Partisans – and they were Communists.

In the North, it was the Communists, therefore, who were given all the major civic appointments, while in the South it was the mafiosi, thus setting the scene for a division that still affects Italy and contributes to the difficulty of establishing nationhood outside the football stadium.

It had been less than 100 years since Garibaldi had invaded Sicily, which the Piedmontese had joined to the conglomerate that they called Italy. The Sicilians still viewed it as treachery and continued to feel that the island had nothing to do with the peninsula, even though they were included in the name.

The rump of the first Mafia considered that their activities were for the overall good of Sicily, even though those from whom they took money (and could probably afford it) might not have agreed. But that was the way it worked. So it becomes understandable that the Mafia saw the disruption of war as an opportunity to rid themselves of their odious neighbours and achieve independence and closer ties with America.

Living in Europe and understanding communism better than the average American, the Mafia realised that any advance of communism in Sicily would be translated immediately into demands for the redistribution of land and a break-up of the estates that by now were mostly Mafia-owned. The better alternative was therefore control of their own affairs through independence from an Italian state that had done nothing for the island since unification – apart from leaving the first Mafia to get on with ruling it!

The first Mafia, essentially based in rural areas, thought in terms of local politics being the important controlling factor, in the same way as rural Italians think today. The important local considerations are who is your mayor and who is on the council of your village or town. What happens in Rome doesn't impact on your life because you can do nothing about it. You can, however, speak to the mayor and try to persuade him of your cause in the local bar, and if your uncle or cousin is on the council of the *Commune* then he will be able to persuade the mayor to support your petition.

People like the old dons were not educated well enough or sufficiently politically astute to open their minds to the possibility of influencing things in Rome by 'placing' their own politicians there; they were almost certainly what would now be considered 'control freaks' who mistrusted anything but their own way of doing things. Thus they were quite happy that the Rome government had never interfered with Sicily because it allowed them to get on with governing from a local base with no outside interference. This was the situation they wanted to continue after the war, but they were probably farsighted enough to realise that things would certainly change. What they feared was that unless they drove the changes, anything thought up by outsiders would not be to their benefit.

Like the British, the population of Sicily has always had an island mentality. In some ways, it was this insularity that allowed the Mafia philosophy and method to develop and prosper. The feeling of being a big fish in a small pond and the twin philosophies of 'honour' and 'respect' were easier concepts to implement if you were shut off from neighbours.

What the Sicilians had voted for after Garibaldi was to associate themselves with people like him – handsome, swashbuckling, red-shirted, gun-slinging heroes who wore an ostrich feather in their hats. They wanted people who looked like removing the palsied hand of absentee landlords from the face of the countryside, but they certainly didn't like what they got, which were the Piedmontese occupying troops, Piedmontese laws, conscription and another layer of taxes. None of these things helped the poor socio-economic situation and, in fact, it worsened their lives: it would have been preferable to have been invaded by a race such as the Normans, the Byzantines, the Saracens or the Spanish rather than the Italians!

Like any island people, Sicilians of all persuasions felt that they could govern themselves better than any outsider, but they faced the question that arises in any nationalist movement: what sort of New Utopia do we want? Is it going to be a left- or a right-wing state? Will your friends govern or will mine? And who will be our preferred allies? In other words, your vision or mine?

And, as with many nationalist parties, that is where it failed. There was no cohesive force because there were too many people involved and no common agenda. The nearest that they got was probably accepting the Mafia way of life on the basis that it had done no great harm in the previous hundred years and they were all part of it.

Like other groups who disagree about many things, common ground can usually be found in a club tie. The Sicilian separatists found agreement on a new flag! They went back to their original Sicilian (pre-Garibaldi) flag, which was similar to that of the Isle of Man, consisting of three legs in three colours on a background of yellow and red.

The original Separatist Party was not a post-war phenomenon. It had been formed in 1933 by Antonio Canepa, a Sicilian professor of economics. As a result of a ludicrous attempt to set up an independent anti-Fascist state in San Marino in 1933, he was declared insane and put into a lunatic asylum. In 1933, this was not an unreasonable response because at that time Mussolini was quite the best leader and reformer ever to have ruled Italy, and if you opposed what he was doing, insanity may well have been part of a differential diagnosis. Canepa stayed in the asylum for ten years until released by British Intelligence in 1943.

It turned out that he had either never been mad or had recovered, because the Allies who freed him used him as a liaison officer to work with the Partisans. As a result, he ended the war as a committed Communist. Canepa's vision was of a Communist Sicily and obviously this cut right across Mafia plans, so, in the best traditions of the island, when he returned he was killed.

If the Mafia were responsible for his death, it was likely in association with the police because there was a botched attempt at a cover-up by the *carabinieri*. On the face of it, there would have been absolutely no reason for the *carabinieri* to have killed a man such as Canepa, who was trusted by the British. But if the orders had come from the CIA via the Mafia, then it becomes more credible.

His place as champion of independence, though, was taken by a much more charismatic figure who became one of the few Sicilians to appear on the cover of *Newsweek* magazine.

II

SALVATORE GIULIANO

The story of Salvatore Giuliano has been filmed, written about by Gavin Maxwell in *God Protect Me From My Friends* and romanticised by the author of *The Godfather*, Mario Puzo, in *The Sicilian*. Articles about him have appeared in *Time* and *Newsweek* magazines, as well as in newspapers all over the world. In an era before celebrity culture, he would have made the A-list anywhere in the world. He photographed well, looked good on horseback and, unlike most other Sicilians, had film-star looks. Had he been Californian, he could easily have been a movie star.

The reason that his story is worth telling yet again is because it shows how the old Mafia functioned and how it took its first unsure steps into national politics. Had Salvatore Giuliano come along ten years later, he might have quietly risen to a high rank in the Mafia; likewise, had some of his actions been repeated, his end would have been uncomplicated and swift. But this wasn't 1953; it was 1943.

If we are to believe the commonly accepted story, then this poor country boy was buying grain for the hungry folk in his village when he was stopped by two *carabinieri*, who first identified him then asked embarrassing questions about the source of the grain. We do not know whether he bought it on the black market or stole it, but in those days when the *carabinieri* asked questions like this two things would be certain to happen: the grain would be confiscated, ending up in the *carabinieri* barracks or being re-sold on the black market, and the carrier would be beaten up.

What happened next, according to legend, is that one of the police pulled his gun to detain Salvatore whereupon our saintly young man knocked the gun away and ran for cover in the undergrowth. In the ensuing gunfight, one of the *carabinieri* was killed and Salvatore was wounded in the leg. This should have made him easy meat for the remaining cop, but here there is a gap in the story – a gap that allowed our hero to escape with no further harm and to go to a safe place to allow the leg to heal. It has never been clear how he got there and where 'there' was.

What was certain, however, was that now there was a reward for his capture, he could not go back to his home, so he adopted the bandit lifestyle, hiding and sleeping in caves, having provisions brought to him by his brother Giuseppe and his cousin (who would finally kill him) Pisciotta.

At this stage the story becomes more fanciful at every turn. He wanted to see his *mamma* on Christmas Day and so, under the cover of darkness, he made his way back to his house, but *carabinieri* (who rather unusually were sober and not celebrating Christmas!) raided the house, capturing his father and brother, the guests and, for good measure, around a dozen other villagers. Salvatore, with his God-given powers, escaped while the others were put in jail. But loyal to the last, he managed to get a metal file smuggled into the jail, allowing a mass breakout. Apart from his father and brother, who seemed to be able to go home and live uneventful lives for the next year, the escapees joined Salvatore in the countryside and became the core of his gang.

If all this seems unlikely, there's more of the same to follow. But before we get there, let me set the scene.

This story takes place in and around Montelepre, which is accessed even today by driving along 15 kilometres of very twisty roads from Palermo. Salvatore was conceived in New York and born in this small town in 1920, the youngest of four children, making up a family of two boys and two girls. The family were at the better end of the peasant class because his father had the fortitude to commute annually between New York and Sicily, each time bringing back money so that the family could buy another piece of ground. This is when Salvatore's love affair with America began: a glamorous dad who spent half his time in what to most Sicilians was Shangri-La; having toys, comics and clothes from America that none of the other kids at school had. There is no doubt that had he not experienced his little spot of bother Salvatore would have ended up on a boat after the war bound for America.

But the war came and the boats stopped – until landing craft brought the Americans back in 1943. By the time the Germans had left, the countryside was littered with ordnance and so military equipment was cheap, making it easy for bandits to become well armed. When, six months later, Salvatore was tried *in absentia* and sentenced to twenty years in jail, the real problem began.

Was he a 'made' man? The answer is probably yes. His schoolteacher was a mafioso and was at his side till the end, and since Salvatore was big, good-looking, popular and above all very intelligent it would be inconceivable for him not to have been put forward to the dons for initiation. He was just the sort of young man to be invited – and Montelepre was a Mafia town.

But instead of serving an apprenticeship for a high rank in the Mafia, he was now a very unwilling outlaw, the sort of high-profile role that any successful mafioso sought to avoid. His Mafia family would also have had problems with this because while they were honour bound to help him, they had to maintain invisibility, which was part of the deal with the authorities. Furthermore, now that he had been sentenced (probably a slip-up), there was no evidence that could be made to disappear and no witnesses to receive offers they could not refuse.

The Sicilian countryside in 1944 was full of bandits – young men who were army deserters, criminals who had fled from bombed jails and anti-Fascists who had been released from jail with nowhere to go. They got weapons from the battlefield and lived from the proceeds of highway robbery, kidnap and extortion from the estate-owners, who also gave them shelter and food in order to avoid further violence in the absence of an effective police force. Giuliano was the most capable bandit and recruited men from the other groups. By the middle of 1945 his gang had taken over all the others either by force or by Mafia persuasion. He thus commanded all the other major outlaw leaders whose gangs had disappeared.

One of the newer bandits who joined Giuliano was the exotically named Fra Diavolo. According to Giuliano's nephew, who now owns the Castello Giuliano Hotel in Montelepre, Giuliano was working only by permission of the Mafia and Fra Diavolo was the man put into the gang to give feedback to the *capo dei capi*, Don Calogero. Putting a 'watcher' into a business in which there is Mafia investment is seen at all levels and we will visit the concept again in the later chapters on Berlusconi.

After Italy had surrendered, the debate about Sicily's future was gaining momentum – was it to be part of a monarchist Italy, part of a republican Italy or independent? Of these choices, the last was the preferred option, at least initially. The concept of Sicilian independence was not new and after 1860 and the disaster (as most saw it) of rule from Piedmont it had always been part of the political agenda.

In Chapter 9, we saw how and why the leader of the independence movement, Antonio Canepa, was shot as soon as he set foot back on the island; but he wasn't shot because independence itself was not popular, it was just *his* type of independence – in other words, communism.

The leadership of the movement was now taken over by a lawyer and small landowner named Concetto Gallo. He had strong support from the aristocrats and big landowners, who were desperate that independence be obtained and were willing to back up their ideas with money.

It is unlikely that Salvatore would have made himself available to the aristocrats, but he was beguiled by Gallo, who promised that should independence be achieved he would be offering him the posts of Minister of Justice and Chief of Police. To the simple country boy, this appeared to be his lifeline because it would result in an immediate pardon (even if it had to be initiated by himself).

Had Gallo succeeded, he would have achieved the fame accorded to Garibaldi, but since he failed, historians now write that he began losing touch with reality. Just as Cavour had stood back from Garibaldi's invasion so that in the event of failure he could mount another horse, so the Mafia stood back from the War of Independence about to erupt.

It didn't last very long.

Gallo's plan was that Giuliano and his army should take over the west of the island while a motley bunch of bandits and students put together under a man called Rizzio should conquer the east. Money for uniforms and arms was supplied by the aristocrats.

When Rizzio's mob was routed by the *carabinieri* in the east, the movement largely fell apart. The Mafia saw which way things were going and withdrew support because there was now no possibility of separatism succeeding. And this was when the Mafia threw their support behind the Christian Democrat Party.

But there was one little problem that had to be dealt with, namely Salvatore Giuliano, who now found himself in an impossible personal situation. His only future was as an outlaw in the service of the Mafia, who would be able to end his reign (and his life) at a moment of their choosing.

Now that the barons had cut off his money supply, he had to finance his group with the traditional methods of kidnap and robbery, and it was during this period that his 'Robin Hood' reputation became established following numerous acts of kindness to peasants and children.

He began to panic. He felt that the more people who knew about him, the more difficult it would be to assassinate him, and so he invited journalists to his hideouts. There were two articles written in major international publications, which were then syndicated: Salvatore Giuliano, with his film-star looks, was on the world stage

– much to the embarrassment of both the Italian government and their new backers, the Mafia.

At school, he had been very literate and articulate and so he brought these skills to his problem, keeping the story going. He wrote letters to the national and international press about the injustice of his sentence, and since he wrote so well and his profile was so high he was assured of publication. He even wrote to President Truman proposing that Sicily become a state of the United States; Truman never replied!

The Mafia were concerned. He was the antithesis of the Sect: high profile – and scared. They didn't know what he would do next, but at this point they did not have the confidence (that would come later) to kill a high-profile character. So in their confusion they played for time, protecting him. In return, Giuliano would certainly have been giving a percentage of his earnings to Don Calogero.

In November 1945, Italy got its first post-war government, led by Alcide De Gasperi. One of its first acts was to make Sicily an autonomous region of what was to become the first Italian republic. This occurred six months after his election and it was almost certainly Don Calogero's gift from the Christian Democrat Party for delivering the votes. This arrangement – votes in exchange for autonomy – gave the Mafia their own fiefdom and virtual immunity from the law. There was now no need for independence.

In June 1946, the monarchy was formally abolished, and by virtue of 13 million votes (largely from the North) to 11 million (from the South) King Umberto II was sent into exile. Although he had done well in disposing of Mussolini, probably saving Italy from unnecessary bloodshed, he had fought a 'dirty' referendum, recruiting one of the Italian-American gangsters deported after the war, Nick Gentile, the Freemasons from the universities and the Mafia.

In the April 1947 regional elections, in spite of the Christian Democrats having been voted in to central government in 1945,

Sicily voted for the Socialists and Communists – apart from Montelepre, Salvatore's town, which voted solidly monarchist!

Giuliano hated communism and so offered his army to the Christian Democrat Party to prevent it spreading in Italy, especially in Sicily. He was not alone in his endeavours and was probably prompted by Don Calogero to make the offer, perhaps as a way of getting the judicial sentence off the books.

The Mafia, through men unconnected with Giuliano, did what it could for the war against communism by murdering all seven Communist mayors who had won support in Sicily in that election. This was a typical rural response to what they saw as an insult. They did not have the political savvy to realise that it was the people's choice – as far as they were concerned, the people's choice was decided by the Mafia.

We will not know the true story until 2016, when classified documents are released into the public domain, but the evidence available now suggests that Salvatore Giuliano was set up as a patsy in an event that shocked Europe. This was the slaughter of Communist families at a picnic at Portella della Ginestra, a plain near the village of Piana del Greci, where Mussolini had had his unfortunate encounter with Don Ciccio Cuccia. The victorious Communists and Socialist voters had planned a May Day family celebration. They all brought the typical Italian picnic – wine, cheese, prosciutto, watermelon, pots for spaghetti and cake. It was a typical Italian family day out. But they were not there just with their friends. During the night 12 masked men of the Salvatore gang had ridden to the park on horseback and were hiding on a hillside overlooking the valley.

At 10.15 in the morning, when the Communist leader Li Causa got on the podium to speak, there were bangs, which people thought were fireworks. It was more serious than that. It was Giuliano's men firing into the air in an attempt to scare both the crowd and the speaker before he started his oration.

After about a minute, there was machine-gun fire. This came from Fra Diavolo, who was disobeying what he had been told by

Giuliano – but not what he had been told to do by Don Calogero on behalf of the CIA. There was then fire from a different level and direction that had nothing to do with Giuliano's men.

In the end, 11 people were killed and 27 seriously injured. There followed a national and international uproar and the blame was firmly laid at the feet of Salvatore Giuliano – as was always intended.

His nephew, however, told me that there had been a cover-up by the Italian government. Giuliano's guns were 6.5 calibre and half the bullets found were 9 calibre, the type used in Berettas and solely by the military. This information was gained after two examinations carried out first by Major Agrisanti and then a couple of hours later by Captain Ragusa. Much of the activity that day was almost certainly choreographed by the CIA because at that time it was far too complicated for the rural Mafia to have organised.

Mario Scelba, who would later be Prime Minister of Italy, was at that time a Christian Democrat Minister of the Interior. Evidence suggests that he may have been complicit in the framing of Salvatore, but when asked questions about Mafia involvement in the massacre, he dismissed them, saying that it was 'ridiculous' to think of a political motive.

With Portella della Ginestra went Giuliano's last chance of a pardon. He probably knew that it was only a matter of time before the Mafia either killed him or arranged to have him captured. He was on his own now, but for the previous four years he had been more than a match for any opposition. He was 26 and there was no future in being both a freelance bandit and a Mafia robber/hit man.

As with many others who are described in this book, as the end was approaching he lost his judgement and on 17 July 1948 he killed five old mafiosi in the little town of Partinico because he suspected them, probably correctly, of plotting his murder.

This was a step too far: he had signed his own death warrant. The Mafia came to a working agreement with the politicians.

Mario Scelba, who had 180,000 police and *carabinieri*, as well as the army at his disposal, set up *celere* (flying squads) to deal with the problem. Within a few days, Giuliano's mother and sister were imprisoned in the Ucciardone prison in Palermo and his father was exiled to the island of Ustica for a period of five years. Two thousand *carabinieri* arrived in tiny Montelepre and four hundred villagers were jailed. The government also forbade newspapers from printing any more letters from Salvatore.

The two policemen who were set the task of ending Salvatore Giuliano's career were Colonel Lucca of the *carabinieri* and Colonel Verdiani of the *polizia*. They were both working to different agendas, however. While Lucca was mopping up Giuliano's gang with the help of Mafia informers, Verdiani was in touch with Giuliano through the Micelli Mafia family of Monreale and also through Fra Diavolo, the Mafia plant who was murdered shortly afterwards by the *carabinieri*.

Giuliano and Verdiani met in a Micelli house in Monreale on Christmas Eve 1949 and three things were agreed. Giuliano would call off his war and disband the gang, his mother would be released and his family would be helped to emigrate. Giuliano also had to sign a confession that he and his group had been solely responsible for the shootings at Portella della Ginestra, which unwisely he did.

On 23 January 1950, his mother and sister were freed from prison while he was moved to the shelter of a Mafia family in Trapani. At first, moves were made to help him flee to Brazil, but when Fra Diavolo divulged that Giuliano had been planning to kidnap not only the Archbishop of Monreale but also his old *padrone* Don Calogero his death warrant was finally signed.

When the bandit realised the end was near, he wrote a complete account of events, including names of all the mafiosi and politicians involved. As far as his enemies were concerned, if this were true, the document had to be discovered and destroyed because it would have fatally damaged them. Giuliano sent one copy away to America with his sister's husband, Pasquale Sciortino, who fled to New York with as much security as he could muster but was arrested on landing by the FBI. It is impossible to uncover anything relating to his arrest; if he ever had the document, the FBI deny all knowledge of it.

Giuliano was then passed into the care of a young Mafia lawyer who lived alone in Castelvetrano, a dull sleepy village in the middle of nowhere, 70 kilometres south of Palermo. This was where Dr Allegra had practised before being tortured and interrogated about the Mafia initiation ceremony by the Fascists.

By now, the Salvatore Giuliano gang was gone. His only friend was his right-hand man and cousin Pisciotta, who knew what was afoot and cooperated in order to save his own skin. Pisciotta drove to Castelvetrano and arrived at the lawyer's house at 9 p.m. on 4 July 1950. He slept in the same bedroom as his cousin. At 3 a.m., two shots were heard and Pisciotta was seen running naked from the house and driving off. The *carabinieri*, who conveniently happened to be waiting nearby (at 3 a.m.!), burst into the house and found Giuliano's body with two holes under the left armpit. They threw the body into the courtyard and pumped in two magazines of bullets – then called in the press to show them how clever they had been in capturing and killing Giuliano.

Pisciotta was arrested for the murder of Giuliano and at his trial he made many allegations, including the fact that he had been forced to kill his cousin by threats from the government. 'We are a single body – bandits, police and the Mafia – like the Father, Son and Holy Ghost,' he said at his trial.

It was probably one of the most perceptive statements made in those years, but it wasn't what important people wanted to hear.

He said that he had not wanted to kill his cousin, by whose side he had been since the very first days, but he realised that there were now other forces at work. He was also suspicious about Giuliano's motives in signing the confession about Portella della Ginestra. Pisciotta feared that the police were going to get Giuliano to Brazil, leaving him to appear in court alone, thus giving the politicians their sacrificial lamb.

He claimed to have hidden the only other copy of Giuliano's testament and refused to withdraw this threat of exposure to the politicians for ten years because he always claimed that he had been double-crossed, having been promised a pardon if he killed Giuliano.

What happened next was similar in many ways to the end of other Mafia stories.

Before being tried for his part in the Portella della Ginestra shooting, Pisciotta was held in Viterbo prison. There he was joined by a cellmate who had been planted in the hope that Pisciotta would tell him something. His name was Polaco, and he was shot the day after he came out of prison.

Pisciotta was found guilty of the massacre at Portella della Ginestra and was sent to the Ucciardone prison in Palermo, where he was killed in classical Mafia style – strychnine in the coffee. Shortly afterwards the poisoner was shot, and some months later Verdiani, the *polizia* colonel, was also poisoned.

This episode was probably the final act in the story of the rural first Mafia. Things were moving on, thanks to the enormous investment made by the CIA in the treasury of the Christian Democrat Party, with one of the other beneficiaries being the Mafia.

The holy war against the Communists was now starting.

12

THE UNHOLY ALLIANCE

The reason that the Vatican, the CIA and the Mafia decided to share a bed was the real possibility of post-war Italy voting for a Communist government. Apart from a common hatred of Communist ideals, each had a different agenda.

Post-war Italy was the European country most likely to support communism because of the hundreds of thousands of Northerners who had either actively supported or actually fought for the Partisan movement that had finally forced the German Army out of Italy. It was the Partisans who had captured Mussolini and who had hung him upside down beside his mistress; it was the Partisans who were still assassinating Fascists long after the war had ended; and it was the Partisans who were the Communists. In 1946, Italy was once again divided: in general, people in the North wanted a Communist republic, while in the South people wanted a Catholic monarchy.

There was also some support for the Communists in the rural South. There, land reform had never really benefited the workers and the Communist Party in their manifesto were offering improvements. Even in central Italy, where a very satisfactory system of land management existed, namely the *contadini* system, there was strong support for the Communists. Umbria, for example, has returned Communist regional government at every election since 1948.

If Italy had become Communist in the 1940s and '50s and had left NATO, the world would have become a very different place. Italy would have become part of the communist bloc, and while there would have been little fear of Russia carrying out a nuclear attack on Western Europe, there would certainly have been danger in a panic reaction from the American government to the positioning of Russian bases in the Mediterranean. But it was the bigger picture that really worried America, namely the threat posed by a massive land mass, stretching from the Alaskan shore to Ireland, the nearest point in Europe to the USA, coming under the control of Russia and setting itself the task of the destruction of capitalism.

The man put in charge of CIA activities in Italy at this time was a tall, thin Anglophile called James Angleton. Born in America on 9 December 1917, his father, Hugh, had fought against Pancho Villa in the Mexican War and for the American Army in Europe in the First World War. Hugh had returned to America after the conflict and had begun work for the National Cash Register company. In 1928, when James was 11, his father was sent to Italy to find out why NCR was not doing better business at a time when Italy's economy under Mussolini was booming. Hugh was entranced by the country, turned the fortunes of the company around and eventually persuaded the parent company to let him buy the Italian offshoot.

James was sent to Malvern College, one of England's best public schools. It made such an impression on him that in spite of an education at Yale University, where he was enrolled in 1937, he was always more attracted to English than American values.

He returned to Italy in the summer of 1940, just after Mussolini had declared war on Britain and France. His father had by this time started a career with the OSS, risen to the rank of colonel and by the end of the war arranged for James to be inducted into their service.

As part of James's training, he was sent to MI6 in London, where he came under the influence of Kim Philby, who years later was found to be a Soviet agent at the heart of the British Secret Service. Philby took a special interest in James, probably because he wanted him to go as high as possible in the OSS so that he had an important source at the heart of American intelligence.

When the war ended, James was given responsibility for all counter-intelligence operations in Italy and also with running intelligence networks throughout southern Europe. In the immediate post-war period, Europe was a very complex place. The prizes were German scientists, whose expertise was needed by both sides in the race to build nuclear weapons. Both sides were trying to capture these scientists and part of Angleton's tactic was to persuade the Vatican, since it was a neutral and independent state, to give refuge to German scientists while passports and other identity documents were prepared for their ultimate destination in either the UK or America.

At the same time, those Germans who wanted nothing to do with either Russia or America had the opportunity to use the operations created by the SS (Odessa and Spider), which were designed to help colleagues escape and rehabilitate in South America, where there was a major German presence. Among those who took this route were Klaus Barbie, Adolf Eichmann and Joseph Mengele, along with a further 30,000 or so other wanted former Nazis.

Once Russia had developed the atom bomb, the Cold War became deadly serious. It was estimated that Stalin had 120 Divisions that could reach the Channel ports in 11 days. When Russia blockaded Berlin, it was clear that the aggressive approach to the West could lead to war and only the nuclear threat prevented a Russian-dominated Europe. Angleton was therefore a very busy operative.

When the OSS changed its name and structure to become the CIA, it had at its head Allen Dulles. For Angleton, this was unfortunate. While in Italy during the war, Angleton got to know of the Holocaust and sent information back to America via the Geneva office of Allen Dulles. He found out some years later that his information had not been sent back to Washington and he blamed this on Dulles, holding a grudge against his boss ever since this episode. During that time, Angleton had also developed strong pro-Israeli sympathies and had begun sharing information clandestinely with Mossad, the Israeli secret service.

Dulles's main role was to prepare a reaction to the Russian takeover of Western Europe, which looked ever more likely. He, with Angleton, created Operation Gladio, which was the foundation of a support system for a number of anti-communist guerrillas who would operate behind Soviet lines until the USA once again came to liberate Europe.

Another of those whom Angleton met during this period was Licio Gelli, who would later come to prominence as the Master of the Masonic lodge P2, which would acquire notoriety in the 1980s, when it was exposed as harbouring treasonable aims. Gelli had fought with Franco's forces during the Spanish Civil War and by the end of the Second World War was a liaison officer with the German SS Hermann Goering Division. It has also been alleged that he was a double agent in the later years of the war, being in the pay of the OSS as well as serving in the German SS.

In 1943, Gelli was sent to Belgrade to supervise the entraining of 55 tons of gold bars labelled with a red cross. The shipment disappeared and 50 years later some of the bars were discovered buried in flowerpots in the grounds of his villa in Arezzo, Tuscany. But the story of Gelli comes later.

Angleton's main role as chief of counter-intelligence in Italy was to make sure that the Christian Democrat Party was elected in 1948. For this job he was massively funded. Of the $300 million sent by the American government for the reconstruction of Italy in 1945, $30 million went directly to the Christian Democrat Party to make sure that they would win the election.

Italian Communism, as expressed by every leader of the party since the 1940s, was always very different from the Stalinist interpretation and implementation. Palmiro Togliatti, the pre-war Communist leader, had fled the Fascist regime in the 1930s and had spent the war in Stalin's Russia, a fact that left him mistrusted for the rest of his political career and also stopped potential support from those who would otherwise have voted for Italian Communism. When the Italian government allowed him to return to Italy, he did not preach Stalinism; he swore to serve king and country and as a reward was given a ministry in the interim post-war government. Unfortunately, he was always labelled a Stalinist so was never really electable; even though he had seen what Stalin really was and despised him, he could never establish trust. Had he succeeded, Italy might well have voted for his party in the first elections in 1948.

Angleton's career was not going well, even though the Christian Democrats won the election. When his old friend and mentor, Kim Philby, defected, it hit him like a hammer blow. He had never suspected Philby of holding Communist sympathies; in fact, he had regarded him as the perfect role model of an urbane English spy. The episode tipped him into paranoia.

As he attempted to destabilise Communism in Italy, he began destabilising himself. He became suspicious of everyone and everything, seeing Communist influences everywhere. His paranoia continued to get worse until it started affecting his daily life. When William Colby became director of the CIA, Angleton was relieved of his post and was retired back to America.

The Catholic Church had the clearest reason for wanting the Communists destroyed. The Communists denied the existence of God and thus, when opposed by a system that was going to abolish God, the Church was facing its greatest challenge since the Goths.

They did not take this anti-Communist stance because they were on the side of the rich against the poor – very much the opposite. Their opposition to Communism was simply based on the fact that the Communists had closed all the Catholic churches in their empire, had imprisoned cardinals and were making things difficult for the Orthodox Church.

In the 1940s and '50s, Catholic masses all over the world used to end with what were called Prayers for the Conversion of Russia. At the height of the Cold War, many people would have thought these prayers to be ridiculous – but they worked! In 1989, the Berlin Wall came down and churches were opened again in countries that had been behind the Iron Curtain.

The Vatican could live with other Europeans quarrelling about who should be Pope, where the papacy should reside or how much of Italy the Pope should rule, but with a system that denied the existence of God there was no product to sell and 'business' would be at an end.

This has to be understood in order to realise the importance that the Vatican attached to the defeat of communism. In this light, their collaboration with the Mafia and the Christian Democrat Party does not appear as corrupt as it might at a distance of half a century. In their view, the basic Jesuit philosophy applied, namely that the end justified the means. The Church probably didn't feel in harmony with either of these two worldly forces, but there was no doubt that if a choice had to be made between the CIA, the Mafia and the Communists, the decision as to who to support was quite clear. The Communists had not only closed churches, they had also prevented the young from being taught that there was a God who should be worshipped. This ignited a Crusader-like spirit in the Vatican and they reasoned that any method of preventing that happening to the rest of the world was acceptable.

Pope Pius XII didn't like Hitler and was not anti-Semitic, but he knew about the Holocaust and did nothing about it, an action that caused the late Pope John Paul II 50-plus years later to visit the Wailing Wall in Jerusalem and deposit a message begging forgiveness of the Jews for the ambiguous role of the Catholic Church at that time. One of the things that enabled Pope Pius to rationalise his stance would have been that Hitler was fighting communism and that to him was more important than anything he might be able to do to save millions of Jews.

Beating communism was the twentieth-century crusade of the Catholic Church. When Italy showed signs of electing a Communist government, the Vatican wholeheartedly sided with the Christian Democrat Party and went to enormous lengths to make sure all Catholics voted that way. There are tales of people being asked their voting intentions in the confessional and there is no doubt that some misguided and zealous village priests may have done this, seeing it as their individual effort to beat communism. It was a very powerful weapon.

The Christian Democrat Party was led by one of the Vatican's own: Alcide De Gasperi. In 1927, Mussolini had sent him to the Regina Coeli prison because he opposed Fascism. When he was released in 1930, it was on condition that he exiled himself in the Vatican, which he did for the next 15 years. Thus the Under Secretary of State at the Vatican, Monsignor Montini, felt able to say to him in 1946, 'Any kind of collaboration with the anti-clerical parties, not only in the municipality of Rome but in the government, is no longer admissible. If the Christian Democrats were to continue with such collaboration, they would be considered a party favouring the enemy. The Christian Democrats would no longer have our support or our sympathy.'

The reason that the Mafia did not want a Communist government in Sicily was that they were totally against land reform; anything that upset the system that they had developed over the previous 100 years was to be resisted. In Sicily, therefore, an accord developed between the Mafia and the Christian Democrats on the basis that if the votes were delivered and they won the majority, the Christian Democrats would show their gratitude by making sure that the custom of giving the important Ministries of Public Works, Public Instruction and Postal Services to Sicilian deputies continued. This in turn would ensure that Mafia businesses got the big government contracts, or at least if a non-Mafia firm was chosen they would certainly know that their success was due to the intervention and influence of the Mafia and appropriate percentages would be paid. By now the Mafia had almost 100 years' experience of fixing elections and so this presented little difficulty.

The Church was not part of this profiteering and corruption. They had their eye firmly on their own agenda, which was the maintenance of a society that believed in God – and, as a vital by-product, made them relevant.

The Church was much more important in the mainland south of Italy than in Sicily, where they were passive partners with the Mafia in the delivery of the vote. It is not, therefore, surprising that this alliance made sure that there was a Christian Democrat Prime Minister of Italy from 1946 to 1982.

The rather ambiguous relationship between the Church and the Mafia is illustrated by the fact that no cleric had ever talked about the Mafia until Pope John Paul II gave a sermon in Agrigento Cathedral on 9 May 1993 after the murder of the magistrate Giovanni Falcone. He said to the Sicilians: 'Begin a new era, without deaths, without assassinations, without fears, without menaces, without victims. The Sicilian people . . . cannot always live under the pressure of a counter-culture, the culture of death. Here it is the culture of life that is needed. In the name of Christ, crucified and risen again, in the name of this Christ who is the life, who shows us the way forward, who is Truth and Life.'

Some months later, the Sicilian Cardinal Pappalardo, preaching in Palermo Cathedral, said that abortion had killed more people than the Mafia and in saying this he more truly reflected the underlying attitude of the Catholic Church towards the Mafia. The jump that the older churchmen had failed to make, along with American movie directors, was that the post-war Mafia had long since sacrificed rustic chivalry in favour of corporate profit.

In Sicily, and also in Ireland in the last 30 years, many priests will have had practising Catholics, who were also gunmen, confess to wounding or killing. What did they do? We, of course, don't know the answer to that question, but I would be astonished if the majority of priests would not have used discretion.

Priests in Sicilian towns or villages with strong Mafia families would either be mafiosi, related to mafiosi or believe that mafiosi were on the side of God. This latter belief would arise from the fact that all mafiosi behaved as good Catholics. They would attend mass and take the sacraments. Their daughters would be married in church as virgins and there would never be any talk of divorce or abortion. They would be supporters of the local church, raising money when necessary and helping a family when recommended to by the priest. They would be accepted as a valuable part of community life and one that the priests could rely on. So could a system that had as members people who were pillars of the Church be anything other than an example for others to follow? If one confessed to a murder, it would certainly have been for the good of the family or the community, and the priest would certainly have believed a mafioso who said that he wished that he hadn't *needed to do* what he had done – but . . . *Ego te absolvo!* (I forgive you.)

Soon, however, they would be saying these words to mafiosi who were running the cities and behaving very differently from their forefathers.

13

THE MAFIA COMES
TO THE CITY

In preparation for the invasion of Sicily, the Allies had
bombed the docks at Palermo. Bombing in those days was
not as accurate as it is today and so the collateral damage was
gross. Many Italian cities had their hearts ripped out and some
fabulous buildings disappeared, but none more so than Palermo.
Streets such as Via della Liberta, once one of Europe's finest, down
which the glitterati of Europe had taken an evening drive or walk,
were stripped bare of their borders of palaces.

What befell Palermo in the post-war building boom was much
the same as happened to cities all over the world, but since it
was just a little bit worse and more drawn out it was christened
the Sack of Palermo and the blame laid at the feet of the Mafia.
People from the poorer areas, whose houses had been lost from
bombing, were more concerned about a roof over their heads than
the view or city centre beauty. The demand for new housing also
came from the tens of thousands who were moving into Palermo
from the countryside, looking for work. And so the politicians
built houses for votes, just as politicians did all over Europe.

In Britain as well as in Sicily, there was a simple, quick and
inexpensive way to build houses; you used concrete and glass
and the result was what present-day architects describe as 'brutal'.

While high-rise concrete blocks promised an airy clean future for former slum families, the political advantage was that the local candidate had his voters and his constituency corralled together, which made gathering the votes for re-election easier. The complaint levelled against Palermo was that while in Britain they pulled down slums to make way for concrete, in Palermo they pulled down palaces. But no one was ever going to rebuild these palaces.

Peasants were not the only people to move to the cities; their masters, the Mafia, followed and either stayed within their own 'family' or joined one of the existing families. By 1953, Palermo and the suburbs were divided by the Mafia into 13 districts, each controlled by one family. By 1987, the number of families in Palermo had risen to 18, while there were 105 in the rest of west Sicily. Each family had a variable number of soldiers, from ten in the smallest family to 120 in the largest, the Bontade family.

There were five construction firms involved in the post-war building programme and while none were openly mafiosi all of them would certainly have had a partnership with a Mafia family. If they did not have this, then they would probably never have been awarded contracts; in the unlikely event that they were, then the work would never have been allowed to be completed.

The way the Mafia functioned in cities was different to the agrotowns, where a single don was visible and responsible for all good and evil. In cities, mafiosi acted as individual units connected by a brand name (the Mafia) and the product they sold (protection). The difference between the Mafia and criminals in other societies was that the Mafia's product was sold with the collusion of the state.

Cardinal Ernesto Ruffini, a very influential man during the 1950s, consistently refused to denounce the Mafia as a criminal organisation and took the view that the same was going on not only in the rest of Italy but all over the world. Superficially, he was probably correct – only the style and the name were different.

By its nature, the construction industry cannot be an honourable one. Major firms must bid for contracts and must have time to prepare their tenders. They will all have a source within local and regional councils to keep them informed of what projects are being considered and in many cases the pitfalls to avoid in that bid.

If the Mafia families had worked as independent units within their own territories, their profits would have been unequal and unpredictably distributed, which would have led to friction between families. They, therefore, developed a method of sharing customers, with buyers being systematically referred to protected sellers. There was no coercion involved because it was presented as part of a wider friendship. This had the added value of defining 'friendship', so that if there was any later treachery it could be identified as a breach of this friendship, with death being the probable outcome. In some cases there would not be enough customers to go round and so the families would take it in turn, not unlike a dealers' 'ring' at an auction.

Twenty years after the so-called Sack of Palermo, Britain had its eyes opened to the wiles of the construction industry. In 1974, John Poulson was sentenced to five years in jail, having been found guilty of bribing public figures to win contracts, with the collusion of a top Scottish civil servant named George Pottinger, demonstrating that the construction industry was corrupt even away from Mafia circles. More recently the Scottish public were astonished by a hearing that exposed the corruption surrounding the choice of contractor for the vastly expensive new parliament building.

Pizzu applies to almost everything in Sicily and is the reason that things cost more on the island. Naturally, therefore, it was applied to the construction industry, and as this boomed so did Mafia wealth.

The first Mafia had gradually expanded the old tradition to arrive at a point where they had become partners in whatever activity was making money. In return for part of the profits, they would supply protection from their own vandalism. This transition from the old to the new saw a complete change in the nature of what was essentially a Sicilian rural way of life. Whether or not the second Mafia was a continuation of the first or a mutation remains to be judged.

Failure to accept a deal related to a money-making venture would not result in murder or bodily harm – at least not at first. There would be damage to property and equipment, and members of the workforce might disappear and easily find other jobs. When the firm re-advertised for workers, there would be surprisingly few applicants. On the other hand, to accept the deal would bring advantages that might increase business, with the activity of competitors being harnessed or even weakened. It was, therefore, in the interest of both the protector and the protected to continue to be successful.

One of the important differences between conducting normal business and conducting Mafia business was that the Mafia were always certain of payment. Ordinarily, if a supplier does not get paid all he can do is to mount a small court action, and even then he might lose out when, and if, the fees are paid. But the Mafia bypassed the courts. Its success as a business was founded on the certainty of violence if fees were not paid. This was at best expensive and at worst fatal.

If the Mafia was not previously in partnership with a firm that won a contract and if there was any subsequent resistance to paying the amount of *pizzu* demanded, the initial refusal to cooperate would not result in personal violence but only in harassment, implied threats and damage to property. Once in the system, a protected firm would enjoy not one but two benefits. First they would not suffer robbery or vandalism; second, and more importantly, they would not have much competition.

La Repubblica newspaper in 1990 reported the story of a coffee firm that took on a Mafia soldier as a salesman. Their sales rose dramatically, but other coffee firms complained to the police, even though the salesman was doing nothing wrong and using neither violence nor threats. When questioned by the police, he said, '*Commisario*, when I wasn't working, you hassled me, and now I'm working you're doing the same. What can I do?'

His employers said that they were helping to reintegrate a convict into society and that it was just a coincidence that those outlets that used their coffee had a quieter life and were robbed less often!

Most of the construction contracts in those years went to a handful of people, none of whom were remotely concerned with building – they were front men used by Mafia-owned firms. There were several ways of making sure contracts were delivered. Here are two examples.

A common system used in local authority work in Italy is to set a price for the job and make a maximum discount, which remains secret. The contract goes to the firm that comes closest to the price minus the discount, the idea being that the secrecy of the process stops firms colluding. The only way this can occur is for information to be given from someone on the inside who knows what discount has been set. The figure is not easy to guess because it will almost always include a fraction. It is a good system in theory because it should mean that a local authority cannot regularly have one firm winning – that would result in the police being brought in or other firms bringing in their own protection.

Another system involves a number of builders who between them decide who is to win the bid. It is essential that only the firms in the cartel are able to participate, but with the system of 'penalties' that apply in Sicily – death, beating or vandalism – this is easily arranged. The other firms submit artificially high bids and it is understood that no one undercuts the pre-agreed winner. The Mafia will, of course, have a controlling interest in the firms allowed to join the cartel and usually their margin is the difference between the successful bid and the bid that would have won in open competition. In this way many businesses end up in the arms of the Mafia because otherwise they would not get any work.

While the payment of a bribe to the correct person in the contract process would be the simplest thing to do, there are too many variables to allow this as a standard crude Mafia ploy.

Although we do not know whether or not the five building firms were Mafia owned, we do know that Palermo was run in those years by four very high-ranking mafiosi; men who were on a separate VIP list, much as future members of the P2 Lodge would be.

The first two of these were the Salvo cousins, Nino and Ignazio, who held the archaic post of tax collectors. It seems extraordinary that in the mid-twentieth century a government of a country within NATO deemed tax collection so complex an act that it had to be outsourced.

The tax collector had been an integral part of culture and life in the whole of southern Italy from well before the time of Garibaldi. If people did not have money to pay their taxes, then some of their livestock or their produce would be confiscated. In today's terms, it could most closely be compared with a debt collection agency.

In 1946, when Sicily was given autonomous regional status, the government chose to keep the old system of tax collection. The thought of raising taxes from Sicilians by means of voluntary donations accompanied by the completion of forms was considered to be fantasy. They believed that it needed eye-to-eye contact and so they had to have real people collecting the taxes, thus providing the Salvo cousins with the most lucrative job on the island from 1952 till 1984.

Even though they were, strictly speaking, government employees, they did not work for a salary; their company was permitted to keep 10 per cent of the tax income raised and they were also allowed a delay of four months before paying the government, which gave large additional interest payments on the huge sums involved. They therefore became rich in a legitimate fashion, branching out into real estate, hotel chains and winemaking. Due to their wealth, they had a controlling interest in the Christian Democrat Party. Eventually, Ignazio and Nino were discovered to be on the secret VIP list of the Salemi Mafia family in Trapani.

As the richest men in Sicily, they acquired influence and had free access to Giulio Andreotti, who was to be the most influential politician in Italy for the next 40 years. The Salvo twins' association with the Mafia was discovered during the investigations of the '80s and they were arrested in 1984. Nino died of metastatic lung cancer before the trial began and while Ignazio was awaiting sentence after having been found guilty of Mafia association he was killed by Mafia gunmen, thus ensuring his silence.

The next man was Salvo Lima, who delivered electoral Sicily to Andreotti and became his right-hand man in Rome. He was ahead of his time in his media skills, wore beautifully tailored suits, had a patrician bearing, impeccable diction and manners, and the type of silvery hair that one usually associates with American senators. He knew his way around the corridors of power in Rome and also how Sicily 'worked'.

Lima was elected mayor of Palermo in 1958, right in the middle of the building boom. Four years later, he moved on to become a deputy minister in the Regional Parliament. He was elected to the National Parliament in 1968 and brought his Sicilian electoral base as a dowry to Andreotti. He was a careful man and, knowing how the press worked, suggested to Andreotti's staff that they check his background carefully before admitting him to government. He had suffered from allegations about Mafia association and he did not want these to be resurrected in the future, creating embarrassment for Andreotti.

He had been cleared of Mafia association in Sicily and the subsequent investigation revealed that he was squeaky clean, allowing him to work for the rest of his life for Andreotti, thus making sure that Sicily remained true to the Christian Democrat Party.

In 1979, Lima was elected to the European Parliament, but he seldom attended Strasbourg because his time was taken up attending to Andreotti's political requirements in both Sicily and Rome.

Although cleared of any Mafia association, it was the Mafia who executed him in 1992, probably as a warning to Andreotti. Lima had done nothing wrong, but they had an important message that they wanted Andreotti to hear and understand.

The fourth man involved in making enormous sums for the Palermo families was Vito Ciancimino. He was quite different from the suave Lima and came from the famous Mafia town of Corleone in the centre of Sicily, a place that bred the worst mafiosi. Ciancimino looked like a caricature of a post-war spiv. He was slim, with heavily greased, slicked-back hair and a pencil moustache, and when he smoked, he used a cigarette holder.

Like Lima, he had joined the Christian Democrat Party in the immediate post-war period and had certainly been in the right place at the right time. Ciancimino was Minister of Public Works in Palermo when Lima was mayor and he followed him into the mayor's office when Lima went to Rome. He was arrested in 1984 but not tried until 1992, when he was convicted of working with the Mafia and money laundering. As part of his sentence, the court ordered the sequestration of millions of dollars of his assets.

Many upper- and middle-class members of the business and professional community were both mafiosi and Freemasons, but that did not imply criminality. They were the glue that held the Sicilian Establishment together, acting as the bridge between the authorities and the day-to-day mafiosi. Many small-town priests, landowners, lawyers and teachers were mafiosi, as were doctors. They would be in the same social set, attend one another's family celebrations and attend the same dinners.

Sicilians (provided you have been vouched for) will today tell you of their Mafia fathers and grandfathers with no shame or embarrassment because in the '40s that's the way things were in Sicily. Mafiosi were in the best clubs in Palermo, such as the Circolo della Stampa (the Press Club) and Circolo di Tiro a Volo (the Clay-

Pigeon Shooting Club). They were also protected because in the '50s and '60s the word Mafia hardly ever appeared in the press or TV and the police and magistrates dismissed the whole idea. Many would have believed that what existed was no more threatening than the old school tie in England or the college fraternity in America.

But in 1958 Vittorio Nistico, writing in the magazine *L'Ora*, noted: 'The topic of the Mafia was like putting your hands on electricity; there is always someone powerful ready to get angry.' To be from a Mafia family in those days was considered to be a status symbol and many Sicilians of the period who went to school with the children of mafiosi told me that they would be admired and envied because of their father's position.

Just as the Sicilian Mafia were making their first fortunes, their American cousins were consolidating an empire funded by the huge financial base established during Prohibition.

PART 2

THE ZENITH

14

THE AMERICAN COSA NOSTRA

Franklin D. Roosevelt was undoubtedly the cleverest President of the United States of America in the twentieth century. In 1940, he understood the significance of a possible German conquest of Europe in terms of both international and domestic politics, especially the effect on his popularity if the massive Jewish population saw that he sat back and did nothing in reaction to what was to become the Holocaust. There were many Germans, especially in the Midwest . . . but there were more Jews in the east.

Roosevelt had also handled the Great Depression well, creating employment for thousands with new public works, while at the same time displaying a social conscience in government that had never been seen before in the United States, the only poor in the country having previously been the black population. His policies came to be known collectively as the New Deal.

He also realised what a terrible mistake the Prohibition laws had been. Not only had they made alcohol abuse a popular and socially acceptable pastime, but a group of criminals, mainly of foreign origin, had become obscenely rich by openly flouting the law of the land.

Rich was one thing, but it was their arrogance that really bothered the President. As their purchase of political power and the corruption of the police and judiciary had increased, so had this arrogance. He knew he had to repeal the Act, but, in spite of the havoc that the criminals had created in the east, it had not really impinged on either the Bible Belt or the Midwest puritans, who didn't like foreigners, blacks or alcohol anyway.

He moved slowly, first asking Congress to merely modify the laws so that beer could be brewed with an alcohol content greater than 3.2 per cent. Once this was implemented, in 1933 he went the whole way and had the Twenty-first Amendment to the Constitution passed, repealing all laws relating to the sale and manufacture of liquor.

But Roosevelt did not repeal Prohibition solely because of the gangsters. He was most concerned at what Prohibition had done to the processes of law, with corruption of the police, federal agents, prosecutors and the judiciary, and thus the entire electoral process.

By repealing the laws, he was saying to the American public: 'You can drink what you want, but I'm going to get the government back on to the straight and narrow.' And America, as it sank its Martinis, drank to that.

To oversee this, he used a man whom he had appointed to his staff a year earlier when he was governor of New York, Samuel Seabury. He had two agendas running when he appointed Seabury: one was the re-establishment of the legal process, but more important was the winning of the Democratic nomination for the next presidential election. He was afraid of a man called Al Smith, who was likely to become his opponent at the Democratic convention. Smith was going to be difficult to beat because he had already run against Herbert Hoover in 1928 and nearly won, and he had the backing of Tammany Hall, who usually backed winners. Smith's only weakness was his religion; he was a Catholic. Seabury's brief was to show that it was not just Negros who misused drink but also the Irish, the Italians and the Catholics who had corrupted the morals of that great nation. In this role, Seabury, a morally strict, white Anglo-Saxon Protestant judge, was the perfect tool.

Seabury and his staff started what would now be called a 'dirty tricks' campaign but which 70 years ago was not recognised as such. He set about framing police, Irish and Italians, making sure that when their case came to court they were highlighted in the newspaper with appropriate moral comment. One of his dirty tricks involved the cooperation of a Chilean-born small-time crook called Chile Acuna.

Acuna confessed that the police used to make him go into a brothel and pay with a marked five- or ten-dollar bill. When the police raided the place, they would find the note and charge the house with prostitution. This charge, however, would be dropped on receipt of a cash payment from the owner. He would do the same with innocent landladies who had nothing to do with prostitution but were merely renting rooms to respectable people. The police would arrive, find marked notes and extort money, which if the woman couldn't or wouldn't pay would result in a 100-day jail sentence.

Altogether Acuna named 50 policemen and detectives with whom he shared the pay-offs, all of whom subsequently received jail terms for extortion. One of them, Tom Farley, sheriff of New York County, was found to have banked $83,000 in cash from an annual salary of $8,500 in 1931.

The tactics worked and Roosevelt was elected.

Apart from making the taking of illegal payments very difficult, and dangerous, the main way in which the New Deal politicians ended Tammany Hall politics was by trumping them. In the past, if someone wanted something, the only way to get it was by the modern Italian method of getting a *raccomandazione* from Tammany Hall. So Roosevelt created an alternative, giving people everything they had previously had to ask for at Tammany Hall: food stamps, jobs and low-income housing.

His masterstroke, however, was his 1944 Servicemen's Readjustment Bill, the so-called GI Bill. This made military service very attractive because if a man had served in the military, he became eligible for education grants as well as special consideration for public housing. Most valuable of all, Roosevelt built VA (Veterans' Administration) Hospitals across the land. They were all attached to university hospitals and doctors signing contracts of employment with the university also had to sign up to do a certain amount of work at the neighbouring VA, thus ensuring a high quality of medical attention. They were built from the same set of blueprints and so the building programme was quick, with each hospital looking the same from the outside and having the same internal geography.

Healthcare, always a fraught issue in America, had huge political and social value because it guaranteed anyone who had served in the armed forces and their families the highest quality of medical care – free! And it was for life. Neither the gangsters nor Tammany could compete with this and so for many of them it was the beginning of hard times.

For the majority of city dwellers, the most important outcome of the Roosevelt reforms was that the streets became safer: random killings between gangs stopped, so there was less chance of being accidentally shot. For the low-level gangster, however, it was a trade recession. Income dropped dramatically, and in the absence of brewing, packing, truck driving, distribution and strong-arm work they had to look elsewhere for employment. Many joined the labour unions as enforcers, others turned to kidnap and bank robbery, while some went into the numbers racket and into 'fixing' sports betting. But a significant number started in the newly developing narcotics trade.

No such problem faced the successful gangsters, who had made so much money in the good years that their present problem was what to do with it. In those years there was no electronic transfer, so in order to place it in a Swiss account it had to be physically carried there, which after 1940 became impossible. Depositing it in banks or investing in stocks was also impracticable because it left a paper trail and, after the jailing of Al Capone on tax charges, being unable to explain where money had come from was a certain way to end up in jail for a very long time. Many just had to keep their cash in various hidden boxes because in the 1930s and '40s money laundering had not become the science that it is today.

Some gangsters, however, did not have the imagination to change direction and felt that the old system should continue. One of them was Dutch Schultz. Like many others, he had been charged with tax fraud, and although he, unlike Capone, escaped imprisonment, by the time he had paid his huge fine and also his professional fees, he was relatively hard up and so had to move into a new area. He chose the numbers game, which was a safe and reliable way to make money.

The winning number was always deemed to be the last three digits of the Tote betting total, so it could not be fixed; it varied each day and was published in the daily newspaper, so it was available for all to see. Unlike the lottery, if no one had the winning number there was no rollover and the organisers took the lot as profit. It was a world populated by the same little old ladies who pull handles today in Las Vegas and betting slips were often registered in apartment rooms, warehouses, street corners and empty shopfronts.

In order to do business, the outlets had to stay open, which meant they were visible and known to the neighbourhood police. This was a viable second-income option for the cops because they had to be bought off.

Schultz needed help from Tammany Hall to square the police and so he approached Jimmy Hines, who was a 'financial adviser' (bag man) to the Hall, a job which entailed making all the arrangements for kickbacks to aldermen and councillors. Hines was a quiet man, the soul of discretion and tact, but it was well known that he had acted in the same capacity as he would for Schultz with both Lucky Luciano and Meyer Lansky. Schultz came to an arrangement with Hines that is reputed to have earned the adviser a downpayment of $10,000, followed by $1,500 per week. What Hines had to do in return was arrange for councillors to keep police in their ward out of Schultz's way. The arrangement only lasted a few years because Thomas Dewey, that other rising star within American law and politics, was still grooming his curriculum vitae for higher office and once he had set his sights on Schultz serious harassment began.

Schultz, being an unsophisticated old-time gangster, could think of no other method to stop the harassment than 'bumping off' Dewey, but he had to clear this with the hierarchy of the Mob. Not surprisingly – because there were people in the group who were not psychopaths and could think ahead – the view was that Schultz's idea was not only stupid but also dangerous, given the climate of reform that Roosevelt had succeeded in weaving into American life. Schultz did not appear to value their judgement; he made it clear to them that he wasn't going to pay a blind bit of notice to their decision because in his opinion they had to get rid of Dewey. But it was Schultz who was assassinated by person or persons unknown, thus avoiding a major public scandal and a brighter searchlight being shone on the Mob.

There was no reason for Dewey to be grateful to the Mob for saving his life and so he continued to pursue Hines. In 1940, he had him convicted on thirteen counts and given a sentence that was to run four to eight years. Hines entered Sing Sing and was paroled four years later to live out his life at home, where he died at the age of eighty in 1957, keeping his counsel to himself.

By the end of the war in 1945, old-style politics were gone, and the era of Tammany Hall was finished. The sons of the second- and third-generation Irish who had filled the jobs in the police and fire service were going into the professions and the base of the poor was diminishing. Even the Italians were moving up in society. As a result street crime became the preserve of the successors to the Jews, Irish and Italians: the blacks, Puerto Ricans and Hispanics.

The only place for the Irish, the Jews or the Italians who had neither the intelligence nor the volition to leave a life of crime was with the group variously called the Mob, the Syndicate, the Outfit or Cosa Nostra – none of which, although dominated by Italians, had any connection with the Sicilian Mafia, apart from a handful of Italian-Americans who had come originally from Sicily and would have been 'made' in the Sicilian Mafia. Although the American Cosa Nostra had a similar initiation ceremony, it gave entry solely to the American Mob and was quite separate from the Sicilian organisation. Entry to one did not confer entry to the other.

American criminals had a head start on the law because at this point the FBI did not accept that there was any such thing as organised crime. According to them, criminals were just dumb gangsters who understood only one language – kill or be killed. It is astonishing that they held this view for 20 years, in spite of powerful evidence to the contrary.

The gangs were multi-ethnic, but when Capone was sent to jail his gang was taken over by a Sicilian, Frank 'The Enforcer' Nitti, who was unique in being one of the only presidents of the Unione Siciliana to have survived assassination. Since the Capone gang was the biggest, it controlled the others, but only in Chicago. In New York, Luciano and Lansky ruled.

While the main activity of the Mob remained gambling and extortion, Lansky was thinking on a bigger canvas. He had had dealings with Cuba during Prohibition, because it was a source of molasses, and during the early '30s had befriended a politician called Fulgencio Batista. When Batista became Dictator-President, he opened Cuba's door to the Mob. In 1937, in return for permission to open casinos legally on the island away from American interference, Lansky arranged a regular income for Batista, reputed to be several million dollars a year.

News film of the time reveals Havana as a favoured holiday resort of thousands of American tourists who enjoyed theatre shows that were an early edition of what we now see in Las Vegas: dancing girls, fruit-loaded headdresses, sex shows, Latin rhythms and exotic colours.

But the main attraction of Cuba was gambling, which was prohibited throughout the entire United States, except in the almost totally inaccessible state of Nevada, which had legalised gambling during the 1847 Gold Rush and had never repealed the law. The centre of the action in Havana was the Hotel Nacional, which was owned by Lansky, whose brother, Jake, worked as pit boss and overseer of the casino. By the 1950s, every major American syndicate boss had a share of Cuban gambling and, as air travel improved and tourism increased, the profits soared and it was back to the good old days of manufacturing money.

But it all came to an end on New Year's Eve 1959, when Fidel Castro arrived in Havana. That night Castro's revolution not only ended Batista's reign but his men also smashed up the casinos, the symbol of the American occupation of their island. Castro did allow some to re-open for a short period, but, with no American tourists, there was no business so he closed them down completely.

Lansky is said to have lost £17 million in cash that was in Cuba awaiting transfer to Switzerland. In the 1960s, he acquired a share of the Colony Club in London but when the Home Office discovered his involvement it was shut down.

During his Cuban experience, Lansky had realised the fortunes that could be made from gambling and so he set his sights on Nevada. The only problem was getting there. Travelling across virtually the whole of the United States was extremely difficult and, once there, there was no attraction other than a casino. The catalyst to development was a Cleveland mobster called Morris Barney 'Moe' Dalitz, who had a vision of developing an old government rest-and-recreation resort which had been used by GIs during the war. Dalitz saw the possibility of building up a town around this place and so Las Vegas was created.

One of the first people that Dalitz and Lansky involved in the development of Las Vegas was Chicago veteran Bugsy Siegel, who was a great friend of the film star George Raft, who specialised in gangster roles. Siegel was involved in building the famous Flamingo Hotel, the first of its kind in Vegas, but as the costs mounted he got into so much trouble with his lenders that he was assassinated in June 1947.

Moe Dalitz and his Cleveland associates had operated illegal gambling in adjacent sites and laundered their earnings into another hotel, the Desert Inn, that also had trouble with construction costs.

Dalitz was always recognised as a criminal. He had originally appeared on the radar of crime investigators during Prohibition because he was associated with the Jewish gangs who smuggled Canadian alcohol across Lake Erie to Cleveland – the so-called 'Jewish Navy'. Later, in 1951, the Kefauver committee had named him as a major figure in organised crime, but he had managed to evade arrest or charge. His association with the Mob was highlighted in the findings of the California Organised Crime Control Commission when they named him as the architect of the money laundering process that developed Las Vegas in the early '60s. But Las Vegas ignores all of that and over the years has showered him with awards; he is still hailed by the city as 'Mr Las Vegas' because of his pivotal role in its development.

The role of moneyman fell to Allen Dorfman, the son of a former Capone gunman. He had become an insurance executive and was developing a legitimate career when he was called upon by the Mob. Basically, he became treasurer of the Las Vegas Development Corporation. The organisation got its main funds from a stupid, ambitious man who wanted to be president of the Teamsters Union so badly that he sold his union to the Mob: his name was Jimmy Hoffa.

Hoffa inaugurated the Teamsters pension fund, to which every member of the union contributed, and this became the Chicago Mob's 'bank'. Dorfman adopted the role of 'bank manager' and Hoffa was ordered to make huge loans to developers when no other institution would lend them money. He financed the Desert Inn and later Caesars Palace, the Dunes and the Fremont.

Truck drivers in America thereafter innocently 'lent' hundreds of millions of dollars to the Mob – and Jimmy Hoffa got the help he needed to become president of the union. From 1958 onwards, he was involved in a bitter running struggle with Robert Kennedy, which ended in 1964 when he was found guilty of jury tampering and getting illegal loans from the pension fund. He was jailed in 1967 but paroled by Nixon in 1971, probably because his union switched their normal Democratic allegiance to the Republicans. In 1975, he told his wife he was going out to have lunch with someone, and then disappeared to be never seen again. But by then Robert Kennedy had also been murdered.

In 1955, the Nevada State Gaming Control Board was set up to regulate gambling, but they had only 300 officials trying to regulate 200 casinos. In contrast, after lessons had been learned, when Resorts International opened Atlantic City as a legal gambling centre (the Mob being excluded), the New Jersey State Control Board had 450 agents supervising ten casinos. It is therefore not surprising that in the first 24 years of its existence not a single casino-owner in Las Vegas was ever investigated.

For 20 years, the Mob was allowed to use Las Vegas both to make and to launder money so that a newly rich America could disburse its excess wealth in gambling, entertainment and fantasy in the western desert.

But it got even better for the Mob when they got into drugs.

15

How the Mafia Moved on to Drugs

This is the story of one of the most remarkable and successful criminals the world has ever known. He survived a life-threatening injury at an early age, recovered from both drug addiction and syphilis, and failed to have his spirit broken by the severest prison conditions to which America could subject him. Prior to being jailed in the 1930s, he managed an industry that gave him an annual income of over $10 million. He possibly made an important contribution to the winning of the war in Europe before developing the modern drug industry to mega proportions while controlling organised crime both in Sicily and New York. He died of natural causes at the age of 68.

He bore many similarities to Yugoslavia's Marshal Tito, who held competing factions together for over 40 years. When both men died, their organisations all but self-imploded. His name of course was Charlie Lucky Luciano.

His early life is covered in Chapter 9, which tells of how he was taken from Sicily when he was ten to become a teenage runner for criminals, eventually joining the Masseria family. He was brutally attacked, almost murdered, then with Meyer Lansky arranged the murder of the boss, Joe Masseria, whereupon Luciano became the new boss.

It was obvious from facts that emerged later that he had used opium and cocaine on a regular basis and recognised their addictive properties – and the business opportunities that this presented. However, in the '30s, only the rich used these drugs. They could afford it, so there was no street crime caused by addicts trying to get money to pay their dealers.

Of all the decisions taken by the post-war American administration perhaps the worst was releasing and deporting Luciano, because it was to cost them dear. Had they known of his key position in organised crime, or indeed that crime was organised, then the future might well have turned out differently.

Although Luciano had worked with multi-ethnic gangs in America, such as Capone's, and although he was a close friend of Meyer Lansky, he was first and foremost a Sicilian. It was he who kept the Unione Siciliana intact during the difficult years of Prohibition after he took over from Masseria. Until then the bosses had given the impression that all they wanted to do was kill one another. Had he failed and allowed a distinct Sicilian 'heritage' in America to die, it is likely that the later link between Sicilian and American cousins would not have been created thus denying them access to the profits that ultimately led, albeit indirectly, to so much Italian corruption.

By the time Luciano was able to apply for parole at the end of the Second World War, he was living in relative comfort in the Great Meadows penitentiary in New York State. Rather surprisingly, the members of the parole board who examined his request were not only sympathetic but also unanimous in recommending it. One of the reasons for this surprising decision to let someone with a thirty-to-fifty-year sentence out in less than ten years was the fact they could get rid of him; Luciano had never applied for US citizenship and so could be deported with neither appeal nor challenge.

Rather ironically, the recommendation for parole arrived on the desk of the man who had jailed him, Thomas Dewey, and there could have been few others who would have known

Luciano better. He approved the request, apparently without any protest, because he had known all along that although Luciano's connection with prostitution was peripheral it could be proved, and that the sentence had not fitted the crime; and so on 8 February 1946 Luciano was put on board the SS *Laura Keene* bound for Italy. It seems that as far as Dewey was concerned he could get up to whatever he wanted as long as it was outside America.

Dewey did not die until 1971 and so had many years to regret the folly of his decision. He would have observed the devastation caused by Luciano's organisation as it not only damaged the lives of tens of thousands of the '60s generation but also, more importantly, the efficiency of the American forces in the Vietnam War. Luciano was only one of many Italian-Americans to be deported at the end of the war, however, and this probably made it easier for Dewey to sanction the decision of the parole board.

As a result of Fascism and Cesare Mori, the Sicilian Mafia was moribund and the deportees were all welcomed home. As we have seen, one of them, Nick Gentile, who went to Eraclea in Sicily (the home of the Canadian Mafia family, the Rizzutos), was even enlisted by the King in an effort to make sure the monarchists won the referendum, preventing Italy from becoming a republic. Like Luciano, the deportees had been sent into internal exile in their towns and villages of origin, but escaping from this was simple and as they became more active they breathed life into a moribund Mafia.

These men were no longer shepherds or farmers; they now had years of experience of America, knew about technology and, more importantly, the possibilities that technology afforded their generation. They had some knowledge of English and knew about all the latest American fashions and trends, transport, films – and some had even seen television! They all had friends and relatives still in America and thus many were sympathetic to Salvatore Giuliano's short-lived attempt to have Sicily made one of the states of America.

Among the other mafiosi to arrive back in Sicily at that time were Joe Profaci, Gaetano Badalamenti and Carlo Gambino, all of whom we will come across again later in this book.

When the *Laura Keene* docked in Genoa after eleven days at sea, Luciano was not met by old mafiosi friends but by the police, who, to his horror, escorted him to the town of his birth, Lecara Friddi, which, although better than cold, damp jails in New York State, did not offer the comfort of the Waldorf Astoria, which he was probably looking forward to. Unknown to him, one of the agreements between the Americans and the Italians was that he would be in virtual internal exile in Lecara Friddi, the same tactic used by Mussolini during the Fascist years.

Once in his home town, he got the sort of welcome he had rather hoped for in Genoa, Naples and Palermo: the mayor with a red sash, the village band with out-of-tune clarinets, the statue of the local saint brought out on display and free pasta, porchetta and wine for all in the piazza. After a few months of village life, however, it was no problem for a man with Luciano's contacts to arrange a move to Naples, where he set up house with a dancer from the famous opera house the San Carlo called Igea Lissoni.

While Hoover and the FBI refused to recognise the danger of narcotics and the organisation of crime, this view was not shared by the head of the Federal Bureau of Narcotics, Harry Anslinger. Had the request for parole landed upon his desk, it would not have been approved. He had the foresight to realise that with his experience of supply and distribution Luciano would become a major player in any future developments in the narcotics industry. Not only did he have numerous contacts in both Italy and America but he was also not the dumb, rough, tough criminal epitomised by Capone and his like. He had 'brains' and was going to be a formidable opponent should he choose to enter the drug business. And Anslinger was sure that he would, because he was quite certain that Luciano would not grow old in Lecara Friddi.

His fears were justified when Luciano turned up in Cuba within a year of his deportation. Batista's Cuba at that time was in the pocket of Luciano's childhood friend Meyer Lansky, who was now using the island's casinos as a cash cow. When Anslinger discovered Luciano's whereabouts, he of course had little chance of persuading Batista to deport him, so he trumped up a charge that Luciano was smuggling heroin into the United States, which immediately had him once again deported to Italy.

Luciano had few of the basic Catholic moral principles held by the dons of the first Mafia, who considered involvement in drugs beyond the pale. At that time, in the late '40s and early '50s, few people in the world understood drug addiction. People were smoking and drinking, usually to excess, and that seemed enough to satisfy most. Drugs had made no impact whatsoever; in fact, they were almost a joke. Tom Lehrer songs about people going around cities selling 'dope' and being known as peddlers in the old-fashioned meaning of the word were laughed at. There was no inkling of the wholesale destruction of society that we see today and most people would have had little idea of the fallout that would occur from the narcotics business over the coming decades.

It has been said that the Mafia wanted to stay away from drugs because it brought too much police surveillance, which would in turn disturb other activities. While this view was certainly held by the older dons, the young ones did not agree and it was only a minority of families who stood back from the activity. Most saw the huge potential to be developed and realised that addicts made a very secure and stable market: curing addiction was so difficult that business could only increase.

Pushing drugs was nothing new. To most Britons, the East India Company symbolised trailblazing the Empire, flying the flag overseas, guarding our interests and making good profits for investors; but they were the original narco-imperialist organisation and the fallout of their creation of a Chinese opium market from Hong Kong is now well known. At the time the narcotics industry was not considered in the same way as it is today: wrong and evil.

Upper-class Victorians used opiates as drugs of relaxation, and cocaine-sniffing was common. Sir James Young Simpson first used chloroform as an anaesthetic in 1847, but it was also commonly used as a pleasant 'sniff'. In fact, there were those close to the discovery of the anaesthetic agent who believed that Simpson and his friends were merely experimenting with chemicals to develop better 'sniffs' when they came across a mixture that put them to sleep! Since it was an upper-class pastime, it is difficult to have an opinion about addiction because addiction is only noticed when there is a problem.

The definition of a 'problem' is also difficult. One of Britain's foremost psychiatrists, an expert in alcohol addiction, once said to me that 'a problem is only a problem when it becomes a problem'. This is why no one knew that Luciano was an addict until he was imprisoned for his prostitution activities and had his heroin removed.

In the 1950s, the drug-smuggling trade was in its infancy. At that time there was no mass market and no social problem, so little effort was made by customs officials in most countries to do anything about it. Joe Profaci, one of the men deported to Sicily along with Luciano, returned to own the Mamma Mia Importing Company in New York, which was a front for the smuggling of drugs in shipments of cheese, olives and anchovies.

The Sicilians and Neopolitans had a long history of smuggling cigarettes from Tunisia. A Corsican, Pascal Molinelli, was the overall boss of cigarette smuggling. He owned a large private fleet that sailed to all the Mediterranean ports. The south coast of Sicily, especially around Agrigento and Sciacca, was only a few miles from Tunisia and there were multiple small harbours and a disinterested customs service. The rocky shoreline, full of natural harbours and coves, between Castellammare and Palermo also gave good cover in the north of the island. Naples was the final distribution point for the smuggled cigarettes and there the Camorra were in charge. Between Tunisia and the distribution point, the price of the cigarettes multiplied by a factor of ten.

The move to drug smuggling was, therefore, simple because all the transport was in place; the pick-ups were made at sea from Turkish boats by Molinelli's fleet and Sicilian fishing boats that he would have commissioned for single jobs.

Luciano chose to make his headquarters in Naples rather than Palermo probably for a number of reasons. First, it was likely to have been safer to live in a large cosmopolitan city that was full of Camorra gangs, who would support him. Second, it had a position of strategic importance in the smuggling business. Finally, and most importantly, it let him stand aside from taking sides in inter-family quarrels in Sicily. In New York, there was a Commission, where every murder had to be sanctioned before it was carried out and the victim might have some idea that all was not well beforehand; however, in Sicily, it was rather like the Wild West, and someone like Luciano could have been killed in a moment because of some perceived slight to someone.

We do not know if or when Luciano made the move from cigarettes to drugs, but he would have had a keener idea than most as to the business opportunities presented by narcotics. Although cigarettes created an addiction that was difficult to control, their general supply was assured in abundance and so the price could never go above the level set by the manufacturers. Obtaining, smuggling and distributing cigarettes, therefore, had a limit on profitability. The market for drugs, on the other hand, was not as confined. There were no manufacturers who would sell them in shops at a fixed price, mainly because it was illegal and, as the Mafia bosses had learned from Prohibition, when something is illegal it becomes a more desirable product.

The one difference from the cigarette trade, however, was that the raw opium which the boats picked up in the Mediterranean and delivered to Naples had to be processed and that meant establishing refineries, which in turn made it necessary to employ chemists – in particular, chemists who would be willing to act in an illegal capacity.

The first refineries were set up by Molinelli in Marseilles, where he succeeded in manufacturing heroin from the raw product for about 15 years. The discovery that Marseilles was the centre of heroin refining was featured in the film *The French Connection,* unforgettably starring Gene Hackman and his pork-pie hat. During these years, the narcotics industry had settled into a well-regulated and well-conducted business built on the primitive arrangements that were once used for cigarette smuggling.

The raw opium that had been picked up in the Mediterranean would arrive in Sicily, be handled by the Mafia to Naples, where the Camorra would liaise with the Corsicans to get it refined in Marseilles. From there it would reach America again via Naples and Sicily by plane, cargo boat, small boats and human carriers. Many outwardly respectable import and export companies in the USA were used to receive the heroin for distribution.

The transfer of drugs in the early days was easy. In the 1950s, there was another wave of emigration from Sicily to America and families carried their possessions in trunks or similar containers, perfect for hiding drugs. At that time no one would have suspected them of being part of the narcotic-smuggling industry. The drugs were also moved to America by body carriers, now called mules. These were village women who wore special girdles that could hide four kilograms of heroin; to deceive security and the sniffer dogs, they drenched themselves in perfume. Men transported the same weight by packing it into special leggings.

Before 'mules' started to receive very long prison sentences if caught, this was a very sought after job for poor villagers because not only were they paid a fee of $5,000 per trip but they also spent a few days in a New York hotel.

Naturally, parcels were commonly sent between families, with sorely missed foods such as mortadella, prosciutto, cheese, panforte, torrone and biscotti going to America and cigarettes, clothes and candies coming back to Sicily. These parcels would be wrapped in cheesecloth, which would then be stitched closed, along with the customs declaration, and the address stencilled on the outside. For more than a decade, these parcels were also used to smuggle drugs across borders, until the narcotic problem became so great that the Drug Enforcement Agency (DEA) received extra finance so that they could employ enough manpower for effective surveillance.

By the mid-'50s, it was obvious to Luciano that he had created a massive industry that would do nothing other than grow and continue to produce massive profits. His management skills at this point came to the fore: he realised that personal, family and informal arrangements had to be better integrated. His American end was also wobbling, and with very good reason.

In 1950–1, Senator Estes Kefauver chaired the Commission on Organised Crime in America. His committee interviewed hundreds of people and many of the Mob were taken into custody as a result of their failure to cooperate. When their hearings were televised from New York, the nation watched spellbound as one after another sleek-haired, squat, podgy-lipped Italian-Americans sat in the witness chair and refused to answer any questions, every one of them pleading the Fifth Amendment, refusing to testify because of the risk of self-incrimination.

The report introduced the word 'Mafia' to a larger audience – at that time it had been seldom used. 'There is a sinister criminal organisation known as the Mafia operating throughout the country,' the committee warned in its final report.

Kefauver concluded that there were two main groups, based in Chicago and New York. He identified that they were involved in prostitution, extortion, gambling and narcotics – and so the risk that the old dons had identified, of involvement in drugs leading to a closer examination by the police of the basic 'family businesses', was proving to be true.

As dissension and uncertainty as to future Mafia involvement was going on among the five New York families, many found that their decision not to deal in drugs was correct, because when the Narcotics Control Act was passed in 1956, it gave the courts power to sentence anyone convicted of a narcotics offence to 20–40 years in jail. It was now getting too risky. Drugs gave a good return, but their basic businesses of gambling, loan-sharking and labour racketeering were keeping them all very comfortable and many reckoned that they did not need the added danger of dealing in narcotics.

And it was at that point, in 1957, that Charlie Luciano arranged a meeting.

16

LUCKY LUCIANO'S SUMMIT

The meeting that Luciano arranged in October 1957 took place in the Grand Hotel Et Des Palmes in the centre of Palermo.

At the end of the nineteenth century, this had become one of the most famous hotels in the world. Palermo, along with Paris and Naples, was the place where the rich and famous went to party throughout the winter and those who did not have a home in the city would stay in the hotel for the season. It was central, opulent, large and full of only the very best people. Nowadays you will not meet duchesses, countesses or even minor *marchese*; you are much more likely to meet busloads of Japanese tourists.

Richard Wagner orchestrated *Parsifal* during an extended stay in the hotel, using a room that has come to be known as Sala Wagner; it was also the room in which Renoir painted Wagner's portrait. At that time Sala Wagner was a sumptuous room decorated in the grandest baroque style with antique mirrors that reflected the vaulted sky-blue and gilt ceiling, but today it is just a sad, dusty barn of a room, with tired and torn wallpaper acting as a backdrop for shabby, disintegrating furniture.

But in October 1957 it had been restored to its original opulence after the wartime bombing and while the aristocrats had gone, never to return, there were plenty of wealthy tourists who regularly used it. One of the regulars was Luciano, who was such a frequent and important visitor that the management reserved a room that opened onto the Sala Wagner for his own private use, called the Little Red Room.

It was here that between the 10th and 14th of October 1957 Luciano did the impossible; he created a set of rules by which the Sicilian Mafia and their American cousins agreed to abide if they were to work together.

Many of the people who met were blood relatives because they had all come from the same group of families in the same area. The Sicilian families who had become the main players at the European end of the drug trade were mostly from the small area around Palermo, places such as Castellammare and Bagheria, and their family names became legends in Mafia folklore: Inzerillo, Bontade, Badalamenti, Greco and La Barbera.

The American delegation was led by Joe Bonanno, a man who was also born in Castellammare. Bonanno fled the Fascists in 1933 to settle in America, where he got in at the tail end of Prohibition, taking over the leadership of Luciano's family in the '40s after the boss was deported. He had already followed Luciano as the head of the Unione Siciliana when the latter was sent to jail, and he had succeeded in persuading his fellow Sicilians to stop vendettas and to use the Unione more creatively. What Joe created was the original American Sicilian family, never allowing anything other than Sicilian dialect to be spoken in his home and hiring only Sicilians. If one New York family could be labelled Mafia rather than the Mob or the Americanised Cosa Nostra, it was the Bonanno family.

When Joe arrived at the old Leonardo Da Vinci airport in Rome (now Ciampino), he was met by the Minister of Foreign Trade, Bernardo Mattarella, a fellow Sicilian from Castellammare and a relative of Stefano Magaddino, who ran the Buffalo branch of the Bonanno family. Joe stayed in Rome for a couple of days to recover from the flight, all the time receiving VIP treatment courtesy of the Italian government.

In his autobiography, he describes his 1957 'holiday' in Sicily, where he had 'a pleasurable time spent catching up with old friends and old memories'. In America, his memoir catalysed a Grand Jury hearing, even though he explained the Mafia in terms of 'the Sicilian way of life' and 'rustic chivalry'. His writing evokes the romance of the first rural Mafia and fails to mention either the meeting or the agenda. As a result of refusing to testify, he spent 14 months in jail.

People who were successful in America did not just visit Palermo for a few days' holiday – even though Luciano had invited them. The flight was long and uncomfortable, and the American police would ask questions on their return. There had to be a very good reason – and, on this occasion, there was.

After the Narcotics Control Act was passed in 1956, over 200 major American gangsters had received long prison sentences. They included Bonanno's right-hand man, Carmine Galante, who was sentenced to fifteen to twenty years, while two ranking men in the Lucchese family each got forty years.

Of the New York families, three out of five members of the Luccheses, two in five of the Gambinos, one in two of the Genoveses, one in three of the Colombos and one in three of the Bonannos had been arrested under the terms of the Act and given long prison terms.

There was no possibility of the Americans continuing in the narcotics trade in the face of these penalties. What they needed was unknown people to come to America to run the business at ground level; people who were unknown to the police, who had no criminal records and whose photographs and fingerprints were not on police files. In other words, young Sicilians were needed if the narcotics business was to continue. If that couldn't be arranged, then the Americans would pull out of the business and continue their traditional businesses, especially the new one of labour racketeering with their new-found friends in the labour unions, through whom they could control and bleed the cities.

Joe Bonanno chaired meetings in the Little Red Room from a script written by Luciano. We know about the meeting not from Luciano, who did not divulge any information to his biographers,

Martin Gosch and Richard Hammer, but from the confessions of Tomasso Buscetta, a young rising star of the La Barbera family who claimed to have been in attendance.

He described the few old dons who had been invited out of respect as being completely out of place both in dress, language and attitude, exemplifying the widening gap between the old and the new Mafia. The demeanour of the old men of honour was low-key and their values modest and rural, and basically they did not want the organisation to get into drugs. But their successors valued profit more than honour.

The meeting was successful because both sides could see that it was a win-win situation. Although the Americans could have settled for a very good future based on their traditional activities, not to have attempted to continue in what was obviously going to be a hugely profitable business would have been foolish, even though some American Godfathers were at one with the old Sicilian dons in disapproving of dealing in narcotics.

The Sicilians, on the other hand, needed a market for drugs because there was absolutely no demand in Sicily, hardly any in Italy and at that time only a small market in Europe. Using drugs was just not part of Italian culture, nor is it today. One has to remember that Italy is a country where people need little help to enjoy themselves and even today some pubs are still shut on New Year's Eve, not out of Presbyterian restraint but because the Italians can enjoy themselves without getting drunk. The police in Italy had neither the experience nor the interest in drugs; there was no problem, as far as they were concerned, at that time.

The basic agreement drawn up in Palermo was that the Sicilians would pay the Americans 'rent' in order to import and distribute drugs on their territory: the New York families were basically leasing their city to Sicily. This was possible because both sides knew that the American police did not communicate with their counterparts in Italy and vice versa. Furthermore, records and information were not exchanged. The American police knew when one of the Mob left the country but paid no attention when a young Sicilian with no police record entered or left the country, and there were hardly any mafiosi in Castellammare or Palermo who did not have a relative in New York.

That is as far as the agreement went. There were no grand plans to merge the Italian Mafia and the New York families, there was no agreement on methodology or management and there was no agreement on strategy or punishments; it was just 'business'. It was agreed that the Sicilian Mafia would send young men to New York to distribute drugs and would also be in charge of drug imports to America. This meant that the Americans could have clean hands and so be virtually immune from the risk of imprisonment. All they would get was a fairly substantial 'rent'.

There were a couple of other small bits of business conducted. Luciano obviously saw tensions developing between the Sicilian families and so, in an effort to defuse these and to avoid the risk of future conflict that might destroy everything, he persuaded them to adopt the American model of a Commission that oversaw all Mafia activity and acted as a coordinator of family activity. In view of what happened after he died, this is a tribute to the foresight and intelligence of this very remarkable man.

It was proposed that each province of Sicily would have its own Commission, but it was not until the '70s that a National Commission for the whole island came into being. The original Commission, as far as Palermo was concerned, involved fifteen families spread over five districts. Each district, or *mandamento*, contained three families, who would choose one of their number to represent them on the Palermo Commission. This member had to be someone other than a *capo*, a move designed to take power out of the hands of *capi*, who from time to time might be psychopaths unwilling to share corporate responsibility. But the first the magistrates heard about this arrangement was when Tomasso Buscetta became an informer 25 years later.

The faultline that ran through this altruistic idea was the representation on the Commission; there was never any possibility of a *capo* delegating important decision-making to an underling.

Buscetta, however, said that he saw it as a way of getting back to the honourable society of the first Mafia, when there was a common thread of brotherhood binding the group together. I think at this point, when he was confessing in the 1980s, he was joking!

From the American point of view, they wanted a Sicilian Commission because it saved them from getting involved with individual families in the event of an inter-family conflict. They insisted that if the Sicilians were going to work in parallel with the Americans, then they had to do it the American way, an attitude still reflected in American foreign policy today. The Americans wanted the Commission to function in the same way as it did in America, laying down major policy, mediating disputes between families and, most importantly, deciding who needed to be murdered.

And just as Americans today do not appreciate that they are not dealing with people with American values, the Mob got the structure wrong even though the idea was good. The embryo Commission had a dummy run before Joe Bonanno finished his so-called holiday and it did not involve drugs – rather the murder of one of their number.

The victim was a psychopathic killer who had been a very useful creation of the Mob's during the 1930s. Alberto Anastasia had the perfect curriculum vitae for his role as head of Murder Incorporated. This organisation was set up by the American Cosa Nostra in order to carry out agreed assassinations. Anastasia had so far performed well and was reliable: phone a number, give a name, agree a price and someone would be killed. However he had started to take on a life of his own and was deciding who to kill without reference to his masters. Given that the situation had worked well for over 20 years, it required agreement among the group to terminate it and the Palermo meeting was the perfect forum for such a decision.

Shortly after the meeting ended and the participants had returned from whence they came, Anastasia was shot in a barber's chair in the Manhattan Sheraton by four unknown men while having a shave. Two of the men were Sicilians and had travelled back with the American delegation.

Vito Genovese, who had attended the meetings, used a rather primitive method to inform the other American families about the arrangement thrashed out in Palermo. He got them to meet a month later, on 12 November 1957, in a country house owned by Joe La Barbera, the head of the Pennsylvania Mafia, in a small town called Apalachin on the New York–Pennsylvania border.

Unknown to either Genovese or La Barbera, the house was already under covert observation by the local police on the grounds that a wealthy man with an Italian name had moved into the white Anglo-Saxon district. While ostensibly running a bottling plant, he also carried a gun and had been noted to have offered police bribes for traffic offences. Sergeant Edgar Croswell of the New York State Police already had Joe under surveillance when his visitors arrived.

On 11 November, three people who did not look like soft-drink salesmen had checked into a local hotel but refused to sign the register. Furthermore, Croswell was suspicious of their expensive cars, all without state number plates, and when he saw them parked outside La Barbera's house, he sent some troopers down to note their car numbers. As they were doing so, they were astonished to see dozens of well-dressed overweight men running out of the house. While some jumped in their cars and drove off, others ran over the fields and into the woods. Since there was only one road out of the complex, Croswell was able to have it blocked; those who had been stupid enough to drive rather than run were arrested and taken to the local police station.

When their records were checked, the full impact of what Croswell had uncovered became apparent to the police. Of the 58 men detained, 50 had been arrested in the past and had police records; 35 had been convicted of a range of felonies; 23 had served prison terms; 15 had convictions for narcotic offences, 30 for breaching gambling laws and 23 for firearms offences.

Since they were carrying no weapons and had done nothing illegal in visiting Joe La Barbera, they could not be charged and were freed. The men turned out to be the cream of the Mob, from New York, Philadelphia, Cleveland, Detroit, Boston, Kansas, Texas, Denver, California and Chicago.

But there was an even more bizarre end to this story. The FBI was, of course, routinely informed of the meeting and the arrests, but they either chose to ignore it or were requested to ignore it because they took absolutely no action and never followed it up. J. Edgar Hoover had apparently still to be convinced that crime in the United States was 'organised' – there is no record of his interpretation of the finding of dozens of known crime bosses from all over America meeting in one place.

Lucky Luciano's summary of the fiasco put all the blame on Vito Genovese:

> What the hell did Vito think would happen when a bunch of guys from all over the country, dressed in fancy clothes, come drivin' up some country road in their big Cadillacs like it was a fuckin' parade. I bet not one of them overfed fat guys runnin' through the woods for their lives had been off the city streets before.

And so, from then on, nearly every Sicilian who went to America, or rather got permission from home to go and work in America, worked in the pizza trade. They were all sent to live in 'Little Sicily', which was Knickerbocker Avenue in the Bushwick district of Brooklyn. Most of the property was owned by the Bonanno family and therefore the Sicilians came from Castellammare. They arrived in America via Montreal, where the Vitale family arranged identity papers for their uncomplicated admission to America.

These young Sicilians acquired the rather derogatory nickname 'zips', the origin of which remains obscure. In true Sicilian style, they kept themselves to themselves and did not socialise with their American cousins, which did not add to their popularity.

It became part of New York culture that just as immigrant Chinese worked in Chinese restaurants, immigrant Sicilians worked in pizza parlours. The difference was that the Chinese were selling chicken chow mein while the Sicilians would be wrapping up heroin with their margaritas and quattro stagiones.

Similar patterns for dealing in drugs were later imitated in many other countries, where outlets such as coffee bars, ice cream vans and snack bars were used for distribution. It was all done so openly that the police never suspected what was really happening. Heroin was being distributed and money laundered right under their noses.

Unfortunately, one of the errors that the inward-looking American police made in those years was that they paid no attention to the fact that nine out of ten Sicilians who were deported in those years worked in pizzerias. Their philosophy seemed to be that things would be OK if they just got these hoodlums out of their backyard.

The late Claire Sterling described the Mafia as an octopus, and it was in these years that the tentacles grew, sucking in many other countries.

17

HOW THE FRENCH CONNECTION BECAME SICILIAN

In 1969, Richard Nixon began his War on Drugs, appointing Henry Kissinger as its leader. He, in turn, hired another young Italian-American, Rudolph Giuliani, and between them they started to knock heads together in an attempt to get the FBI, the DEA, the Internal Revenue Service, customs and immigration, and the metropolitan police forces to work together, sharing information under the umbrella organisation the Crime and Drug Enforcement Task Force.

Although Turkey was the main source of drugs in these years, due to the ease of delivery from its neighbours, Afghanistan and Iran, its main role was in the transportation of these drugs to the rest of Europe. It was overtaken, however, by Bulgaria, a country which at that time was known for little else other than its blind allegiance to the Soviet Union, winning all the weightlifting medals at the Olympics and usually ending up in the quarter-finals of football tournaments.

The reason for the Bulgarians' entry into the drug market was that in 1968 they had set up an organisation called Kintex, which acted as a government arms supplier. At first the market was confined to Lebanon, supplying Palestinians and Syrians, but soon it expanded to include the Yemenis, Pakistani terrorists, Filipinos and the ANC.

The arms were bought from Italy, Czechoslovakia, Hungary and Poland and sold for dollars or gold – or drugs.

Bulgaria was a good site for the distribution of drugs because in those days Transcontinental TIR trucks could, by international agreement, be sealed in the country of origin and travel freely by road across all European borders. In the 1960s and '70s, nearly three-quarters of the opium reaching the West came via this route. The man in charge of the operation in Bulgaria was the head of Turkish organised crime, Abuzer Ugurlu, who became better known when one of his former employees, Mehmet Ali Agca, attempted to assassinate Pope John Paul II in 1981.

The first move Kissinger made was to pay drug-growing countries such as Iran, Turkey, Mexico and Afghanistan to outlaw growing poppies and marijuana, giving the farmers what they would have earned for their crop had they sold it to drug agents, in the hope that they would see it as a bonus because they could then make more money growing another crop. The Vietnam War had ended by this time, thus temporarily stopping the supply from the Golden Triangle.

The Crime and Drug Enforcement Task Force put pressure on the French government to find and close the eight refineries in Marseilles, leaving Pascal Molinelli with a lot of out-of-work chemists for hire.

Molinelli's first move was to offer a partnership with the Camorra, but this did not play well with the Mafia and, after a short and bloody war, the Mafia converted the Camorra to the role of junior partners.

Ugurlu then approached the Sicilian Mafia to offer three key things: a supply, a protected delivery service and immunity at the start point. The work would be shared by the Sicilian Mafia families, either running the refineries, arranging transport and distribution, providing mules or laundering the money. The embryonic east Sicilian Mafia families would be in charge of importing the drugs and distributing them to the west of the island because the narcotics coming by sea would be landed in the region of Catania.

The agreement was concluded on Camorra territory, on the estate of the Nuvoletta brothers near Naples, by the leaders of the main families: Michele, Salvatore and Pino Greco, Gaetano Badalamenti, Stefano Bontade, Salvatore Inzerillo and Bernardo Provenzano, who was acting for and under instruction from his jailed leader, Luciano Leggio.

When the French connection was broken and the short war with the Camorra was won, the Sicilians started building their own refineries, as did most other criminal organisations in other European countries, but Sicily had the major share of the market, with 15 refineries. The Alcamo laboratory near Castellammare was producing one and a half tons of refined heroin a year and, with the introduction of a new electronic pressure pump, invented and manufactured in Bulgaria, they could have increased this to four and a half tons a year, had the laboratory not been discovered and closed.

Many refineries were built within the grounds of the estates of Mafia *capi*. For example, Michele Greco, also known as 'The Pope', was a pillar of Palermo society, sitting on the board of 18 companies, including banks and insurance firms. He had a large estate at Ciaculli called La Favarella, where Palermo's Establishment, including police and politicians, lunched, shot pigeons and wild boar, and partied. Even though from the earliest days there was a long family history of Mafia involvement – some Grecos had gone to jail for absolutely barbarous murders – Michele seemed above it all, with his stately bearing, shock of silver hair, perfect manners and lack of showiness. But it was all a front.

When he was arrested years later, his double life was exposed when dozens of tunnels and passageways were found at La Favarella, ensuring a quick getaway in the event of a raid. He had also bought all the nearby houses in Ciaculli so that he would be surrounded by 'friends'. This was important not just for personal safety but in order to protect another building on his estate – a heroin refinery.

By the mid-1970s, the Sicilian contribution to the American heroin market was 60 per cent, with the rest coming from Mexico and South-East Asia. For each of the first five years of the decade, they were exporting six tons to half a million *known* addicts. These were those who had registered, had got into trouble or had sought help: there were probably three times this number actually using heroin in America, with no social, medical or financial problems. With a selling price of $250 million per ton, the output from the Alcamo refinery alone translated into $400 million, which, when multiplied by 15 to convert it to street value, became a $6 billion-a-year industry, which today would translate as $50 billion.

The other source of Mafia-controlled drugs was from South America. Even though it might sound unlikely to other Europeans, Mafia involvement there was as natural as summer following spring.

Between 1820 and 1924, six million Europeans emigrated to South America and, of these, 47 per cent came from Italy.

Although Italians now form the new aristocracy of Argentina and Brazil, their great-grandfathers went to replace the then-freed slaves on the coffee plantations. Between 1880 and 1900, 800,000 Italians arrived in Brazil and, although some were seasonal workers, the majority stayed. This meant that by 2000 the majority of the white population was of Italian extraction, with the Portuguese in second place, in spite of the fact that Portuguese is the national language. In Argentina, 40 per cent of the population have Italian surnames. In 2004 in Brazil and Argentina alone, the Italian diaspora numbered almost four million.

Although Argentina and Brazil were the destinations of the original Italian immigrants, those with a criminal bent discovered Venezuela, a country that the original Spanish colonists had called 'Little Venice' because of the stilt villages built by the Amerindian tribe on the Orinoco River. If you want to hide from someone, Venezuela is the perfect place, for many reasons. As well as having a very varied geography, it has a 1,750-mile coastline. In the north-west there are the Andes and on the north coast are myriad islands, formerly called the Dutch Antilles, among which are Aruba, Bonaire and Curaçao. In the south there are the Guiana Highlands while in the centre of the country are Los Llanos, the extensive plains that extend from the Colombian border on the west to the river delta of the Orinoco in the east.

Mafiosi on the run could obtain citizenship with very little problem and, once there, for $500 they could also create a completely new identity, including birth certificate, driver's licence and passport. The great value of citizenship was that Venezuela had no extradition treaties with any other country. There were also no exchange controls. Dollars could be brought in, changed to bolivars, deposited in a local bank and used to underwrite ghost companies. The money could then be withdrawn, reconverted to dollars and exported.

In the 1970s, as a result of US pressure at the height of the marijuana boom, Colombia was paid to spray with pesticides all the fields that grew the drug, thus opening up the cocaine market. The centre for the export of cocaine was the island of Aruba, which is equidistant from Venezuela and the Colombian town of Maicao on the La Guajira Peninsula. Aruba had been a smuggler's paradise since colonial times, when it was used to circumvent the Spanish trade monopoly.

By 1983, it had achieved *status aparte*, meaning that it was semi-autonomous. The Netherlands agreed that it take on independence by 1996; however, this was postponed upon the request of Aruba's then Prime Minister and the island reverted to colonial status. In March 1993, *Corriere della Sera*, one of the main Italian newspapers, described it as 'the first state to be bought by the Mafia bosses'. It has been alleged that at the end of the 1980s and the beginning of the '90s, the Mafia invested heavily in Aruba.

The report was probably inaccurate because if any family 'owns' Aruba it is the Mansurs. As part of their portfolio, they own Interbank, as well as the licence from Philip Morris for the distribution of Marlboro cigarettes throughout the Caribbean and South America. They own the biggest hotel, The Cabana, and the casino, plus the largest island newspaper, *Diario*. They are also the backers of the AVP Party, led by a former Prime Minister, Henny Eman. In December 1996, when President Clinton put Aruba on the list of major illicit drug-transit countries, the Mansur family were mentioned.

One of the most important vehicles for smuggling cocaine in the 1980s was tuna fish. In Sicily, the centre of tuna fishing is Agrigento and so it is not surprising that Mafia expertise was transferred to this industry in the Caribbean. They bought up most of the tuna fleets and canneries in Latin America and used these to smuggle cocaine and heroin by sea to the United States. So much cocaine was shipped out of Venezuela and Colombo in cans and frozen blocks of tuna that the colloquial name for cocaine in the Caribbean became *atun blanco* – white tuna.

Ironically, it was the conservationists, not the police, who killed off this method of smuggling. Tuna fishing involves chasing, capturing and killing dolphins for bait and because the tuna fleets were killing off more than 50,000 dolphins a year in the east Pacific, a US Federal Court in 1991 ordered embargoes of tuna from the Caribbean nations that refused to adopt adequate dolphin protection measures. The Italian custom of signing up to something and then ignoring it might have seemed the easy way out, but in this case signing up meant allowing outside observers on the boats, and, for obvious reasons, this was not acceptable. The response in Venezuela from the large numbers of people making a living from cocaine was so vitriolic that two leading conservationists who had absolutely nothing to do with either drugs or the Mafia were forced to flee the country.

The Mafia's connection with Venezuela continues today. On 28 February 2005, there was a snippet in *Corriere della Sera* that read as follows:

Eight persons have been arrested by *carabinieri* from Osti and police officers of Rome's 'Fidene Serpentari' charged with leading a criminal organisation devoted to drug smuggling. The drugs came from Venezuela via different European and South American countries. There are two Italians, three Venezuelans, two Lithuanians and one Dutchman held in custody. Among them is a lawyer and a member of the Venezuelan Prime Minister's bodyguard troop.

. . . but the link had been forged more than 40 years before this rather anodyne news story.

Two of the people present at the signing of the agreement between the Camorra, Kintex and the Mafia were Pasquale and Liborio Cuntrera from Agrigento province on the south coast of Sicily, where, in 2002, a Ministry of the Interior report stated there were 47 Mafia families and 580 'made' men. The Cuntreras started as guards for estates, like most low-level mafiosi, and their early police records show that they had no compunction about killing, thus demonstrating their essential psychopathic personalities. Two clans intermarried over the years to the extent that in Mafia history they are referred to as one, the Cuntrera-Caruanas. They all came from Eraclea Minoa, the small town near Agrigento.

Giuseppe Tomasi di Lampedusa set part of his novel *The Leopard* in Agrigento province and it is the birthplace of the playwright Luigi Pirandello and the writer Leonardo Sciascia. Just outside the town is the most complete set of Greek temples outside Greece itself, which sit on a small hill surrounded by almond blossom. The site is overlooked by an awful sprawl of a town on a hill that appears to represent the outcome of deliberations by a panel of demented town planners. On one side you see the temples and the sea, on the other a motorway on stilts and a cement factory, and in the east is an incomplete highway started almost fifty years ago.

Pasquale and Liborio emigrated to Montreal in 1954, took Canadian nationality in 1957 and formed the nucleus of a Mafia family that aligned itself to the Bonanno clan in New York, with

Carmine Galante acting as 'viceroy'. After Galante was killed in Brooklyn in 1979, the Montreal family was taken over by Paolo Violi and the Cuntreras worked for him. It was an uncomfortable period because the Sicilians from Agrigento had to share power with the Calabrian Contornos. Inevitably, there was a shooting war, which ended when Violi was assassinated.

The Cuntreras had seen this coming and, sensing trouble, had moved out of Montreal and gone to Venezuela with their other brother Gaspare. There they joined up with Salvatore Greco, who was living in Caracas under the alias Renato Martino Caruso. With the support of the Cuntreras, he ran the drug trade from Venezuela for the next 16 years until he died of liver cirrhosis in 1979.

Liborio later moved to England and bought a house in Guildford. Those investigators who have attempted to follow up Cuntrera with a view to establishing whether or not London was used for money laundering for this particular family have never proved anything. Like Salvatore Greco, Liborio too died at home from cirrhosis of the liver, in 1989.

After Liborio had been domiciled in London in the '70s, his two sons, Pasquale and Alfonso, arrived and made the UK capital their base for frequent commutes to Montreal and Zurich. Alfonso bought Broomfield Manor in Godalming, Surrey, while Pasquale invested in an estate in Hook Heath, Woking. The brothers also shared a lakeside villa in Lugano, which is the banking centre for those Italians who want to hide their money from the tax authorities.

In 1976, they recruited a man from Altofonte, a town midway between Corleone and Palermo, a place that hadn't had a Mafia family until it was encouraged by the Corleone Godfather Luciano Leggio, from his jail cell. This man, who 29 years later, in 2005, would be tried but acquitted for the murder of Roberto Calvi, was Francesco Di Carlo. Shortly after he arrived in London, Di Carlo bought himself a Ferrari and invested in the full range of service industries, as well as creating a string of dummy import and export companies. The police caught up with him for his drug-related activities and on 11 March 1987 he was sentenced to 25 years in jail for drug smuggling.

The final identifiable man to join the group came from the other renowned Mafia town near Palermo, Bagheria. Michelangelo Aiello set up an import-export company called Industri Derivati Agrumi (IDA) that dealt in citrus fruits, but which made no deliveries, since it was used as a pathway for money that moved between Palermo, London and New York. It was eventually discovered that, as well as money laundering, Aiello had swindled the financial arm of the Italian government's fund for the regeneration of the South and Sicily (Italtrade) out of $350 million.

At the beginning of September 1992, while still a colonel in the army, the present Prime Minister of Venezuela, Hugo Chavez, led an abortive coup attempt. This failed and led to his imprisonment, but it catalysed another important event: the removal of Pasquale and Gaspare Cuntrera from Caracas.

In order to give them no time for delaying tactics, they were removed from their houses in the middle of the night by the secret police and held incommunicado for two days in order to prevent them from having any contact with influential people on the outside who might get them freed. They were then secretly smuggled out of the country, as if they were a drug shipment. On arrival at Fiumicino, Rome, on 8 September 1992, they were arrested by Alessandro Pansa, the head of the economic crime section of the Italian police.

Gaspare Cuntrera had obtained Canadian citizenship and when he was released from prison with a three-year probation period in 1998 he applied for a Canadian passport, but this was refused, probably because the embassy was unsure whether or not he would be allowed to travel while on probation. He filed a lawsuit against the Canadian government in Federal Court in January 1999, claiming that he had been unfairly denied a passport when he had Canadian citizenship. He eventually won and regained his passport on the basis that he had been a Canadian citizen before leaving the country in 1980. The affair brought to unwanted prominence another Sicilian who had been an immigrant from the small town of Siculiana and who had risen to become the 'bagman' for Prime Minister Jean Chrétien's Liberal Party, also raising money to fight the historic 1993 election that saw the Canadian Conservative Party demolished. His name was Alfonso Gagliano, the representative of Montreal's Little Italy constituency, Saint Leonard.

Chrétien recommended him for a Cabinet post, but he failed his screening by the Royal Canadian Mounted Police. A little later, the Montreal daily, *La Presse*, clarified his background. His accountancy firm had only one client, Agostino Cuntrera, a nephew of Pasquale Cuntrera, who had been implicated in the killing of the former *capo* Paolo Violi. Gagliano, however, retained the support of the then Prime Minister, who was quoted in response to the allegations as saying, 'This Parliament would be much better off if we had more Gaglianos,' a sentiment that astonished the country. He continued to back Gagliano, who became Minister of Public Works (redolent of post-war Sicily).

But many years before this, an event had occurred in Italy that drove many mafiosi over the Atlantic to North and South America, and one of those to flee would eventually bring the organisation to destruction.

18

THE FIRST CRACKS APPEAR

In the early 1960s, three things happened that spelled the beginning of the end for the second Mafia.

The first took place at Naples airport on the cold morning of 26 January 1962, when Charlie 'Lucky' Luciano dropped dead with a massive myocardial infarct. The Mafia thus lost its most effective and respected leader in both Sicily and America. He had coordinated all the branches and had done so without opposition because he had that indefinable quality shown by all natural leaders, demonstrated in politics by Churchill and Kennedy; in sport by Martin Johnson, Roy Keane and Mike Brearley; and in crime by his predecessor Al Capone.

Criminals obeyed Luciano for 30 years, following his instructions even when he was in prison, from 1936 to 1945. When he was freed, he took over seamlessly from where he had left off, and his decision to set up home in Naples indicated that he needed the protection of neither the Camorra nor the Sicilian Mafia, and it was perhaps a shrewd move: since he was living outside Sicily, the police would not connect him to the Mafia, nor would he get involved in inter-family disputes on the ground. Far away in Naples, he was in a much better position to find solutions to problems and have them implemented.

I have made little mention of the Camorra in this book because they are quite unlike the Mafia. Probably the best marker of the difference is the fact that their leaders have always been 20–30 years younger than their equivalents in the Mafia. The Camorra is a 'thug' organisation; they always pick the strongest and nastiest of the group to be leader – get old in the Camorra and you're moved on. It is the perfect organisation for the *now* mentality of the psychopaths who are always at its head. They do not come from a tradition of social acceptance and political infiltration in the same way as the Mafia and the leaders find the creation of a long-term strategy – other than to rule their area forever – impossible.

They were quite incapable of managing a business as big as the international drug trade and function on a local basis. The philosophy is: take the profits, beat up or kill the opponents – and avoid the same being done to you.

Luciano lived among them and at first coordinated cigarette smuggling with them, managing to persuade the Camorra and the Mafia to work together. It was he who secured the drugs from Turkey to kick-start the narcotics trade in the Mediterranean and it was he who persuaded the Corsicans to cooperate with both the Camorra and the Mafia. From the time he returned to the time he died, 1946–62, although the various Mafia families might have had grievances, there were no major inter-family feuds. After 26 January 1962, things changed – and quickly.

The second event to hasten the downfall of the organisation was a bomb that exploded in Sicily exactly a year after Luciano died. For 100 years, the Mafia had been accepted as part of Sicilian life, and as long as there was nothing more than *pizzu*, people just got on with their lives because *è così*. The Mafia were an integral part of society, they were accepted, were admired and envied by many, and probably they did no more harm than a corrupt English regional council getting their 'snouts in the trough'. The agreement had been made with the American cousins; the young were going to and from the American pizza parlours; lots of money was being made and the families were adjusting to a change from their normal business of extortion, protection and abuse of public-works contracts to the hitherto undreamed of profits from narcotics.

This was a major step up in money-making but, as always in these situations, some were greedier than others and were beginning to feel disappointed at the profits. They had expected to enter an established market in America, but initially that did not exist, since there were fewer than 50,000 American addicts. Their part of the agreement was to expand what was then only a small market by creating a demand and organising the supply. Had Luciano been alive, this would have happened in a controlled, graduated way, but in his absence the only 'governing body' was the newly formed, toothless Commission. The reason that it was not giving a lead was that there were no bosses on the board and the uncertainty of decision-making was reflected in leadership tensions between the families.

There were also some old scores from the construction era awaiting settlement, which acted like sores between the families, especially the Grecos of Ciaculli and the La Barberas of Palermo central. What ensued was choreographed in a typical Mafia fashion – but it went wrong.

Given the imprecise nature of the drug trade, there was always the opportunity for personal initiative and a little private enrichment. The usual method of explaining 'missing' cash was to persuade people to believe that some unlikely event had occurred, such as portions of a consignment being rejected because of poor quality or the buyers reneging on the complete payment. This was a card played by the stupid, the greedy and those who felt they were not having their full worth recognised.

The Sicilians could live with a permanent atmosphere of mistrust and suspicion because that was a way of life; without an intermediary, you were bound to be cheated. They could tolerate small scams – but when most of a shipment went missing, it stretched even their tolerance. The man who 'lost' this particular load, worth millions of dollars, was Greco underboss Calcedonio Di Pisa. His fate was discussed by the Commission and, while the majority view was that he should be assassinated, the Grecos who sat on the Commission wanted him spared and a less final punishment administered. The La Barberas disagreed because, in their view, he had clearly overstepped the mark.

In spite of the impasse on the Commission, the La Barberas launched a vendetta against the Greco family which resulted in the La Barberas being expelled. The Grecos then killed Salvatore La Barbera, and in return his brother Angelo killed a Greco, and after that it continued in true Sicilian style, with a murder a day – until the bomb went off.

No one knows why a bomb was introduced to the usual game of gunfire and kidnap, but it was probably to act as a warning to the Grecos since it went off very close to their huge estate and homes in Ciaculli. Go there today and you see no one, but everyone sees you. The houses have no numbers and the streets seem to have no names, apart from the one through which Garibaldi marched his men in 1860 when they entered Palermo.

On a hot day in June 1963, an Alfa Romeo with a flat tyre was reported to the *carabinieri* because it seemed to have been abandoned. Who reported it and why remains obscure, but the *carabinieri* duly arrived to tow it away. As they were attaching the car to a tow truck, they noticed what turned out to be a dummy bomb with a burnt-out fuse sitting on the back seat. One of the seven officers then opened the boot to investigate further and detonated 200 pounds of explosive. It was a booby trap. Flames leapt fifty feet into the air and the seven *carabinieri* were vaporised; all that remained of the men was a pistol, a wedding ring and a cap.

This was a killing too far even for the Sicilians and the waves rippled right up to the beach of the Italian parliament in Rome. Action was required and so the Christian Democrats gave what they hoped was a meaningful response.

Ten thousand police and *carabinieri* arrived in Palermo and the surrounding districts, arresting 1,903 suspected mafiosi. A dozen dons were sent into internal exile on the remote islands around Sicily and another 114 were sent for trial. The first Anti-Mafia

Commission was established and, within five days of the bomb, the first anti-Mafia law was passed. From then on, anyone even suspected of being associated with the Mafia could be held on remand.

A year later the double-cross came to light. The greedy Di Pisa had not been killed by the La Barberas but by a relative of the Grecos, Michele Cavataio, in order to throw suspicion on the La Barbera family, thereby allowing the Grecos to legitimately escalate the war, deplete the La Barberas and get a bigger share of the market.

This crackdown on the Mafia resulted in thousands fleeing to the Americas and the Commission being disbanded. The massive exodus of young Sicilian pizza workers to Brooklyn meant that the hippie generation would have a regular supply of drugs and those who went to fight in Vietnam could continue their habit by obtaining Asian drugs.

The third, and most important, event that would hasten the organisation's demise was that in the aftermath of the bomb Tomasso Buscetta fled from Sicily. He would one day become the vital witness at the trials that heralded the end of the second Mafia.

Buscetta, an underboss of the La Barbera family, left his family, took a girlfriend and made his way in a roundabout fashion to New York via Germany, London, Paraguay, Mexico and Canada, entering the United States on a Mexican passport under the name Manuel Lopez Cardena. He had also obtained a Paraguayan passport under the name of Thomas Roberto Felice and almost certainly had another clutch of passports and identities.

Once settled in New York, he was looked after by Carlo and Paolo Gambino on the understanding that he would not function independently within the city. Together they came to an agreement which defies explanation, given the standards of morality expected in Mafia family life: Buscetta's estranged wife and daughter were taken in and looked after by another Gambino, Rosario, and Buscetta's two elder sons, Benedetto and Antonio, were given work in a New York pizzeria owned by the three

Gambino brothers. Buscetta's wife and daughter worked in a firm called the Lisa Wig and Wiglets Company, which was run by a man known as Antonio Napoli, who would eventually become another weak link in the chain. Napoli owned many pizzerias, and Buscetta, who had registered for agency employment as an apprentice pizza-maker, was placed in one of these, the La Dolce Vita Pizza Company, in Brooklyn.

For the next six years, Buscetta commuted between Mexico City and Napoli's pizzerias in New York. He might have continued to live like this, doing some drug dealing around the Americas, had it not been for an ordinary New York cop, Officer Mike Minto, who stopped him because of a minor traffic offence on the Brooklyn Bridge. When he was processed, the police found that he was an illegal immigrant and so in 1971 he was deported to Brazil. Of all the bad things that happened to the Mafia in those years, the flight and survival of Tomasso Buscetta was the worst because he would return to bring down the organisation.

Buscetta took his son, Benedetto, and his partner in the narcotics trade, Carlo Zippo, with him to Brazil. He knew exactly what he was going to do there because it was a major centre for drug supply and distribution, and he knew that he would fit in seamlessly. Shortly after his arrival in Rio, Buscetta displayed another Italian weakness by falling for and marrying a beautiful beach-blonde, Maria Christina Almeida de Giumaraes, 20 years his junior, who came from a very well-known Rio family. The whole family – including father-in-law Homero Snr, who left a successful legal practice – went into drug dealing with Buscetta. We shall leave Buscetta at this point but will return to him later.

Meanwhile, back in Sicily, events had moved on from the Ciaculli bomb and the previously rural family from Corleone was now planning to enter the big time. Its leaders, Luciano Leggio, Toto Riina and Bernardo Provenzano, were in jail together from 1963 till 1969: even though they had had nothing to do with the bomb, they had been rounded up and jailed as part of a general Mafia crackdown that followed. Leggio, Riina and Provenzano, along with another 114 mafiosi, finally went on trial in a Bari court presided over by Judge Cesare Terranova. Among their co-defendants were a number of men who had fled to the Americas and were being tried *in absentia*, including Badalamenti, La Barbera and Buscetta.

It was a very difficult trial for Judge Terranova because while all witnesses displayed collective amnesia (a common failing among Sicilians), he and the other judges all received letters signed with a cross and including the warning, 'We simply want to warn you that if a single gentleman from Corleone is convicted, you will be blown sky high, you will be wiped out, you will be butchered and so will every member of your family . . . A Sicilian proverb says, "A man warned is a man saved." It's up to you. Be wise.' It turned out to be an apparent Mafia triumph because all but ten of the 114 were acquitted, including Leggio and his sixty-three friends from Corleone.

There were now hundreds of rather angry mafiosi back on the streets with a lot of old scores to be settled. The most violent affair was a re-run of the St Valentine's Day Massacre. Almost exactly 40 years after the event, on 10 December 1969, in a real estate office in Via Lazio, Palermo, six men dressed as *carabinieri* burst in and killed the man who had started the original war by framing the La Barberas for the assassination of Calcedonio Di Pisa, Michele Cavataio, along with seven others.

This was when the Mafia re-awoke after the Ciaculli bomb. And the clarion call came not from Palermo but from a small town in the middle of Sicily – Corleone.

19

Corleone –
The Mafia Heartland

When Mario Puzo wrote *The Godfather* in 1969, it would have been doubtful if any non-Sicilian had ever heard of the name he used for his main character and his family: Corleone. When the book was first published, Corleone was just another Mafia town which for many years had been headed by a very respectable old-style *capo* who was also the town doctor, a not unusual and a very acceptable arrangement. No one knows why Puzo chose Corleone out of all the other places, such as Trapani, Agrigento or even little Villalba, that were full of Mafia associations. However, his decision was prescient because the Mafia in Corleone would mutate from an old-fashioned rustic organisation into a collection of psychotic individuals who would unleash a trail of murder and destruction never before seen in the history of the Mafia. This violence, accompanied by a complete lack of judgement, would eventually cause the whole Sicilian Mafia to self-implode.

Corleone is a small town in the centre of Sicily, equidistant from Palermo in the north and Agrigento in the south. It takes about 90 minutes to travel from either town and after driving through what used to be the Bourbon hunting grounds of the Ficuzza oak forest you start climbing up to a tall escarpment called Montagna

Vecchia, which rises 600 metres above sea level. There, in between two huge rocks, lies the town, guarded by a much-photographed signpost saying merely CORLEONE. Not 'Welcome to Corleone' or 'Corleone Twinned with Bruges' or 'Corleone, Historic Centre' – just Corleone, in crude black-and-white.

On top of each escarpment is a castle: on one side, Castello Sottano, an old Bourbon prison that was turned into a Franciscan Hermitage in 1960; and on the other, Castello Soprano (perhaps the stimulus for the name of the TV Mafia family). The town is home to 11,000 people, who, as is usual in towns of this size, have a choice of five churches, all Catholic. Corleone was chosen as the original site of filming for *The Godfather*, but the film-makers found it to have so little beauty or charm that they had to move south-east to Taormino.

Look down from the town and you see low hills, desolate scorched fields and the Corleone, a small river that seems to reflect the sadness of the past. Much of the Sicilian landscape is very photogenic, if you can avoid the motorways and concrete: there are fields full of colour, with poppies, wheat or sunflowers, depending on the season, and low roadside walls enclosing fields of olives and almond trees and bordered by wild fennel and thyme. It is, however, a waste of time taking film on a visit to Corleone – unless it's to photograph the sign.

The name Corleone comes from the Arab word *kur liyon*, meaning lion's heart. It possibly became a strong Mafia centre after the peasants' strikes in 1893, organised by a new socialist group called Fascii (as opposed to the entirely different future Fascists). This was, of course, crushed, but it sent shockwaves through society and posed a threat to the status quo, and when the founder, Bernardo Verro, was elected mayor in 1915 the Mafia had him shot. The killer, Antonio Gagliano, was acquitted due to lack of evidence and collective amnesia.

Michele Navarra, the town doctor, took on the role of Mafia *capo*. He was old-style Mafia – well respected, a fixer, a confessor and an intermediary. He would have brought many of the population of Corleone into the world and looked after those who survived their childhood illnesses. He would have been well experienced in the common ills of that time – malaria, typhus, tuberculosis and pellagra – and he would certainly have been involved in trying to save the life of the father of the future *capo* (and his assassin), Toto Riina, when he was fatally injured in 1943 while trying to defuse a land mine.

Navarra had the appearance of a well-loved small-town doctor: overweight, corpulent and florid – an obviously healthy, prosperous man. He would enjoy the traditional Italian card games of *scopa* and *tre sette* both at home and outside a bar, hunting boar and game birds and playing *boccia*. Like Don Calogero, he would be available every evening in the piazza to give advice on a whole range of subjects from health through to infidelity, financial problems and landownership. He was not an obviously wealthy man and up until the 1950s travelled by horse to see those patients who lived outwith the town. He, like most other men of his age, would wear a collarless white shirt and suit trousers held up by braces held on with button fastenings. He was called *u patri nostru* – 'Our Father' – and mention of his name would always have been accompanied by the sign of the cross.

He moved upwards in the Corleone world of medicine when the director of the local hospital, Dr Carmelo Nicolosa, was shot on 29 April 1946 and Dr Navarra was appointed to take his place.

It was the end of the war, the Allies were leaving and from their cache of stolen American vehicles the doctor and his brother set up Corleone's first bus service, which had an enormous social impact, given the fact that prior to this anyone wanting to travel outside the town had to do so by mule. The collection of American Army vehicles would no doubt have been facilitated by the fact that his cousin was a US Army captain who had led the bloodless occupation of the town in 1943. It was natural, therefore, that Navarra was elected as the head of the local branch of the Christian Democrat Party. Thus he was the embodiment of Church, family and goodness, which combined in a single package to fight the advance of godless communism.

At the time of the 1948 local elections, when the Communists made such big gains, the position of the Mafia was still uncertain because the question of independence was still unresolved. The peasants had a sound legal claim to take over all uncultivated land on the big estates and this presented a major threat to the established order. Furthermore, these were not the beaten, cowed peasants of the early twentieth century; they were more experienced, better travelled and well organised, and were now getting the advice of politically savvy trade unionists. One of the reasons the Mafia opted to side with the anti-Communists was exactly this question of landownership and the increasing power of the trade unions.

In the following years, Communists were being murdered all over Sicily, but the slaughter was especially bad in Corleone province, where, in the five years between 1943 and 1948, fifty-seven murders of left-wing politicians took place – quite remarkable for a town of fewer than 15,000 people. One in particular caused a profound change in the social order of the town.

One night in 1947, a young shepherd boy was brought to the hospital in a state of hysteria. He had run for miles down the mountains to tell people that he had seen two men take another and hang him from a tree and that he knew one of the men was called Luciano Leggio, one of the Navarra family's enforcers. In order to calm him, Dr Navarra gave him an injection. Unfortunately, the boy died. His death was written off as a tragic accident and all believed that the good Dr Navarra would only have been doing his best to calm down the fear excited by an imagined apparition; after all, everyone reasoned, if you spend all your days looking after sheep alone in the hills, you start to imagine things.

However, the truth emerged 18 months later when the remains of several human corpses were discovered at the bottom of a huge ravine within Montagna Vecchia. One was identified as that of the trade-union organiser Placido Rizzotto and it appeared that the cause of death was hanging.

Marching someone out of a crowded piazza holding a gun in his back would create some discussion in most towns, but not in Corleone. No one had remarked on the disappearance of Placido Rizzotto, who had been marched out of the piazza in just such a way, but when his remains were discovered they had to pay attention. Normally, an unenthusiastic police force would 'lose' evidence, but a new police chief, Alberto Dalla Chiesa, had arrived in Corleone and he was different. In 1947 he was just starting his career, but by the 1980s he had become an Italian hero as the *carabinieri* general who had destroyed the Red Brigades that had terrorised Italy for a decade.

It turned out the shepherd boy had been quite correct. Leggio, who had been the man with the gun in Rizzotto's back when he had marched him out of the piazza 18 months previously, had been the one to hang him.

Navarra's protégé Leggio had risen to high rank in the Navarra Mafia family, as had a younger man who would eventually take over the leadership when Leggio died, Toto Riina. The name Toto is dialect for 'Shorty' (*curtu*), the name he was given because of his small stature.

Leggio had the typical characteristics of a Mafia recruit: he was a fixer, a tough, and apparently without morals or scruples. He had obviously come to Navarra's notice and had been employed as a mounted guard on the local estates before being promoted to hit man.

After the Rizzotto investigation, Dalla Chiesa arrested both Leggio and Navarra. Leggio absconded, but Dr Navarra was tried, found guilty of manslaughter and sentenced to five years of internal exile in Calabria, a sentence which, like all exile sentences, lasted only a few months, thanks to the influence of his friends in the Christian Democrat Party.

Like all young men, Leggio and Riina soon became intolerant of their leader, with his old-fashioned ways, his satisfaction with his position in society and his apparent economic fulfilment with his bus service. They heard of the riches being made in Palermo, realised that they were being left behind like country bumpkins and wanted to explore and take advantage of the new post-war opportunities. They had also seen their well-off kinsmen and neighbours come back from the United States with stories of wealth, riches and opportunities.

With instincts nurtured by years of nuance, subtle looks and glances, Navarra was well aware of what was in the air. He clearly understood the danger from his younger associates and decided to abort any attempted coup by getting rid of them. So one summer morning in 1958, when Leggio and Riina were riding to their abattoir outside Corleone, they were ambushed – but apparently the gunmen shot from too far away (perhaps a tribute to the courage and firepower of the duo) and both were only slightly wounded. Riina evidently behaved with such courage at the time that he was credited with saving Leggio's life, but after an incident like this it was inevitable that Dr Navarra would be assassinated.

About a month later, he was coming back in his car from nearby Lecara Friddi, birthplace of Lucky Luciano, when he stopped to give a fellow doctor a lift back to Corleone. As the car stood stationary, it was riddled with several magazines from a machine gun. Navarra died with 112 bullet holes in his body and his unfortunate passenger suffered the same fate.

After escaping arrest following the investigation of Rizzotto's murder, Leggio took to the hills and was basically on the run in one way or another until his final imprisonment in 1974. Apart from his sojourn in jail after the Ciaculli bomb, he spent an impressive 26 years without being uncovered. In all that time, he seldom left Sicily, a feat that has been replicated many times, most recently by Bernardo Provenzano, one of Leggio's *picciotti* and future *capo dei capi*.

In the first Mafia, Leggio would never have risen beyond the rank of *capodecina* (in charge of ten soldiers) because he functioned on the level of a typical sadistic psychopath. Such was his record of violence, trying to engage him in discussion or logic would have been useless and so people both feared and avoided him. Like all the young men brought up during the war, he did not share the old Mafia values and forced the State to hunt him down. People like Don Russo and Don Calogero killed when necessary, quietly and effectively, with little public involvement; if a death was required, it was strictly business. Leggio, apparently, could not rest unless he was creating suffering and making money – preferably simultaneously.

The rule of the Mafia that Leggio had broken was *thou shalt not kill thine own boss without permission.* Thus a five-year vendetta began. In that period, 29 of the Navarra side were killed, while Leggio lost less than half that number.

Corleone became so much like the Wild West that it gained the name Tombstone, which of course is where the famous Gunfight at the OK Corral took place in 1881. The cemetery in Corleone, very conveniently, is near the centre of the town and luckily did not get the sobriquet of its counterpart in Tombstone, Boot Hill, but it contains many more victims of murder.

Even though Leggio was not suspected of having anything to do with the bomb at Ciaculli, he was one of thousands rounded up in 1963, probably because of his distant relationship to the Greco family at Ciaculli. When half the Mafia disappeared to North and South America, Leggio moved up the pecking order, mainly because of his kinship with the Greco family. When he was arrested, he was found right in the middle of Corleone in the house of the widow of Placido Rizzotto, the union organiser whom he had hanged. This was a tribute to the power of *omerta* in the town, because the *carabinieri* were supposed to have been looking for him for years!

Leggio had suffered from tuberculosis of the spine as a child and gradually his spine was twisting, a condition known as scoliosis. Today he would have had spinal surgery with rods placed through his vertebrae to keep it straight, but all that could be done 40 years ago was to use an external spinal brace to try to stop the curvature increasing. He probably also had a disease known as Reiter's syndrome, the symptoms of which are urinary problems, arthritis and eye trouble. He went from clinic to clinic looking for treatment for the incurable Reiter's syndrome and also to try and get better braces for his gradually twisting spine. He travelled quite openly, and in some clinics the staff even informed the police that he was in their clinic, but action was never taken by the police, possibly to avoid embarrassing politicians who did not want the Mafia question resurrected. He was arrested after the Ciaculli bomb event and was jailed until 1969.

The Bari verdict, which acquitted almost all the mafiosi, was appealed in 1969 and by this time the press had found out that Leggio had been travelling quite openly with the knowledge of the police on the mainland and that he was continually interfacing with doctors. Since his crimes had been so blatant and his guilt so apparently clear, he was hastily given a sentence of one year in prison *in absentia* by a court in Palermo.

In 1970, this verdict was further appealed by the prosecution. By this time those covering up for him could no longer be of any help and he was given a life sentence for the murder of Dr Navarra; but at this point he fled to Milan and lived there under the alias of Baron Osvaldo Fattori, working as a diamond merchant. In reality, he had fallen back on the old Mafia business of kidnapping. This was a method of raising money that was getting less frequent in the early 1970s because it was risky and all worthwhile targets had either bodyguards or Mafia protection, especially in the South and Sicily, so the opportunities for big ransoms were getting fewer. In those years, if somebody was kidnapped, it was done more as a symbol than for ransom money.

For example, in Palermo in 1972 Toto Riina kidnapped the son of Count Arturo Cassina, a rich local businessman who was a friend of Stephano Bontade, and as such under his protection. Although the kidnap got Riina a sizeable ransom, the real motive was to insult Bontade and almost challenge him for Mafia leadership. Riina was indicating to Bontade that not only did he find him unworthy of respect but also that if he wanted to start a 'war', Riina was ready. To underline the insult, it is said that Riina distributed the ransom money to charities for the poor in Palermo.

But in 1973, when Leggio kidnapped the luckless son of J. Paul Getty, Eugene Paul Getty III, at that time aged 17, he did it for the money. The ransom, however, was slow in coming because Getty's mean grandfather was only persuaded to pay up the $2.5 million when he received by post part of his grandson's ear and hair. This was given worldwide publicity and there was no possibility of further protection by the politicians for Leggio, so when he was captured in Milan in 1974 and tried for the Getty kidnap, he was convicted and another life sentence was added to the one he had already received. This time, however, the police had their hands on him and his political friends could not save him from spending the rest of his life in jail – but he would never let go of Mafia control.

Like Don Cascio Ferro, he became an honoured prisoner and was able to run his family until his death in a Sardinian prison from a heart attack in November 1993 at the age of 68. The day after his death, his right arm in the outside world, his former number two, Toto Riina, was also arrested and imprisoned.

Riina, however, proved to be the maddest psychopath of all time and his lunacy and lack of old-fashioned Mafia values eventually brought down the whole organisation but not before they had the chance to launder billions into the world's financial markets.

20

HOW THE MAFIA LAUNDERED MONEY

The true extent of money laundering around the world will never be known. The practice is so widespread that the number of people actually caught must be miniscule compared with the number of players in the business. One of the more interesting stories to come out of the second Mafia period is that of their two main launderers, Michele Sindona, who caused the largest bank crash experienced in the United States until recently, and Roberto Calvi.

Money laundering in Italy in the '70s and '80s was easy because of the lax banking laws and even laxer bank regulations.

The Bank of Italy serves the same function as the Bank of England and has only one customer, the government. The bank separated from the Treasury in 1981 and ten years later it received full freedom to control interest rates, six years before the Bank of England received these powers. The Bank of Rome is merely one of the bigger branch banks and, like the others, only answers to the Bank of Italy.

On a first visit to Italy, it is impossible not to wonder at the plethora of bank names. In the UK, we see branches of the Scottish banks, the Hong Kong banks, Barclays and Nat West, but we seldom see private banks that function as branch banks. There is no Bank of Devon or Bank of Newcastle, but in Italy such titles are common. Go to Genoa and you'll see the Bank of Genoa; go to Bari and there, in front of you, is the Bank of Bari.

There are 20 regions in Italy (including the islands) and each region is divided into at least two provinces. Every region will have a bank (e.g. the Bank of Umbria, the Bank of Liguria, etc.) and these banks will have many branches in most small towns in the region. There, they have to compete with provincial banks, which in turn have branches in the provincial small towns. But in addition to the bank that claims the name of the town or the province, there are lots of small banks that have some name that relates them vaguely to the region; for example, as well as the Bank of Cassino, there is also the Bank Cassinate Popolare. This is one of the thousand or so private banks that until recently carried out branch banking all over Italy.

It is not a structure designed for efficiency and this is reflected at branch level. It is every Italian's nightmare to have to do any business in a bank, as it will usually mean a wait of perhaps an hour because of queues, inefficient tellers and a mountain of form-filling for even the simplest transaction, such as paying an electricity bill.

The fact that there are so many banks means that they are unable to compete at an international level. In the '60s and '70s, if they had been bigger, they would have had to submit to external audit, which would have been most unwelcome, given the banks' ties to various political parties. The insurance system is just as primitive, with 30 per cent of the companies being foreign-owned and premiums very much higher than in any other European country.

Today, everyone in Italy must have a *codice fiscale*, or a financial number. This essentially follows every financial transaction that an individual makes; without it you cannot pay an electricity or gas bill. Similarly, if someone decides to send 1,000 euros outside Italy, or even to another town in Italy, then their number is on the transaction and it can be traced back, especially if the tax authorities want to know how the money was acquired. But these *codice fiscale* were only introduced in the 1980s, by which time the bird had flown.

Michele Sindona was born on 8 May 1920 in Patti, a little town near Messina in Sicily, only a mile away from the toe of Italy. There was no tradition of Mafia in Messina in those days and his upbringing would have been just the same as if he had been born in Naples or Rome. His father was a florist who specialised in funeral wreaths and floral decorations for tombs, a lucrative business in Italy not only because funerals tend to be lavish but also because there are a number of other holy days, especially in November, which demand that plants and flowers be taken to cemeteries. He was educated locally by the Jesuits and took a law degree at Messina University.

Sindona somehow avoided conscription and in 1943 got an entrée to the black market through Vito Genovese, one of the Italian mafiosi deported from America after the war and who became an interpreter for Colonel Poletti, head of the Allied Military Government. Sindona's initial foray into business was in 1944, when he started trading in lemons and wheat in the interior of Sicily.

Armed with a *raccomandazione* from the Bishop of Messina to Cardinal Montini (later Pope Paul VI), he went to Milan in 1946 and worked for a business consultancy firm that specialised in guiding overseas investments through Italy's complex tax laws. He was extremely successful not only because of his financial ability, but also because he spoke good English at a time when hardly any Italian spoke foreign languages.

He developed a powerful network of contacts and also got into real estate development, where he met the American Gambino family and their Sicilian cousins, the Inzerillos. They admired his financial and social skills and after the meeting in the Grande Hotel et des Palmes in Palermo in October 1957 between the Sicilians and their American 'cousins', he was offered the job of laundering the profits from the anticipated enormous market in heroin.

Given this opportunity, his first act was to establish a holding company called Fasco AG in Lichtenstein that immediately bought the Banca Privata Finanzaria (BPF) in Italy. If someone wanted to open a private bank in the 1970s (adding to the 1,041 that already existed), all he would need was a licence from the Bank of Italy. In order to get this, he needed the signature of two deputies from the Lower Chamber and if these politicians were in his pay or that of the Mafia, then it became a 'do-it-yourself' money laundering system, at least for small amounts of money. It was Michele Sindona who, in an unguarded moment, said, 'The best way to steal from a bank is to buy one!'

He would have to go through various other steps before final permission would be given, such as declaring the identity and interests of the directors and the details of the operating capital. If the bank was set up as an Italian bank, then it would be subject to external audit, which would be submitted to the Bank of Italy; if, however, it was a bank owned by a foreign group, it would still have to present its audit to the Bank of Italy but the rules would not be as stringent. Thus all money launderers worked through banks owned by foreign subsidiaries.

Within a few years, Sindona was laundering around $1 billion a year and he continued to do so for the next 15 years. With his massive new wealth, not only did he start creating new companies (always using Fasco AG as the babushka in which to hide them), but he also became a well-known philanthropist. One of his first benefactions was to the Vatican with a donation of £2.4 million for a Church-run retirement home in Milan, thus eliciting approval from Pope Paul VI.

It was a moment the Vatican would later rue.

Sindona bought his first Swiss bank in 1964 in Geneva and changed its name from Banque de Financement to Finnabank. This became pivotal in the laundering process because money would go into Finnabank and then to the Vatican Bank before being more widely dispersed. The money was distributed through shell companies into real estate corporations, insurance companies, industrial concerns, hotel chains and even more banks all around the world. One of these was the Bank of Messina, which, very conveniently, provided the Sicilian Mafia with their own local Sicilian bank.

By the end of the 1970s, Sindona owned six banks in four countries, a hotel chain (CIGA) and 500 other corporations. His financial company, Moneyrex, which had been the means of inserting him firmly within the Vatican structure, had 850 client banks whose combined turnover was $200 billion each year.

He speculated against foreign currencies and one of his most brazen coups was to carry out a $650 million speculation against the lira. As the lira was plummeting, he told the President of the Republic, Giulio Andreotti, that he would discover what the markets were doing to the currency and sort it out. In 1972, the *Wall Street Journal* described him as 'Italy's Howard Hughes'; the next year, Andreotti described him as 'Saviour of the Lira'; two years later, John Volpe, American Ambassador to Rome, named him 'Man of the Year'.

He knew David Kennedy, chairman of Continental Bank, from the days when they were involved in joint investment, and when Kennedy was appointed Treasury Secretary under Nixon, one of his first acts was to use Sindona as a conduit to get covert CIA funds into Greece for the Colonels' Coup, the money passing through Finnabank.

From the testimony of former CIA agent Victor Marchetti, we know that Sindona again became involved with the CIA in 1972, when he arranged for $11 million to pass to 21 anti-Communist politicians in Italy for electoral support. This money came in two tranches: one was dispersed to the Christian Democrats and their allies and the other went directly to the Italian secret services.

It was probably because of Sindona's association with the CIA that no action was taken on either side of the Atlantic in 1967, when a file on his possible association with drug suppliers was passed from the CIA to the Italian police. Even at that time the CIA had a large file on his association with the Inzerillos in Palermo and their 'cousins', the Gambinos in New York, but since he was part of their network in the fight against communism they did not pursue the matter.

In 1971, Sindona attempted to take over the two biggest Italian holding companies, Bastogi and Centrale. He was successful in his takeover of Centrale and replaced the entire board with his own people, among whom was the relatively unknown Roberto Calvi. But the Bank of Italy blocked his takeover of Bastogi, which, if the deal had gone through, would have made him, and vicariously the Mafia, almost as powerful as the Bank of Italy.

A year later, however, he went a step too far. He bought the tenth-biggest bank in the United States, the Franklin National, for $40 million, which appeared to be a very low price. The reason for this apparent 'bargain', though, was that the Franklin was in deep trouble, and as it died it took Michele Sindona with it.

After he bought the Franklin, Sindona left Italy to live in New York, but this did not stop the confidence ebbing from previous supporters of the bank. The Americans do not like their banks being taken over by foreigners and there was a run on the funds from investors, among the biggest of which was Hambros of London. The final *coup de grâce* was the Yom Kippur War, which caused the price of oil to escalate and the stock market to plummet in April 1974.

Instead of keeping calm, he speculated wildly and lost a further $350 million from his Milan banks. As the end approached in the middle of 1974, he merged the two Milan banks into one, but each of them had a big hole in its accounts. The new organisation was called Banca Privata, but all he had accomplished was to convert two big holes into one enormous hole. Although he was obviously on the point of going under, he maintained his sense of Italian priorities and gave $3 million to the Christian Democrat Party!

While in prison in Caracas years later, a former employee of BPF, Carlo Bordino, told of the vast number of overdrawn accounts without any real guarantees and of BPF transferring large amounts of money from accounts of depositors without their awareness.

In May 1974, for the first time ever, the Franklin bank failed to pay a dividend. Both Italian and American regulators moved in to prevent a possibly calamitous collapse of banks in both countries. There was a 200-billion-lira hole in the Banca Privata, half of which was filled by the Bank of Italy. Similarly, the Franklin National was given access to Federal funds; the day before it went under, the Federal Reserve Bank loaned it $1.7 billion, but to no avail.

Within a few days of each other, the Banca Privata and the Franklin were declared bankrupt, creating one of the biggest-ever banking crashes both in the USA and in Italy. At the time, it cost the Italian government $1 billion, the Federal Reserve Bank nearly $2 billion, the Vatican an unknown amount and, most importantly, the Mafia a lot of money from drug profits!

Four days before the Franklin crash, two days before the Banca Privata bankruptcy and the day before an arrest warrant was issued, Sindona fled to Hong Kong and from there to Taiwan, knowing that there was no extradition treaty from there to either America or Italy. However, on the advice of David Kennedy, by now US Treasury Secretary, he returned to New York, where he was arrested and bailed for $3 million.

For the next few years, he lived in a suite in the Hotel Pierre in New York and fought his threatened extradition to Italy, employing as his lawyers Richard Nixon and John Mitchell's law firm, Mudge, Rose, Guthrie and Alexander.

In 1975, a court in Milan had tried him *in absentia* and sentenced him to three and a half years in jail. One man spoke in his defence, a president of a division of the Supreme Court in Rome, who argued that Sindona had been framed by the Communist Party because he was a well-known anti-Communist and had financed the Christian Democrats.

He was successful not only in fighting extradition but also in delaying any action by the US justice authorities, but by March 1979 he had run out of ideas, as had his friends. His case was heard and the indictment cited him on 99 counts of fraud, perjury and misappropriation of bank funds. Worst of all was the decision to have him extradited to Italy after his American trial. He could have been sentenced to 25 years in jail in America, and although the same sentence would await him in Italy, he had a few extra enemies there, namely the Mafia, who had lost a lot of money.

There seemed to be no way of avoiding extradition and a trial in Italy, so he fell back on the well-worn Italian tactic of threatening to tell everything he knew about high-profile politicians – and he knew plenty about their illegal money laundering and overseas investments because he had been their banker.

But it didn't work. With his trial set for 10 September 1979, he broke bail on 2 August and, wearing a white wig, a false beard and a moustache, he boarded flight number TWA 740 to Vienna, with a passport in the name of Joseph Bonamico, accompanied by someone called Anthony Caruso. This had been arranged by the Gambino family in New York.

The story that was issued for public consumption suggested that he had been kidnapped by the romantically named organisation 'The Proletarian Committee for the Eversion of an Improved Justice', a Red Brigades organisation. Ransom notes were delivered to his lawyers, but he was not suffering any of the discomforts of the usual kidnap. Of the 90 days of his 'kidnap', he spent 70 in Sicily being looked after and ferried round by the doctor Joseph Crimi. During this time, he even arranged to be anaesthetised and shot in the thigh! A ranking Freemason, Crimi was different from the usual 'Mafiosi Masons' in that he took the craft seriously and this was reflected in his high degree; he had neither need nor desire to use the craft for networking, knowledge and influence.

Sindona also spent some time at the Excelsior Hotel in Catania, where the bill was paid by the local *capo*, Gaetano Graci, and also at the Spatola villa outside Palermo. For two months, everyone was prepared to believe that Sindona was in the hands of kidnappers and that he was merely an unlucky rogue financier; then things went quiet.

The Mafia connection was discovered when the last ransom note was in the process of being delivered to Sindona's Rome lawyers.

The courier was Vincenzo Spatola, the nephew of Rosario Spatola, who in turn was the cousin of the New York don John Gambino. Vincenzo had risen from his first job as a milkman to become Palermo's biggest builder in a period of 20 years. This important link between Spatola and Sindona was discovered during a bugged telephone call and once it was discovered the police moved in.

The Mafia realised they had to get rid of Sindona: hanging on to him was merely going to result in greater police pressure and more problems. Also, even after two months of Sindona's threats to 'tell all' about the politicians, it didn't look as if the lost money was going to be recovered.

Roberto Calvi, Sindona's protégé, was being pressed very hard to replace the lost money and one payment of 30 billion lire was deposited into Rosario Spatola's account. This could be traced back to Calvi's bank, the Banca del Gottardo. We do not know if there were others, but it was at this time that Calvi's banks also started getting into trouble.

How Sindona, with a healing thigh wound and an expulsion from the Mafia, arrived back in New York remains a mystery, but in November 1979 he was found at the corner of 10th and 42nd Streets in New York.

As the ring tightened around Sindona, so his vengeance increased against individuals whom he felt were either threatening or not helping him. Giorgio Ambrosoli, the man who had been appointed by the Bank of Italy to investigate Sindona's Italian banks, was getting close to asking the questions that could result in the rest of his life being spent in jail.

Soon after Ambrosoli was appointed by the Bank of Italy in September 1974, he had started working closely with the Assistant District Attorney in New York, John Kenney. They had identified many of the devices used to export money illegally and had also found the links to the Vatican Bank. Among the devices he found were: paying over the odds for a company owned by a friend and having the surplus deposited in a Swiss account; manipulating the share price of a company upwards, paying even more for it and then skimming off the surplus to another account; and the use of offshore banking. He uncovered the extensive use of double invoicing, where exports would be invoiced at a much reduced cost via the Bank of Italy, passed on to the tax authorities and the balance paid by the receiver to Finnabank. If a loss was made, this would be converted to tax credits by the Italian government. Imports would similarly be invoiced for a much higher sum and the difference would again be deposited in a Finnabank or a Swiss account.

As Andreotti had publicly hailed Sindona the 'Saviour of the Lira', it was no surprise that he should make strenuous efforts to support his friend. He brought pressure to bear on Paolo Baffi, governor of the Bank of Italy, to bail out Sindona's banks, but Baffi refused.

Sindona became more desperate as time went on and attempted to buy back his banks from the liquidator. He started to contact Ambrosoli directly, offering him large bribes, but to no effect. He also approached and threatened Baffi and another major financial figure, Enrico Cuccia, the manager of Mediabank, who was so angered that he went to New York to challenge Sindona.

Ambrosoli meanwhile had almost completed his investigations and was preparing to give evidence to various hearings in both Italy and America when he started to receive threatening phone calls. Although he was not too alarmed, he took the precaution of recording them. In one, which has been replayed many times in various trials, the unknown caller alleges Andreotti is the 'big boss'. The transcription reads as follows:

> *Unknown caller:* They're pointing the finger at you. I'm in Rome and they're pointing the finger because you're not cooperating.
>
> *Ambrosoli:* But who are they?

Caller: The big boss.

Ambrosoli: Who's the big boss?

Caller: You understand me. The big boss and the little boss, everyone is blaming you. You're a nice guy. I'd be sorry . . . the big one, you understand? Yes or no?

Ambrosoli: I imagine the big one is Sindona.

Caller: No, it's Andreotti.

Ambrosoli: Who? Andreotti?

Caller: Right. He called and said he had everything taken care of, but it's all your fault, so watch out.

On 9 July 1979, Ambrosoli swore a statement in front of an Italian and an American judge in the presence of Sindona's lawyers, which was prepared in order to be read out at Sindona's trial in New York.

On 10 July, he talked to the head of the Palermo police about the cheques and phone numbers that had been found on the body of Mafia enforcer Giuseppe Di Cristina, who had been murdered in Palermo in May 1978 around the time that abandoned suitcases containing heroin and half a million dollars had been recovered at Palermo airport – an event that had led to the murder of Boris Giuliani. These were strong indications that Sindona was involved in recycling the proceeds of heroin sales in the usual pathway, which was from source to Finnabank, then to the Vatican Bank and finally overseas.

Later that day, Ambrosoli talked to Lt Col. Antonio Varisco, head of the security service in Rome, and the two men talked again the next day, this time about the purchase of the Banca Cattolica di Veneto, a sale which had caused Pope John Paul I much grief. He had found out that Sindona had paid a brokerage fee to a Milanese banker and an 'American Bishop'. The spotlight shone on Calvi and Marcinkus, but when they were later interviewed Calvi denied it point-blank and Marcinkus denied ever having met Sindona, in spite of having publicly stated in April 1973:

'Michele Sindona and I are very good friends, we've known each other many years'!

Unknown to Ambrosoli, from 8 to 11 July, he had been tailed by an American hit man, William Arico, who had checked in to his hotel four days previously under the alias of Robert McGovern.

When Ambrosoli had completed his testimony on 11 July, he went home, but as he was letting himself into his front door, he was shot and killed. By 6 a.m., Arico was in Switzerland and later that day $100,000 was deposited in his account, number 415851-22-1, at the Credit Suisse in Geneva, paid from Calvi's Banca del Gottardo.

But the killing was not finished.

On 13 July, Lt. Col. Varisco was shot. He was driving in his Alfa Romeo when another similar car pulled alongside and a gunman shot him. A week later, Boris Giuliano, who was handling the Sicilian end of the investigation, was killed while having his morning coffee at the Lux Bar (Chapter 27). Judge Alessandrini, who was investigating the connection between Calvi and the Vatican Bank, was shot by five gunmen in Via Muratoni in Rome. Not surprisingly, another investigator, Gratizano Verzotto, got the message and fled to Beirut.

Sindona's Italian trial began in February 1980. Bishop Marcinkus and two other officials of the Vatican Bank, Bishops Mennini and de Stroebel, said that they would give video testimony from within the Vatican but would not attend the trial. At the last minute, Cardinal Casaroli, the new Vatican Secretary of State, intervened, telling the court that they would not be permitted to give depositions. Casaroli had taken over from Cardinal Villot, who had the good fortune to die before he was implicated in either a Pope's death or a financial scandal. Casaroli took this stance because he anticipated a guilty verdict and this would have meant that three high-ranking Vatican officials would have been at risk of arrest.

After a five-month trial, Sindona was found guilty of 65 of the 99 charges and, knowing what awaited him, attempted suicide with a few superficial cuts and some Digitalis, a possible cardiac poison.

In July 1980, he was sentenced to twenty-five years in jail for the fraud charges and three years for arranging his own kidnap.

In January 1981, he arranged for an attempted jail break with a helicopter. In July that year, he was charged with arranging the assassination of Giorgio Ambrosoli. And from then on, the charges kept mounting.

He was tried for the Ambrosoli murder in 1984 and again said he would use the opportunity to tell all and name names but, while awaiting trial, he received a visit from some members of the P2 Lodge. As a result of this he made the decision neither to attend his trial nor instruct any defence, entering a guilty plea. He was therefore sentenced to life imprisonment, having been found guilty of arranging the murder of Ambrosoli.

By the time he was charged, along with some of the Inzerillos, Spatolas and Gambinos, of running a $600 million heroin trade between America and Sicily, he knew that he would die in jail either from natural or unnatural causes.

It turned out to be the latter. He was held in the Voghera jail on 24-hour watch, his every movement recorded on CCTV, but on 20 March 1986 he was poisoned with cyanide in his coffee – a traditional Mafia prison execution. It was not suicide because his last words were '*Mi hano avvelenato*' (They've poisoned me).

He died two days later at the age of sixty-seven, having spent more than half his life as the most brilliant manipulator of Italian financial services, while doubling as the man who was the Mafia's banker – but who failed them.

He not only lost his bank and his companies, but with them went millions of Mafia money, and that is why he was murdered. But how had he involved the Vatican?

21

Why the Vatican
Needed a Bank

Much of the Mafia's money laundering was done with the innocent connivance of the Vatican. From the early '70s until the late '80s, the Sicilian Mafia had the world monopoly on the supply and distribution of heroin and the profits became part of the world's capital markets in such a way that the money could not be traced back to the Mafia. Merrill Lynch has estimated that 30 per cent of the world's wealth was generated from illegal activity and it is this money that has funded many legitimate businesses in today's world, with or without the knowledge of the investors. That it travelled from the point of issue of the drugs to the world's financial markets is down to a handful of very clever men who used the Vatican Bank and took advantage of lax Italian banking regulations and supervision.

Money laundering is about hiding the proceeds of illegitimate activity; it can range from an individual's attempts to avoid taxation to the hiding of hundreds of millions of dollars from illegal activities, but whatever the amounts involved, the laundering is usually a three-stage process.

The first step is 'placement', which involves getting the money into the global financial system and away from its origin. The second step is usually referred to as 'layering', where the money is passed through multiple transactions using a number of countries and shell companies, with nominee directors standing in front of whoever is going to benefit from the money. The final step is 'integration', which is getting the money back to the originators, or their collaborators, at a place and in a form in which it can be used.

The commonest method is to use the offshore financial facilities available in, for example, the numerous Caribbean and Pacific islands that have very stringent privacy laws to prevent not only foreign investigators but also local investigators from knowing who really controls a bank or a company. As well as the numerous islands, Switzerland, Lichtenstein, Luxembourg and the UK have institutions that will collude with the process.

Any investigator thus has to go through the millions of wire transactions that are carried out each day and has to rely on banks, insurers and other financial institutions to tip him off about suspicious data. Until recently, any transaction above $10,000 had to be reported, which led to 'smurfing', which is pushing through multiple money transactions of just over $9,000. This limit was lowered to £500 per day in order to counter smurfing but, in spite of new obstacles for the criminals, money laundering continues to increase.

If criminals want to launder money outwith the Western banking system, they find it easy to use systems such as the *hawala* in India, the *hundi* in Pakistan and the *chop* in China. None of these involve records that can be traced, using instead tokens, perhaps a password in an email or simply instructing someone to deliver a given amount of local currency to its destination. This whole system relies on trust between brokers, but, as it has been functioning for many years through the various diasporas, it works and is a godsend to criminals and, these days, also terrorists.

If an Italian citizen wanted to take $10,000 out of Italy to avoid taxation, he could put the cash in his pocket, travel to another European country, most conveniently Switzerland, and deposit it in a bank. If he wanted to move $100,000, then the sheer bulk of the load might require some sort of hand luggage and similarly $1 million would require a suitcase. These actions would not attract a fee or a fine, provided that all went well during the journey and customs officials did not take too keen an interest in what was being carried. For generations, the town of Lugano in Switzerland has been the favourite destination for Italians wanting to 'hide' money. Although it has a population of only 30,000, it has 400 financial institutions, which represents a bank or credit institution for every 75 people! Even though border checks for smuggled money are very stringent, Italians have been exporting their money there since the 1920s, hiding it sequentially from Fascists, Nazis, Communist threats, criminals, tax authorities and the Red Brigades.

In the 1970s, if money went from the Vatican to a company (which might be a shell company) in Peru, Nicaragua or some other distant place, no questions would be asked because to consider the Vatican to have been involved in laundering would have been unthinkable. But, due to their financial advisers, this is what actually happened.

But why did a state like the Vatican, with its agenda tied to the aims of the papacy and Catholicism worldwide, even need its own bank? As an independent state, of course it had every right to establish a bank, but equally it could have used the Bank of Rome, which functioned on its doorstep. In addition, the purpose of a bank, apart from keeping money safe, is to make money by investing and lending, and neither is an activity that should have been needed by the Vatican. The reason for the bank might become clearer when we review how the Vatican became wealthy.

The Vatican acquired its first tranche of wealth on 28 October AD 312, when the Emperor Constantine summoned Pope Miltiades, the tiny leader of the Christian Church. Since Christianity was outlawed and many believers had been slaughtered between AD 298 and AD 305, poor Miltiades presumed he was going to be put to death, but instead he had a nice surprise waiting for him.

Constantine was the son of a pagan father and worshipped

Sol Invictus, but his mother was Christian. When he won the battle at Milvian Bridge against his rival Emperor Maxentius in October 312, he ascribed it to a symbol of a cross he saw in the sky and therefore converted to Christianity. It was one of the more important visions of the millennium because it resulted in Constantine embracing the astonished Miltiades, putting a purple robe around his shoulders and kneeling before him.

He gave him not only the title of Pontifex Maximus but also the wealth of Byzantium, and made his own nobles convert to Christianity and donate a proportion of their wealth to the new church. To share in his astonishment would have been a rich experience.

The treasures Miltiades received were mostly in the form of jewellery, icons, mosaics and paintings, and as such they were not a source of wealth that could be used to maintain a papal court. In AD 756, in exchange for the title Patricus Romanus, Pepin the Short, King of the Franks, gave Pope Stephen II all the Italian city states that he had conquered, which consisted of much of today's Lazio, Umbria, the Marches and part of Emilia Romagna, a land mass representing about 20 per cent of present-day Italy. Tributes and gifts in the form of jewels and art would regularly be donated by other Christian states and their rulers, and so gradually the Vatican, the name applied to the new court of the Pope, became extremely wealthy. But the Vatican was asset rich and cash poor.

By the time of the Renaissance, the Vatican was able to use its wealth to sponsor some of the great art of the world through artists such as Michelangelo and Leonardo and it filled Rome with priceless beauty in the form of gates, buildings, statues, frescos and paintings. Several centuries later, after the Church had survived the Reformation, Pope Pius IX reacted to the further post-revolutionary unrest in Europe after the French Revolution by publishing in 1854 an encyclical, *Quanta Cura*, which denounced freedom of speech, unrestricted comment by the press and the concept of equality of status for all religions. What was troubling him in his own backyard, however, was not French Revolutionaries but the anti-clerical speeches being made by the father of the concept of Italian unity, Giuseppe Mazzini.

In 1860, had it not been for Cavour fearing a French backlash, Garibaldi would have invaded Rome because he too was fiercely anti-clerical, but he was ordered to stop by the Piedmont Army. After the unification of Italy, the Vatican was confined to Rome and was protected by a French garrison. When this was withdrawn in 1870 to fight in the Franco-Prussian War, the Piedmont Army marched unopposed into Rome, entering on 20 September, and incorporated into the new Italian State not only Rome but also all the papal lands.

In response to this, Pius IX summoned a Vatican Council. He was horrified when it initially overthrew the dogma of Papal Infallibility because this was his defence against the removal of the Vatican land and income. Soon afterwards, he summoned another Council, but, due to the difficulties of travel, it was poorly attended and he was able to persuade those who turned up to reverse the decision and once again he claimed infallibility. The Pope was offered a grant from the State, but he refused to accept it. He withdrew within the walls of the Vatican and for the next 60 years no Pope ever emerged from his seat.

Never a forward-looking man, Pope Pius IX excommunicated everyone who had been associated with the unification of Italy and also threatened to apply that sanction to any Catholic who voted for anyone in any future election.

The Papal State was confined to the Vatican, the Basilica of St Giovanni in Laterno, his church in Rome and a summer residence in the hills outside Rome at Castel Gandolfo. The Vatican State in Rome covered 109 acres – the size of a golf course, the size of St James's Park in London, and one-eighth of the area of New York's Central Park.

Although the temporal power of the Vatican was abolished, it was allowed some vestiges of statehood in return, such as the right to print its own stamps, to run a postal service and have diplomatic representation.

The unhappy Pius IX was followed by the equally unhappy Pius X, who remained just as unenlightened and enclosed. During his term, he excommunicated writers of 'unsuitable' books and coined a new word for all that he opposed: 'modernism'. Only those who swore to oppose modernism were permitted to teach in seminaries. Furthermore, seminarians were forbidden to read newspapers or magazines.

By 1929, the Vatican was broke, but Mussolini came to the rescue. His reasons for bestowing wealth on the Vatican were not hard to fathom because if he could get the Church onside, even though he was not a believer himself, he would be all-powerful. All the other possible sources of opposition, such as the trades unions, the press and Parliament, could be beaten either by force or legislation, but not the Vatican.

In his turn, although Pius XI held the same inward-looking and suspicious attitude of his predecessors, he fully realised the power he held over Mussolini because he knew that the Church still held huge sway across the country, especially the South. When the Lateran Treaty was signed between the Vatican and Mussolini on 11 February 1929, the Vatican became a separate state with full diplomatic rights. They were given three-quarters of a billion lire in cash and another billion in government bonds as compensation for their lost lands. Religious education was to be taught in all schools, not only Catholic ones, and Church marriages were brought under canon rather than state law, thus making divorce impossible. Mussolini agreed to shut all brothels and to restore damaged churches, and decreed that the crucifix be displayed in all schools and government buildings.

This was a triumph for both parties: for the first time in its history the Vatican was cash rich, while Mussolini was now all-powerful and seen in world terms as the defender of the Catholic faith. Nationally, he received the full support and blessing of the Vatican.

After the Vatican became a separate state, with all the rights and privileges that go along with that, it could claim diplomatic immunity and used this to great effect towards the end of the Second World War for the benefit of not only the many escaping British prisoners of war but also Nazis who wished to escape to the UK or America. It was also to prove invaluable in the 1980s in protecting members of its own staff, who were being sought for financial offences.

The Catholic student movement was the only non-Fascist organisation to be allowed to function in the 1930s. Among its presidents were the future Prime Ministers Aldo Moro and Giulio Andreotti as well as a man who at the time was the student chaplain, Monsignor Montini, and would one day become Pope.

Hitler was a lapsed Catholic and was delighted with Mussolini for bringing the Vatican onside; even when writing *Mein Kampf*, he had realised the importance of the Catholic Church. There was a Catholic Centre Party in Germany that opposed national socialism, but the papal legate to Germany, Cardinal Eugenio Pacelli (later to become Pope Pius XII), persuaded them to change their stance and support Hitler.

Hitler further cemented relations with the Catholic Church by giving an undertaking that there would be no criticism of the Church, that Germany would be bound by canon law and that Catholic social work would receive State support. But the most profitable part of that concordat was that Hitler decreed that the Vatican would get part of the *Kirchensteuer*, the Church tax, which was deducted from all pay packets. By the time Italy left the Axis alliance in 1943, the Vatican had received over $100 million from this source.

Prior to getting the money from the Lateran Treaty, the Vatican did not have its own bank. After it inherited almost a billion lire from that treaty, it set up a structure called the 'Special Administration of the Patrimony of the Holy See' and the funds were administered by the Bank of Rome because at that time it was considered improper for an organisation such as the Vatican to be involved with anything so 'worldly' as a bank.

When Cardinal Pacelli became Pope Pius XII, he changed this

rather unwieldy name to 'The Institute for Religious Works', the IOR. He did this because he felt that while the Vatican should not be seen to be involved in banking practice and lending money, it had amassed a considerable fortune and it needed an investment policy. An agreement was therefore reached with Mussolini that the IOR would not pay tax on its dividend income and this was to prove enormously costly for the Italian State, as well as enormously profitable for the Vatican.

Holiness is not an essential requirement of a bank chairman and so the Vatican was able to appoint someone from outside the Church to this post and the man they chose changed the Vatican's finances spectacularly.

Bernardino Nogara came from a prominent Catholic family, had trained as a mineralogist, was fluent in eight languages, had a photographic memory and an amazing aptitude for mathematics. Between 1924 and 1929, he had successfully reorganised the Reich bank on behalf of the Inter-Allied Reparations Agency after the First World War. The Pope asked him to take over the investment policy of the IOR in 1931 and Nogaro accepted on condition that he had a completely free hand and did not have to answer to committees of cardinals. He also persuaded the Pope to forget about reacquiring land in favour of becoming an economic force. These were the years of the Great Depression, but Mussolini, like Roosevelt, was investing heavily in the reconstruction of his country, therefore Nogaro invested heavily in Mussolini's Institution for Industrial Reconstruction and in a short time the Vatican was the largest shareholder in any State-secured businesses, which included Italgas and the overarching company of all government business, the Società Generale Immobiliare (SGI). His investments were so successful that, had they come to light, the Vatican would have been embarrassed, therefore much of the portfolio was transferred to Switzerland, a perfectly legal and very astute move.

The IOR was not only involved in international investment, it also had a deposit bank within the Vatican. Ostensibly, it was for the Vatican staff and their families, but, as war alliances changed and Italy's future became uncertain, many Italians who wanted to protect their wealth from confiscation by the Germans were allowed to use the bank.

By the 1980s, the Vatican deposit bank had 11,000 accounts, of which only about 1,000 served an ecclesiastical purpose, the remaining 10,000 or so being 'slush funds'. Journalist Umberto Venturini wrote in *Il Mondo* that the IOR was the best offshore bank in the world because it had no unsavoury Caribbean background, no central bank governor, total secrecy and the moral backing of the Church.

Nogaro set about investing Vatican funds in every major world corporation, some of which would not have been appropriate had the Vatican followed what in recent years has come to be called an 'ethical investment policy'. After Nogaro died in 1958, it was discovered that investments had been made in arms manufacturers, publishers of pornographic books and magazines, and even the pharmaceutical company that went on to manufacture the contraceptive pill. Although this was inappropriate, Cardinal Spellman of New York said on the occasion of Nogaro's death, 'Next to Jesus Christ, Bernardino Nogaro was the greatest thing that has happened to the Catholic Church.'

Nogaro's initial successor was an ailing octogenarian, Cardinal Alberto di Jorio, who in 1970 asked to be relieved of the job because of his ignorance of banking; he was followed by Paul Marcinkus.

Born in Cicero, Chicago, on 15 January 1922 to Lithuanian parents, Marcinkus was ordained in 1947 and had been an altar server at one of Al Capone's funeral masses. He was sent to Rome for further education at the Gregorian Institute and came to the notice of the hierarchy not only because of his size – he acquired the nickname 'The Gorilla', standing at six foot three inches tall and weighing over 220 pounds – but also because of his intelligence and ability to speak five languages fluently.

He was brought into the Vatican State Secretariat in 1952, where he worked in the English section of the Secretary of State's office.

He was put in charge of organising the Pope's overseas visits and was used as a clerical bodyguard, being constantly at the Pope's side. On one trip in 1964, he prevented the Pope from being crushed by a crowd and in the Philippines he saved him from an assassination attempt. He became a major figure in the Vatican hierarchy and was consecrated as a bishop in 1965, the same year that he acted as interpreter when the Pope met with Lyndon Johnson.

When he was offered the job, Marcinkus at first expressed a reluctance to take over the IOR because of his ignorance of banking. He requested the assistance of Michele Sindona, a man we shall meet in the next chapter and who was fast becoming the best-known financier not only in Italy but also internationally.

Sindona was already known to the Vatican because, in the brief period in which Cardinal di Jorio was in charge of investments, the Italian government had revoked the terms of the 1929 Lateran Treaty and ordered the Vatican to pay tax on their Italian dividends. Initially, it looked as if there would be a tax bill of $270 million, but Sindona managed to have the portfolio transferred out of Italy and at the same time got out of the unethical investments that Nogaro had made. He was given the title Mercator Senesis Romanam Curiam, the equivalent of controller of the Vatican Bank.

Sindona basically abused his trusted position within the Vatican financial system to give an appearance of respectability to his dealings, which were primarily to 'launder' the drug money of the second Mafia. In 1965, Sindona created an international brokerage company called Moneyrex, which within two years of its foundation was dealing annually with $40 billion.

Marcinkus almost certainly did not know what he had got into and his failure to comprehend was to cost the Vatican millions of dollars and also his own elevation to archbishop; in fact, he ended up as the model for Bishop Frantisek in Morris West's book *The Salamander*.

When the Vatican wanted to get rid of its half-billion-dollar holding in the SGI, the owner of all nationalised industries, Sindona offered to buy it for double the market value and subsequently used this not only as part of the laundering mechanism, but also to funnel costs to political parties: the remaining Vatican holding of 5 per cent gave outsiders the all-important factors in any financial dealing – confidence and trust.

If the Vatican bank was involved, then it must have been OK!

Except that it wasn't, and when a pope was on the verge of finding out, he died.

22

The Death of a Pope

In 1958, Cardinal Angelo Roncalli was elected Pope and chose the name John XXIII. His predecessor, Pius XII, had hoped that he would be succeeded by the arch-conservative Cardinal Siri, who had at one time said that voting Communist was incompatible with being a Catholic. He was talked out of trying to 'fix' this by the French Cardinals, who saw that it would lead to even worse persecution of the Church behind the Iron Curtain. Roncalli was old and was supposed to be merely a caretaker – but he surprised everyone.

John XXIII was the son of poor farmers and was called a 'true socialist' by Khrushchev's daughter, probably because prior to being elected Pope he had often expressed left-wing views. He had identified the positive features of the Russian Revolution in 1917 and had enjoyed his time as Apostolic delegate to Bulgaria. Her view of his left-wing credentials was underpinned by the concern expressed by the CIA when he was made a cardinal.

He had taken over a Church that had always been the soul of conservatism. The story is told of the couple in the '50s, in Prato, a suburb of Florence, who married in a registry office and were branded as 'concubines'. They sued the Church and won and, in response, the Cardinal of Bologna, an enlightened and Communist-run city, ordered his cathedral to be dressed in mourning for a month!

The Christian Democrat Party also had to seek the approval of the Church when they made an alliance with the Socialists (*not* the Communists, who were beyond the pale) to bring them into government.

The number of Catholics attending mass was dropping alarmingly, mainly because of the birth-control issue, and one of the first things that Pope John did was to summon an Ecumenical Council, which came to be known as Vatican II. He was trying to lift the palsied hand of conservatism from the Church because he saw that to carry on as before would lead to its becoming irrelevant. He once said, 'We are not born to be museum keepers but to cultivate the garden of life.'

He appointed 23 cardinals, most with left-of-centre views, from the developing world and this was one of the things that kick-started the marriage of Catholicism and Marxism in Central and South America. He also invited Khrushchev to the Vatican and published the encyclical *Pacem in Terris*, calling for a rapprochement between communism and the Church. He certainly started the reawakening and modernisation of the Church, but unfortunately he died and missed the bitter struggles that were to take place both in his Church and in Catholic society, especially in relation to birth control.

The work of Vatican II, which the present Pope, Benedict XVI, the former Cardinal Ratzinger, had a big part in planning, was carried on by John's successor, Pope Paul VI. As the former Cardinal Montini, he had been the chaplain to the Catholic student group that was allowed to continue being active in the Fascist years as part of the Lateran Treaty. He died in 1978 after a 15-year reign in which he published the encyclical *Humanae Vitae* that forbade birth control, especially in the form of the newly available contraceptive pill. This encyclical had been cobbled together in 1968 by the arch-conservative Cardinal Ottaviani, whose motto, *Semper idem*, exemplified the way he thought: No change! *The Economist* got it right when it said: 'Although it will become the focus of bitter controversy, the encyclical within days of its issue is intellectually deader than a dodo.'

The future Pope John Paul I, Alberto Luciani, was born on 17 October 1912 in a mountain town 120 kilometres north of Venice, to Giovanni and Bartola Luciani, who, while being stalwarts of the Catholic Church, were also Socialists. He was sent to a seminary at the age of 14 and wrote his thesis on a book that had resulted in its author, Rosmini, being excommunicated, *The Five Wounds of the Church*. The book had been banned because he had listed the 'Five Wounds' as the remoteness of the clergy from the people, the low standard of education of the priests, disunity among the bishops, unhealthy interlocking of power between the Church and the State, and massive unused Church wealth.

Luciani took the view that Rosmini had based his arguments on incorrect scripture and his thesis was highly commended. He was made a bishop in 1958 and although there is some evidence that the future Pope did not wholeheartedly support the encyclical *Humanae Vitae*, he did not break ranks and criticise it, as many of the clergy had done. Perhaps this was one of the factors regarded in his favour when he was made Patriarch of Venice in December 1969.

In this post, he abandoned many of the ceremonial traditions that were supposed to reflect the power and the glory of the Church, and lived a frugal and simple life. He took special interest in the needs of the handicapped and disabled and it was this work that led him first to have doubts about the IOR, or Vatican Bank.

Like the other clergy in Venice, he used a bank called Banca Cattolica di Veneto, otherwise known as 'the priests' bank'. Traditionally, it had offered low-interest loans to priests and their parishes, and many parishes even had small stock holdings in the bank. The Vatican sold the bank to Roberto Calvi without consulting the Patriarch, and once again Luciani kept a low profile and did not complain because he had no direct interest in the bank. But when the new owners stopped the traditional low-interest loans to priests and parishes, demanding the full rate of interest, he was moved to speak up. Furthermore, he found out that the parishes that had bought shares in the bank had neither received any of the profits nor even had their original stake returned: the Vatican had kept the entire profit.

Luciani went to see Marcinkus personally but was sent packing, with Marcinkus telling him, 'Eminence, don't you have anything better to do?'

Towards the end of his reign and as he was getting old, Pope Paul unwisely interfered in the Divorce Referendum, calling for a 'No' vote. Luciani knew that it was a lost cause as far as the Church was concerned but supported the Vatican line and rather half-heartedly campaigned for a 'No' vote in Venice. As expected, the Italian people voted six to four to allow divorce and the Vatican, instead of being pragmatic, took the result as a major snub.

Before he died on 6 August 1978, Pope Paul had made changes in the way his successor would be chosen. All cardinals over the age of 80 were excluded and, fortunately, this ruled out the *éminence grise* Cardinal Ottaviani.

The initial favourite was the protégé of the dead Pope, Cardinal Pignedoli, but a 'Stop Pignedoli' campaign was launched and the support moved behind the Archbishop of Genoa, Cardinal Siri, the arch-conservative who had hoped for election when Pius XII had died. He failed to get the required level of support and so, after two days in conclave, the cardinals settled on Cardinal Alberto Luciani, who basically came down the middle between the conservative and the moderniser. He chose the name John Paul to reflect the admiration he felt for his two immediate predecessors.

He brought his unconventional lifestyle habits from Venice to Rome, failing to grasp the fact that he was no longer an individual but a symbol that was supposed to reflect a consensus within the Curia of the Vatican. He started to dispense with ceremony, which was thought of as essential to the Vatican, and his attitude towards tradition caused confusion among the 3,000 staff, both lay and clerical. His idea of projecting the profile of the Church as 'poor' did not sit well with the Curia, but he stuck to his guns, rejecting their protests.

Very few 'new boys' in any organisation make good impressions with their staff because of the tension caused by threatened changes. John Paul was no exception because in his thirty-three days in office he made four, or possibly five, sets of enemies.

The first were the supporters of *Humanae Vitae*. He made it clear that he was in support of artificial birth control and he expunged all references to *Humanae Vitae* from a speech written for him by his Secretary of State, Cardinal Villot. He refused to go to a conference in Milan to speak in support of the encyclical and made it clear that he wanted the debate reopened. In this he showed great political naivety because it would have been virtually impossible for the Vatican to do a U-turn so soon after issuing such a dramatic document that had disappointed so many young Catholic couples worldwide, who had expected to be permitted to use contraception. A Pope who was showing signs of recognising the worldwide disappointment created by the encyclical was causing serious concerns within the Vatican Establishment.

The second group was his State Department. Cardinal Villot wanted to retire and be succeeded by his close colleague, Cardinal Baggio. John Paul had pencilled in Baggio to succeed him as Archbishop of Venice, but Baggio had flatly refused to leave the Vatican. That tension was at its height when John Paul died.

The third was Cardinal John Cody of Chicago, who was a man who saw himself not only above the Vatican but also beyond the grasp of the US government. He was a close friend of his compatriot, Paul Marcinkus, and controlled a budget of over $250 million a year. There was a big Polish Catholic congregation in Chicago and he started sending diocesan funds to Lech Walesa, the leader of the Polish Solidarity. This would probably have had the approval of the Vatican had they known because it was part of the fight against godless communism, but he did it on his own initiative.

But it was Cody's close friendship with Helen Dolan Wilson, a divorcee, that was upsetting both his congregation and his priests. He had bought a house with her in Florida and she was the beneficiary of his $100,000 life policy. In addition, all the diocesan insurance work was handled by her son, David, and Cody kept no traceable accounts, refusing even to answer to the US Federal tax authorities.

The scandal became so open that when his priests complained to him he refused to acknowledge that he was doing anything wrong and also refused all efforts at reconciliation. As a result, 30 per cent of the clerics in the Chicago diocese left the Church.

The new Pope was incensed at the scandal and so he sent Cardinal Baggio to see Cody with a very generous retirement package, but Baggio got a very hostile response and was basically thrown out. But the message that this new Pope meant business had been clearly heard and understood by Cody: sooner or later, he was going to go.

The fourth group comprised those who were using the Vatican Bank as a conduit through which to launder money. John Paul did not suspect laundering, but he had previously crossed swords with both Calvi and Marcinkus about the sale of the Banca Cattolica di Veneto and he had concerns about the way Vatican finance was functioning. Certainly Marcinkus would have dealt differently with the visit he received from Luciani had he known of the future election result!

The new Pope stated his intention to look into the Vatican Bank structure and it was strongly rumoured that he intended to replace Marcinkus with Cardinal Bellini. Had this happened, the money laundering venture might have been exposed, resulting in massive Mafia losses.

The fifth group to be involved in the theories about the Pope's death was the Freemasons. The relationship between the Vatican and Freemasonry is long and complex and many people will be surprised to hear that there is a Lodge that meets regularly in the Vatican today. Some authors suspected that the Freemasons were associated with the death of Pope John Paul I on the basis of a letter he received on 12 September from an investigative journalist called Mino Peccorelli. The letter included a list of 100

Vatican employees who were Freemasons, including Cardinals Baggio, Villot and Marcinkus. Although on the face of it this seems scandalous, it is very credible because members of the Vatican have often joined Italian lodges on a 'need to know what's going on' basis. Therefore none of the information that Peccorelli had alleged would have been very surprising and it is thus very dubious as to whether Freemasons had anything at all to do with Pope John Paul's death.

When, at around 4.45 a.m. on Friday, 29 September, he was found dead in bed, logical explanations were outnumbered by conspiracy theories. Die young in any great office (and 65 is positively juvenile for a Pope) and two things happen: your memory is immortalised and conspiracy theories abound. This applied to Mozart, President Kennedy and Pope John Paul I. If the death occurs in Italy or America, and if there is the remotest possibility of a conspiracy, then the Mafia and the Freemasons are first in the line of suspects.

Certainly John Paul's death was surprising and totally unexpected. He had a good family medical history, with both his parents and his brother living into their 70s and 80s. There was no family history of stroke or heart disease, and he was brought up in a healthy mountainous area of Italy. He was five foot nine, weighed eleven and a half stone, was not obese and was a non-smoker and a moderate wine drinker. He took regular exercise and, until six years before his death, had been a rock climber.

He had suffered from TB as a child, but this came from unpasteurised milk and was a not uncommon condition in most European countries at that time. It might also have been the reason for his subsequent tonsillectomy. In 1964, he had his gall bladder removed and also had an operation for piles. Two years before his election, he had had a venous thrombosis in his eye, but it was resolved with the simple treatment of vasodilators and warfarin (to thin the blood). He had three check-ups by the Vatican doctors in his thirty-three days and the records show that his blood pressure and chest X-ray were normal.

As part of his reduction of protocol in the Vatican, John Paul had dismissed the Swiss guard who would normally have stood outside the door of his bedroom all night. His immediate household consisted of three nuns, Sisters Clemenza, Vincenza and Asunta, and two priests, Fathers Lorenzi and Magee.

The night before he died he had dinner with the two priests. Sister Clemenza had cooked clear minestrone, veal, fresh beans and salad, and it was served by Sisters Vincenza and Asunta. The curates drank red wine and the Pope had mineral water. At 8.45 p.m., he spoke to Cardinal Colombo of Milan by telephone for 45 minutes and at 9.30 p.m. he said goodnight to the curates and went to bed. He did not complain of feeling unwell in any way.

As usual, Sister Vincenza left coffee on a table outside his room at 4.30 a.m., knocked on his door and left. The Pope would normally then open his door, take in the coffee, say his breviary and emerge at around 6 a.m.

Sister Vincenza returned at 4.45 a.m. and found the coffee still on the table, untouched. After knocking, she entered the bedroom and found the Pope sitting upright in his bed, with the light on, wearing his spectacles and holding a sheet of paper. He didn't move and so the frightened nun ran to call Father Lorenzi, who rushed to the room with Father Magee. They called Cardinal Villot, who arrived at 5 a.m. and reportedly took away not only the Pope's spectacles but also some medicines that were on the bedside table and the sheet of paper that he was supposedly holding.

Villot swore the three clergy to silence and called the Dean, the head of the Diplomatic Corps, the Pope's doctor, Renato Buzzonetti, and finally the head of the Swiss Guard, Hans Roggan.

Roggan had returned to the Vatican at 10.30 p.m. the previous evening and had noticed that rather unusually the light in the Pope's apartment was on.

After a superficial examination, Dr Buzzonetti announced that the Pope had died of a myocardial infarction at around 11 p.m. the previous evening, but the embalmers, the Signoracci brothers, did not agree. Because of the lack of rigor mortis, they thought that the death would have been no earlier than between 3 a.m. and 4 a.m.

There was no death certificate with a cause of death lodged in the records, no autopsy and no definite time of death recorded. Some of these errors could be explained by the sheer panic that hits an organisation when the leader dies unexpectedly: normal protocols go out of the window and things that would be done routinely for any lower member of the organisation are left undone, thus opening the way for conspiracy theorists to have a field day.

This was the case in Dallas when Kennedy was killed. Among the facts that breed continual suspicion are that paperwork is missing from the hospital where he was taken and that the autopsy was done by a junior naval medical officer, who had evidently never carried out an autopsy previously.

Embalmers are far more expert in assessing how long a body has been dead than non-forensically trained physicians because that is their everyday job. In this case, there is a huge difference between the physician's estimated time of death and the embalmers'. The difference between 11 p.m. and 4 a.m. is crucial.

There are three cardinal signs that have to be considered when determining the time of death – temperature, lividity and stiffness. The most important thing in determining rigor mortis is the ambient temperature – the warmer the room, the quicker the three cardinal changes set in. Cooling does not start for an hour after death because the liver goes on metabolising after the heart stops. Thereafter the temperature drops by one degree an hour until it reaches 34 degrees, when the body becomes cold to the touch. There was no mention of the Pope's temperature or what the body felt like.

A dead body displays lividity when the blood is no longer circulating, draining to the dependent parts, causing darkness and blotching. This is normally well established in three or four hours, but again there was no information about this.

When death occurs, the body is flaccid, but gradually the muscles lose their ATP (adenosine triphosphate) and become filled with lactic acid. The face is affected first, and the eyelids go up and the jaw opens, thus the old custom of putting a bandage round the jaw to keep the mouth shut and putting a penny on each eye to hide the grotesque eye opening. The rigidity is palpable in two or three hours and if the temperature is high, then the changes will be quicker.

The Pope died in September, when the temperature in Rome is still high. There were thus no likely factors that would have delayed the onset of rigor mortis and so the embalmers are far more likely than the doctor to have been correct in estimating that he died between 3 a.m. and 4 a.m. Had he died at 11 p.m., he would have been cold, livid and totally rigid, with an open jaw and staring eyes. On the other hand, he was obviously reading when he died because he had a paper in his hand and his spectacles on. His light was also on, as it had been when Hans Roggan returned the previous evening, an hour after the Pope retired to bed.

It is very unlikely that he had either a brain haemorrhage or a heart attack. He could have had a blockage of the conducting mechanism of the heart, but this also causes acute pulmonary oedema, which results in blood-tinged foam coming out of the mouth.

The diagnosis of the sudden death syndrome from stress is now legally accepted, and there have been at least two cases in the UK where people have been jailed, having been found guilty of manslaughter without even touching the deceased.

In his book *In the Name of the Father,* David Yallop argues that the piece of paper the Pope was holding was a list of the changes he was intending to make in the State Department and the bank, but his evidence for this remarkable and key claim is not presented. John Paul, according to Yallop, had evidently argued about this with Villot earlier in the afternoon. If this is so, it could explain why Villot took the paper away, and it could have been the reason for a 'delayed' heart attack because at the end of the period of stress, when catachol amines are built up, adrenalin is released and this can lead to metabolic changes in an atheromatous plaque that might be in coronary arteries resulting in sudden death with no pathological changes of either clot or damaged heart muscle.

It is very unlikely that he was poisoned by anything that he ate or drank at his last meal. There are, however, three other poisons that could have been administered that would have caused almost instant death with no signs. The first is potassium chloride, the second is insulin and the third is diamorphine.

They would all have had to be injected into a vein and this means that at least two men would have had to enter the Pope's bedchamber, one to restrain him while the other injected him. He would die within minutes and the bed could be remade, any signs of a struggle obliterated and the scene set to indicate natural causes.

It is quite possible for even a trained pathologist, never mind the Pope's physician, to miss an intravenous injection. Indeed Dr David Bee, a consultant pathologist in England, was called before the General Medical Council to explain why he had missed an injection site in one of Harold Shipman's victims.

If we hypothesise that Pope John Paul I was murdered, then one has to ask: who benefited?

The issue of birth control would not warrant murder, nor would a very angry and anxious Archbishop Cody; and while a Masonic plot always plays well to the tabloid press, it is hardly realistic. Bishop Marcinkus would lose his position in the bank, if Yallop is to be believed, but again while he was clearly being duped and flattered by Sindona and Calvi even he would not have contemplated murder.

The real losers would have been Sindona and the Mafia because any investigation of the bank would have certainly exposed how they had duped Marcinkus. Subsequent events in the colourful life of Sindona demonstrate that he certainly had the capacity to arrange a murder through the Mafia, so it is conceivable that it might have been a Mafia assassination. However, we shall never know.

The Vatican Bank carried on being used by the Mafia financiers and Marcinkus continued in post. When Sindona fled to America, his successor as Vatican finance adviser became so famous that he will forever be known as God's Banker. And he was in a rather special 'club'.

23

PROPAGANDA MASSONICA DUE

Freemasonry in Italy has as much resemblance to Freemasonry in Britain as this book has to cookery! In Scotland and England, there is one Grand Lodge to which many provincial lodges answer. Not so in Italy. Such is the independence of the Italian that there are over 60 Grand Lodges. Some are religious, some are mixed sex, some are ecumenical and some are traditional.

Freemasonry is an admirable charity and, although I am not a Freemason, I have been associated with organisations that have benefited enormously from the charity of the Freemasons and I think that I understand their true purpose. Yasha Beresiner, who was of great help in informing me about the P2 Lodge, told me: 'Freemasonry is what is in a man's heart.' This is undoubtedly so, but the truth is that not everyone who joins the Freemasons has that understanding.

There are probably more Freemasons in Italy than in any other country in Europe, but they are not all true Freemasons. People join the organisation for many reasons, even though all who are admitted will swear to the underlying principles. There are those who join out of curiosity or to delight in the 'secrecy', and those who want more contracts or promotions – but they are not Masons. Freemasonry is basically a charitable, non-religious craft that tries to do some good.

Most people are very surprised that it thrives in Italy because the commonly held view is that Catholicism and Freemasonry are mutually incompatible. The Papal Bull issued by Clement XII in 1738 was probably a warning shot across the bows of fledgling Masonic activity. The Carbonari were a true anti-clerical political secret society and were confused with the Masons, which resulted in yet another confrontational Papal Bull in 1821 by Pius VII.

The first official Italian Lodge was the Ausinia Lodge in Turin, formed in 1859, and these Freemasons were among the financial backers of Garibaldi and the invasion of Sicily. When Italy was united in 1860, both Garibaldi and the new King, Victor Emmanuel II, were Freemasons and they each exhibited the characteristics that cause such confusion about the involvement of Freemasons in conspiracies.

Victor Emmanuel was a Freemason – and Garibaldi was a 'voyeur'. He is recognised as such within the Freemasonry movement and his standing as a Mason is very low, even though his rank was high, having moved from third to thirtieth degree in one evening prior to being made Grand Master of Italy!

The suspicion and antagonism that Freemasonry had created in political and government circles in the mid-nineteenth century continued into the twentieth. To be identified as a Mason at that time would have had disastrous effects on anyone's career in Italy because of the mistrust that was felt towards the Freemasons by both the Church and society in general.

Because of this, the Grand Orient of Italy formed a special Lodge in 1875 that would not keep membership lists, was totally secure and that the leaders of the country could join. They called it Propaganda Massonica and it was formed in order to allow prominent Italians to become Masons with no fear of being 'outed': its existence was to be kept secret from all apart from the officers of the Grand Orient, at that time the supreme body. The arrangement was successful, but the Grand Orient in time became more concerned about the implications for the craft if this elite lodge was uncovered and decided to dissolve it in 1907. The problem, however, became administrative and they never quite got round to doing anything about it, even though the decision had been taken. Thus at the end of the First World War it was still in existence and there was a body of men who were all for keeping it. Prominent politicians and eminent individuals continued to be initiated and the Grand Master of the Grand Orient was invariably elected Master of the Lodge.

The re-numbering of the lodges that took place in 1950 gave Propaganda Massonica Lodge the number 2 and thereafter it was known as Lodge P2. In 1967, the then Grand Master of the Grand Orient of Italy, Giordano Gamberini, invited Licio Gelli, then merely a prominent businessman, to become Secretary of the P2 Lodge. It was a step the craft would later regret because Gelli behaved with an independence that he had not been granted. But who was this mastermind Mason who corralled the elite of Italy into a Masonic lodge that even the Grand Orient had doubts about?

Licio Gelli, who later acquired the nickname 'the Puppetmaster' (he told a journalist this was what he had originally wanted to be when he grew up!), had been a fervent anti-Communist from an early age. He was born in Pistoia, a suburb of Florence, on 21 April 1919. He was expelled from the local school when he was 15 and shortly afterwards went to fight with the Blackshirts on Franco's side in the Spanish Civil War. During the Second World War, he fought in Albania and became a member of the German SS. In the Partisan versus Fascist struggle at the end of the war, he was a double agent. In conjunction with US counter-intelligence services, he facilitated the escape of many high-ranking Nazis to South America, including Klaus Barbie, known as 'the Butcher of Lyons'.

After the war, he found himself an extraordinary 'day job' as general manager of the Permaflex mattress company in Frosinone, a dowdy town halfway between Rome and Naples, and then, after a period, as manager with Remington Rand nearer Pistoia. The Permaflex motto was not inappropriate for the life that Gelli led: 'The Whole World in Your Dreams'. He joined a conventional

Masonic lodge in 1963 and was only a third-degree Mason, which is as high as many Italian lodges aspire.

Just four years later, he received Gamberini's call to re-establish this special Lodge, which he understood was also to be a bulwark against communism, given the fears of the time.

At the same time, he gained access to the highest echelons of the Vatican through Umberto Ortolani, who was the son of a railwayman but had managed to graduate in law from Bologna University. When he met Gelli, Ortolani was 60 and had been an adviser to Pope Paul VI (formerly Cardinal Montini); he was known as 'the Vatican's Kissinger'. For his work with Catholic charities and other organisations, he had received many papal honours and so was able to introduce Gelli to Pope Paul. In subsequent years, Gelli, a non-Catholic and a known prominent Freemason, was admitted to the Order of the Knights of Malta and the Holy Sepulchre, an order that is the successor to the Knights Templar.

Ortolani also owned enormous ranches in Uruguay and, in 1970, he placed Gelli on the board of his bank, Banca Financiero Sudamericano, also known as Bafisud. He then brought him to Argentina and, within a remarkably short time, Gelli had become a friend and confidant of Juan Peron, who in 1971 gave him Argentinian citizenship.

When Peron was overthrown, Gelli remained untouched because he was working with the head of the navy, Admiral Massera, on an arms deal with Italy and had the protection of the military. He then helped Peron get back into power and in 1973, at Peron's inauguration, Giulio Andreotti, who was present, remarked on Peron's almost reverential regard for Gelli. 'I saw Peron kneel in front of Gelli,' he said.

One of the other legacies that Gelli left in Argentina was a P2 Lodge. He subsequently built similar power bases that extended through Brazil, Uruguay, Colombia, Bolivia and Venezuela, and in 1973 became Argentina's adviser on Italian affairs.

When Giordano Gamberini, Grand Master of the Grand Orient, had asked Gelli to be Worshipful Master of Lodge P2, he had empowered him to initiate any apprentices whom he thought suitable, and with this power he began to introduce the good and the great of Italy into the Lodge. One of the early entrants was Roberto Calvi, but very soon a thousand of the Italian Establishment were signed up. It was then that the Grand Orient saw the potential for great harm with Gelli in sole and complete control and acting as a loose cannon in the craft.

Fearful of the consequences of a 'rogue' lodge, the Grand Orient dissolved P2 in December 1974, with the vote at the General Purposes committee being 400 to 21. But Gelli had great resilience. Within a year, he had succeeded in getting a new warrant for his Lodge and persuaded the Grand Orient to record that it had 'suspended' rather than 'dissolved' his Lodge.

What the Grand Orient had failed to realise was that this manoeuvre of dissolving the Lodge to get rid of Gelli had backfired. Gelli would still be in a position of power: although 'suspended', he was in total control of a Lodge that was now answerable to no one. When he refused to furnish the names of his members to the legitimate Masonic authorities in August 1976, the Grand Orient expelled him for a period of three years. But that only lasted six months because he again persuaded the Grand Orient to reverse their decision! And it was this error that damaged Freemasonry in Italy more severely than anything Mussolini had ever done.

Gelli would hold court three days a week in rooms 127, 128 and 129 of the Excelsior Hotel in Via Veneto, Rome. He took these three rooms so that there could be separate entrances and exits. Initiates would come into number 127, do their business in 128, where Gelli held court, and would exit through 129. At initiations, Gelli would wear a black cloak, a blue apron bordered in red, and a gold Masonic triangle around his neck. He saw the Lodge as an anti-Communist league and it was almost certainly funded and encouraged by the CIA, even though James Angleton had long since departed.

Gelli, of course, did not invent conspiracy and corruption, but the vehicle of Freemasonry struck that chord in the hearts of

Italians who, even at the highest level of society, distrusted the State and its organisations and fell back on that basic Italian reflex: the safest and best way forward is to know the right people, keep it in the family and to look after oneself.

The biggest 'growth years' of the Lodge were 1970–80, when it was run by Gelli virtually as a private domain. It was established on a platform the legs of which were bankers, politicians, the media and the military, all of whom were fundamentally and enthusiastically anti-Communist.

When the denouement came, the Grand Orient was caught with its pants down. They knew that the original creation of the P2 Lodge was for the good and the great, and when it became the private domain of Licio Gelli they did not act with sufficient resolution, perhaps being satisfied that so many of Italy's Establishment had been initiated into the craft.

Meanwhile Gelli was pressing ahead with the project given him by the Grand Master and, armed with his South American experiences, modelled his *raggrupamento* on the many similar right-wing groups in South America. The aim was extreme right-wing control of Italy and in this regard he was supported by the CIA, who saw him as the perfect vehicle through which to achieve its aims of fighting communism and keeping Italy in NATO.

The existence of this rather strange and exotic lodge was uncovered as part of the fallout from the Sindona affair. One of the magistrates investigating the Ambrosoli murder, Gerardo Colombo, was also investigating the movements surrounding Sindona's kidnapping. He had discovered the pivotal role played by Dr Joseph Crimi, and as he uncovered the doctor's movements he discovered that he had made numerous visits during the 90 days that Sindona was 'missing' to the town of Arezzo in Tuscany.

In March 1981, along with Giuliano Turone, Colombo organised police raids of all Gelli's addresses. In a clothing factory that Gelli managed near his home town of Arezzo, they found the membership list of a Masonic lodge, but while this revealed sensational details of the previously unknown affiliations of 962 high-ranking people, the real discovery was 30 sealed envelopes detailing information that concerned many illegal financial transactions.

When the names of the members of P2 were published, they both titillated and alarmed Italians, but most people who took an interest in politics will now say that they were not in the least surprised because 'this is how it was'. Of the 962 names, numbered from 1,600 upwards, there were twelve generals of the *carabinieri*, twenty-two army generals and eight admirals. There were another 52 *carabinieri* officers, 50 army officers, 29 naval officers and many members of the Italian secret services. There were 11 police chiefs, including the chief of police from Palermo, and 37 from the Financial Police. The government was represented by five ministers, thirty-eight ordinary Members of Parliament, the secretary of the Social Democrat Party, Pietro Longo, and fourteen judges. From the financial world, there were ten bank presidents, including the Mafia banking 'twins' Michele Sindona and Roberto Calvi. And finally from the media there were the owner, as well as the managing director, of the biggest selling daily, *Corriere della Sera*, two other editors of large newspapers and an up-and-coming media man, Silvio Berlusconi, whose number was 1,816.

It is likely that Gelli 'persuaded' some influential people to join with the threat of blackmail. In his book *Italy and its Discontents*, Paul Ginsborg quotes from a document revealed by the Parliamentary Commission of Inquiry on P2:

> Ubs Lugano, current account no. 633369, 'Protezione' number corresponding to the name of the Hon. Claudio Martelli on behalf of Bettino Craxi into which has been paid by Dr Roberto Calvi on 28 October 1980 the sum of $3,500,000, subsequent to the drawing up by Dr Fiorini of the agreement with ENI [the Italian State Energy Company]. On the signing of the agreement by Dr CR [Calvi, Roberto] and DDL [DiDonna, Leonardo] on 20 November 1980, there will be a further payment of $3,500,000.

At that time it was quite unclear why a banker was depositing $7 million in the account of the Socialist Party or why the information should have ended up in Gelli's safe. As important, however, was the document that the police found when they stopped Gelli's daughter at Rome airport. In her briefcase was a report entitled 'A Plan for the Rebirth of Democracy', which called for the rewriting of the Italian constitution, control of the mass media, removal of parliamentary immunity from prosecution and the suspension of union activity. The following is a quote from the Parliamentary Commission from a document entitled 'Economic and Financial Manoeuvres': 'Sums not exceeding 30–40 billion lire would seem sufficient to allow carefully chosen men acting in good faith to conquer key posts necessary for overall control.' There is thus a strong inference that acting behind the facade of a supposed Masonic lodge, Gelli was planning a *coup d'état*.

These envelopes containing membership lists were taken from the two magistrates, transferred to Rome – and never seen again! They were last traced to a locked drawer in Prime Minister Arnaldo Forlani's desk. But *è cosi*.

The discovery of a secret Masonic lodge with the good and the great as members set off a huge public outcry and parliament set up a Board of Inquiry chaired by a remarkable politician, Tina Anselmi. She produced 115 volumes of evidence and her conclusion was that P2 had devoted itself to 'the pollution of the public life of a nation'.

Gerardo Colombo became such an expert in the creation and distribution of 'hot money' that he spent many years on the US lecture circuit. Later in his career he would also instigate the case in which Berlusconi was accused of bribing judges.

After the publication of the list, Ortolani fled to Uruguay and when he returned to Italy in June 1989 he was sentenced to a jail term for bank fraud; however, he was permitted to go free after a week, on payment of a 600-million-lira fine. He died peacefully in Rome in January 2002 at the age of 87 after a long illness.

Gelli also fled to Uruguay but wanted access to the $100 million that Calvi had deposited in one of his Swiss accounts. He asked that the money be transferred to Uruguay but the Union des Banques Suisses refused because the sum was so large; Gelli was told that he would have to appear in person with proper identification if he wanted to access the remaining $53 million. He was arrested on arrival at the bank and put into the high security Champ Dollon prison in Geneva. There then followed several months of negotiation between the Swiss and Italian governments about where he should be tried, and finally it was agreed that he would be extradited to Italy.

On the eve of his extradition, however, Gelli simply walked out of jail, having bribed a guard. On 10 August 1983, he went to Monte Carlo and from there to Uruguay.

But by then the man he had helped to destroy, Roberto Calvi, had been dead for a year.

24

The Man Who Duped the Vatican

There are many people who are remembered for their deaths rather than their lives and Roberto Calvi is one. Although he was known as God's Banker because of his association with the Vatican, his nickname in Milanese banking circles was 'the man with the eyes of ice'. It may have been that he preferred a poker face when doing business, but it may also have reflected his shyness, and especially his paranoia.

Born in Milan on 13 April 1920, he was one of four children of a reasonably wealthy family, with his father becoming the manager of the Banca Commerciale Italiana. He was educated at a private school, and instead of taking the soft option of going to university he joined the army at the beginning of the war. He had a good war, serving and surviving on the Russian front and keeping his troop intact after the confusion of the surrender and fall of Mussolini. For this he was given awards by both the Italians and the Germans.

When he returned after the war, he joined the bank in which his father worked and was sent to a branch in Lecce in the South. But instead of staying with this mainstream bank, in 1946 he joined a peculiar little Catholic bank whose clients were small artisans, shopkeepers and parish priests. It was a bank with an interesting history.

In the late 1880s, Giuseppe Tovini, suspecting that all lay banks were controlled by Freemasons, led a group of Catholics to form the Banca San Paolo in Brescia. In 1896, he transferred it to Milan and changed the name to that of the patron saint of the city, Ambrosiano. The aim of the business was to be a truly Catholic bank, with an ethical lending policy, and 150 Catholics each put up one million lire. To become a customer of the bank, it was necessary to show not only a baptismal certificate to prove that you had been born into the Catholic Church but also a letter of *raccomandazione* from your parish priest. Since all the Milan parishes were clients, it acquired the same name as the Venetian bank, which the dead Pope had once used, 'the priests' bank'. It was certainly *not* the sort of organisation that an upwardly mobile, ambitious young banker would join.

In 1952, Calvi married Clara Cancelli, a chemistry student from Bologna, and they had two children, Carlo, born in 1953, and Anna, born in 1959. Calvi was a workaholic and within half a dozen years he had risen to the position of personal assistant to a man who became not only his patron (essential in Italy), but was destined to become president of the bank, Carlo Canesi.

Calvi set up the first mutual fund in Italy, which allowed small investors to enter the stock market. Perhaps it was this that brought him to the notice of Michele Sindona, who, although a great deal better known, was only a year older. They met through an old university friend, but the interpersonal chemistry must have clicked because from the start they got on well. It was a meeting that Calvi would live to regret.

Some time in 1971 Sindona introduced him to the poisonous triumvirate of Paul Marcinkus, Licio Gelli and Umberto Ortolani. They agreed to help Calvi in his career, as long as Sindona acted as his partner and watchdog in business deals. He should have said no, but he didn't. It looked like a good deal in the first years because within six months he had become general manager of the Banca Ambrosiano and within a year he was managing director.

There was a law dating from 1936 that prevented banks

from actually owning industrial companies, but Sindona had circumvented this by setting up holding companies in Luxembourg and Lichtenstein and he showed Calvi how to copy his tactic. He sold him one of his holding companies in Luxembourg, which Calvi christened Banca Ambrosiano Holding (BAH), and made it the parent of the Ambrosiano Swiss bank, Banca del Gottardo.

In 1972, Calvi bought another bank, this time in the Bahamas, changing its name from the Cisalpine Overseas Bank to Banca Ambrosiano Overseas (BAO). He appointed Bishop Marcinkus to the board because the Vatican had received a minority shareholding and this rather unusual bishop, of course, did not turn down the opportunity of visiting Nassau two or three times a year for board meetings. At one of these, he is reported to have embraced Calvi's wife Clara, singing *'Arrivederci Roma'*!

Sindona was by now using the IOR, the Vatican Bank, as a virtual offshore bank, with a branch in the Vatican City. Money deposited in an IOR account or directly in cash from a suitcase at the IOR itself could be transferred anywhere in the world with no questions asked due to the esteem in which the Vatican was held. The clerics involved in the bank never questioned what was going on. In this way, the Vatican Bank was used to bypass Italy's increasingly severe exchange controls.

Both Sindona and Calvi became major players in the Milan stock market, which at the time was tiny, with fewer than 150 listed companies. It is also astonishing that none of these companies needed to produce consolidated accounts. There was also a smaller and more secret market called *mercato ristretto,* meaning 'restricted market', which they used for marginally dubious deals. Since his brokerage fees were becoming expensive, Calvi started his own dealing company, Suprafin.

The basic tactic used by Calvi and Sindona was to move large sums of money out of Italy to overseas shell companies that they owned either directly or indirectly. From there, the money might pass to further offshore investment companies that they also owned, which would come back to buy shares in Italian businesses through the Milan markets. An asset, once bought, would then be shunted around the shell companies at even higher prices, thus 'liberating' more cash. In this way, they were able to smuggle billions of lire out of Italy (a billion lire was then worth £200,000).

By consenting to work in this way with Sindona, Calvi, the managing director of a small, apparently sleepy bank, was indicating that he was 'bent' and willing to join forces with the Mafia money launderer.

The constitution of the Banca Ambrosiano laid down that no one company or individual could own more than 5 per cent of the stock, which was merely following Italian law. Perhaps Calvi flouted this rule because he felt that his bank would be better protected from a takeover or from government interference, but by setting out to acquire a majority shareholding he was breaking the law. Through Suprafin he amassed more than 15 per cent of Banca Ambrosiano shares, which were held by his dummy overseas companies. Since he had become the largest shareholder of voting stock, he was now the de facto owner of his own bank.

But he then became even more devious. In November 1974, through Banca del Gottardo, he set up a Panamanian company called United Trading Company in the name of the Vatican, which not only made this a holding of Suprafin, but vicariously made the Vatican the unwitting part-owner of Banca Ambrosiano.

When Sindona crashed and fled from Italy and then America in 1974, Calvi became the Vatican's preferred financial adviser and was also honoured by the President of the Republic with the title Cavalieri.

A year later, Canesi retired from the Ambrosiana bank and Calvi became president; he decided to stay on as his own general manager and so neither had to groom nor share his actions with a number two. He had good reason for playing his cards close to his chest. First, he was in breach of a clutch of banking laws, both by exporting capital and by owning the majority holding of a bank of which he was president, and second, Sindona-in-exile looked like turning 'nasty'.

When the initial crash came, Sindona asked Calvi to bail him out, but the sums were so enormous that this was impossible. But knowing of Sindona's Mafia connections, instead of being delighted at being made a bank president and getting his photo in magazines and papers, he became frightened and increasingly insecure. His family later said that he changed: it was as if he knew that fate was waiting round a corner to destroy him. He increased security at the bank, putting in bulletproof glass, installing scrambler telephones and employing bodyguards. He did the same in his three homes and always travelled in an armoured car with bodyguards, carrying a briefcase with his most secure papers with him at all times.

The insecurity and fear made him increasingly unbalanced. He was not wrong in believing that Italy was really run by *potere occulto* (hidden powers); all Italians believe in this concept, possibly because of centuries of living in an occupied country that has fostered secret societies. Not only did he donate generously to all three main political parties but he also did something that would have had the bank's founder, Tovini, turning in his grave: he became a Freemason, being initiated into the P2 Lodge on 23 August 1975.

Sindona, meanwhile, saw things differently. To him, Calvi was a provincial banker whom he had plucked from obscurity and whom he had introduced to the powers and Establishment of Italy. It was Calvi's duty to bail him out, and if he didn't, Sindona was going to make sure that they both went down together.

Sindona hired an agent provocateur, Luigi Cavallo, to plan a campaign against Calvi that began on 13 November 1977. The walls in streets around the Banca Ambrosiano were plastered with posters printed in white, blue and yellow, claiming that Calvi had illegally exported millions of dollars to Swiss banks in both his own name and that of his wife. The posters carried details of the banks, the account names and the account numbers in Switzerland. Calvi capitulated immediately and that same day sent Sindona half a million dollars, claiming that it was the proceeds of the sale of a villa. But that wasn't nearly enough to buy off Sindona.

Ten days later, Cavallo wrote a powerful polemic to Paolo Baffi, governor of the Bank of Italy. This contained allegations against Calvi that the Bank of Italy could not ignore because he also attached the evidence for his charges. As a result of this, a team of 12 inspectors arrived at Banca Ambrosiano on 17 April 1978, led by the head of banking surveillance, Mario Sarcinelli. This marked the beginning of the end for Calvi.

Towards the end of 1978, their report was published, showing that Calvi had run the bank virtually as a personal fiefdom, with its compliant board being used merely as a rubber stamp. They found the link with the Vatican and devoted 25 pages of the initial report to the relationship between the Banca Ambrosiano and the IOR; they also described the way in which billions of lire had been exported from Italy using the Switzerland–Vatican–overseas pathway.

That should have been that. Calvi should have been arrested. But this was Italy and *poteri occulti* were at work.

On 24 March 1979, Judge Antonio Alibrandi, a right-wing Rome magistrate, indicted not Calvi but Baffi and Sarcinelli! Not because of the current case but because of one from years earlier. It involved the case of the Credito Industriale Sardo bank, which the Bank of Italy should perhaps have reported for prosecution because of a minor irregularity. It later turned out to be a non-event, but it sufficed to put an end to the Ambrosiano inspection.

It soon got worse for the main players. Sarcinelli was arrested on charges of misconduct and was remanded in detention in the Regina Coeli prison in Castel Sant'Angelo, the setting for Act 3 of the opera *Tosca*. Baffi was spared incarceration on account of his age but had to resign as governor. Both were later cleared, but it was a truly astonishing act of intimidation and vengeance on the part of the Christian Democrats.

But Sindona terrified Calvi far more than the Bank of Italy inspectors: they could only hurt him, whereas Sindona and the

Mafia could kill both him and his family anywhere in the world at any time. So Calvi looked to Licio Gelli for protection. This initially cost him $100 million, which he deposited in Gelli's Geneva account; but all that did was to transfer him from the frying pan of the Bank of Italy investigators to the fire burning in Gelli, who had spotted a cash cow.

The first thing Gelli asked of Calvi was to buy the ailing publishing firm Rizzoli, which owned *Corriere della Sera*. While Rizzoli was at the time a sick company, the purchase fulfilled two objectives. The first was to get the owners, also Freemasons, out of a spot of bother; the second was to give Gelli some control over a major newspaper.

Further financial lunacy followed. Calvi invested heavily in South and Central America, no doubt at the behest of Gelli and Ortolani. In 1977, he had bought 5 per cent of Ortolani's Uruguayan bank, Bafisud, through his Bahama company and now he followed Gelli's advice to open Banca Andino in Lima, Peru, putting Filippo Leoni, one of his Milan heads of department, in charge.

He then opened a third bank in Argentina, which was, thanks to Gelli's influence, licensed not only to function as an offshore unit but also to act as a local savings bank. It opened to a great fanfare of publicity and was christened Banca Ambrosiano de America del Sud, with an old friend of Gelli, Admiral Massera, resigning from the ruling junta in order to sit on the board!

At this point, the Bank of Italy made foreign holding companies illegal unless they made their accounts available for inspection in Italy. They set up the equivalent of the Securities and Exchange Commission that regulates Wall Street and the City of London. They also ruled that the Banca Ambrosiano shares should be traded on the Milan stock market rather than the *mercato ristretto*, which meant that the Banca Ambrosiano had to publish consolidated accounts, including all foreign operations, which up to now had been totally secret.

Calvi faced two further dangers. Under the new laws, the Italian magistrates were now able to look at illegal money exports, and his ghost company loans were beginning to cause a strain. If the value of the dollar and the lira remained stable, then all might be well, but if the dollar rose sharply against the lira, the ghost companies would be unable to pay the interest on the loans. And that is what happened, with full repayment of the loans being impossible, since the loans exceeded the value of the Ambrosiano shares.

In response to this danger, Gelli offered protection from the judiciary, but it required more money to be transferred from the Banca Ambrosiano to the P2 Lodge. It was typical of Calvi's state of mind at this point that the more he felt the financial strain, the more protection he felt he needed.

Not unexpectedly, other senior staff at Banca Ambrosiano, who were unaware of the extent of the president's dealings overseas and who did not know that the Vatican owned their bank, became concerned at the constant attention that the bank was receiving from the Bank of Italy and its regulators. They were now beginning to doubt the years of unconcerned reassurances that they had received from 'the boss'.

While Calvi was undergoing these trials and tribulations, Gelli came under threat. Mino Pecorelli, the editor of a scandal sheet called *OP*, had begun publishing information about Gelli's alleged traitorous actions in the war. It was ironic that Pecorelli should even think about doing this because most of the rumours he had published in the past had been fed to him by Gelli himself, but the angle he took in his first article was that Gelli had been a Fascist who had informed on his colleagues to save himself from Partisan revenge. The second article, published on 20 March 1979, concerned some secret service dossiers on Gelli that had disappeared, and within six hours of publication, Pecorelli was shot dead but no one was ever charged with his murder.

Earlier in 1979 another Calvi investigation was started by the Milan magistrates led by Emilio Alessandrini. He too was shot dead, supposedly by a Red Brigades group called Primea Linea but in reality it was probably arranged by Sindona and the Mafia.

The case passed over to Lucca Mucci, who, when he asked for the Bank of Italy's initial report, was told that it was not available. He asked the Financial Police to investigate Calvi's share transactions, but what he received six months later obviously had the hand of Gelli behind it because it completely cleared Calvi of any irregularity.

Mucci persisted, however, and in September 1979 his officials went to Lugano and found that Banca del Gottardo executives were connected to ghost companies in Panama and Lichtenstein that had bought shares for Calvi.

By March 1980, the Financial Police, carrying out their own investigation, reached the same conclusion as the Bank of Italy two years previously, namely that in order to buy control of the shares of the Banca Ambrosiano, Calvi had illegally exported capital.

By June, Mucci had completed the investigations and ordered Calvi to hand over his passport, but, after much pleading, he got it back on the basis of having to travel for the 'good' of the Italian economy. Although this claim was false, Gelli took the credit for the favour, which put Calvi even further into his debt.

The Calvi case was then handed over to Gerardo D'Ambrosio, who took a very hard line. He arrested Calvi and 11 others on 20 May 1981 and charged them with the illegal export of $20 million. Calvi was denied bail and kept on remand in a white-collar jail in the town of Lodi, where he stayed until the end of July.

As the trial started, Calvi got more and more depressed, and halfway through, when things were looking black, he said that he would talk to the magistrates investigating P2. They questioned him that night from 10 p.m. till 3 a.m. He told them of the influence that Gelli and Ortolani had over him and that he needed both political and financial protection. When the news that he had talked got back to the Socialist Party, they contacted Clara, his wife, and told her that if he didn't retract what he had said about secret donations they would make sure he stayed in jail for life.

Calvi then attempted suicide by taking barbiturates and cutting his wrists, but the latter was a rather superficial gesture. The attempt did, however, get him sympathy from the politicians, who now realised he wouldn't speak. Suddenly, they all gave speeches of fulsome praise.

He was found guilty and sentenced to four years in prison, together with a $10 million fine. He was freed from jail, pending his appeal, but the two-month experience of the white-collar jail, sharing a cell with two other prisoners, was one that scarred him so much that he resolved never again to go inside a jail.

Everything that happened after this, finally leading to his death, reflected his determination never to serve another jail sentence, especially as he realised that the next sentence would not be served in the 'comfort' of a white-collar prison.

Calvi's defence, and one that he persisted with from the outset, was that he had done everything for the good of the Vatican Bank. He had hard evidence that the Vatican owned a huge part of the debt because when Coopers & Lybrand had audited the Bahama Bank in 1978 and had asked for an explanation of the loans to the Panamanian companies, they were told that the companies were owned by the IOR and this was stated in their audit notes. While this was embarrassing for the Vatican, and potentially very expensive, it was not a 'get out of jail free card' for Calvi. Even though there was evidence that the Vatican 'owned' a whole raft of companies in South and Central America with massive debts, in the background was the ticking bomb of their proxy ownership of the Banca Ambrosiano for all these deals. The real owner, however, was Calvi and in 'buying' his own bank he knew that he had committed a crime that was going to see him serve an even longer jail sentence.

He thought that if he could persuade Marcinkus to admit that the debts were the problem of IOR rather than the Banca Ambrosiano he could buy some time that might allow him to find other investors to fill the hole. But Marcinkus was just as scared as Calvi because he now appreciated that he had been duped and had possibly bankrupted the Vatican, even though at this point he did not know the full extent of the Vatican's involvement – especially the debts!

Knowing that it was unlikely that Marcinkus would ever have anything more to do with him, Calvi played the 'Polish' card. These were the days of the rise of Solidarity and since it was the first possible breach in the wall of communism, the 'Polish' Pope, John Paul II, was minded to help. It was done very secretly because if it had come to light that the Vatican was supporting an anti-Russian organisation within the Russian empire, there would have been massive diplomatic consequences. Calvi knew what was going on because the first tranche of $12 million for Poland, sent to the Vatican by the CIA, went through his bank.

What he needed Marcinkus to sign were called letters of comfort. The name is misleading because they are not comforting, supporting letters but official documents that indicate that the signatory stood behind those companies under threat. By signing them, Marcinkus was admitting to knowing all about the 11 companies in Panama and Lichtenstein and would be underwriting their debts, which he knew to be greater than a billion dollars. Even with the threat of the Polish connection, Marcinkus would never have taken it on himself to sign these letters had he not received in exchange another letter signed by Calvi releasing the Vatican from the whole of its potential debt. For Calvi, the clock started ticking, because these letters had a three-month time limit.

His options for filling the hole were diminishing. In the early 1980s, the main source of investment of this size was Arab money and everyone was chasing it. In the 1970s, the world had become accustomed to stories of huge Arab wealth from 'oily sheikdoms' being dispersed recklessly around the world, often on whims, but by the time the '80s had arrived, the Arabs had learned from their mistakes and were neither as generous nor as naive as they once had been.

The first problem he had to face on getting out of jail was the board of his bank, where his deputy, Roberto Rosone, realising that things had gone badly wrong, was minded to depose him.

The first board meeting was only eight days after his trial and he chaired it as if nothing had happened. He did not tell them that he had given the Vatican a letter clearing them of all responsibility for a billion-dollar debt, but this was not going to remain secret for very long.

The share price stayed up and a successful rights issue was made. The branch managers were instructed to sell shares to small depositors and this was a tactic that worked because, in a peculiarly Italian way, people had faith in Calvi because his trial had publicised the extent and importance of his contacts. He wasn't a crook – he was *furbo*.

Even though he knew that what he was doing was unrealistic, he persisted in holding up the value of the stock, spending another $40 million in the process in the hope that some fairy godfather would buy the bank, if for nothing other than control of the newspaper *Corriere della Sera*, which Calvi now owned.

His first action was logical, namely to shore up his base at the Banca Ambrosiano. He was obviously going to have trouble from Rosone and the rest of the board, especially since they would now realise that many of the bank transactions to which they had agreed had not been as straightforward as they had been led to believe.

To get what he thought would be additional support, he invited a prominent Italian financier and future opponent of Berlusconi, Carlo De Benedetti, to be joint deputy chairman with Roberto Rosone. Everyone was delighted – apart from De Benedetti, who quickly realised that he was being set up, so Calvi had to buy him out after only two months.

On the second attempt, Calvi got what he wanted, namely a 'sleeping' deputy chairman. Genoese businessman Orazio Bagnasco purchased 1.5 per cent of the stock at a cost of $20 million, and when the final crash came, he lost the lot.

Meanwhile Filippo Leone, the general manager of the Peruvian bank Banca Andino, realised that he was sitting on a potential time bomb and that when it exploded he would be severely damaged. He therefore extracted a written promise from Calvi that the shell companies would repay their debts to Banca Andino by 13 July.

The Bank of Italy, under parliamentary pressure, next decided to make sure that the board fully realised their responsibilities. They wrote to each board member, as well as Calvi, asking each of them to sign a letter declaring that they were personally aware of the overseas structure of the bank. The minutes of the board meeting showed that they all agreed to confirm that they were aware of the overseas structure and their reply to the Bank of Italy was robust. But it was the end of the road for Rosone, who told Calvi he had had enough and was resigning. Calvi knew that Rosone's resignation would have a huge public impact and managed to persuade him to hold on a little longer, even though he knew the writing was on the wall.

A week later, while walking home, Rosone was shot. Like Calvi, Rosone had a bodyguard and although he was hit in the legs, before the gunman could get off a second shot the bodyguard got lucky and killed the assassin with a shot in the chest. The man the bodyguard killed was identified as Danilo Abbruciati, an employee of the gangster Domenico Balducci, who in turn was employed by Flavio Carboni, who was on the surface a Sardinian property developer. The *carabinieri* had no alternative other than to include Calvi in the extended dragnet and issued a warrant for his arrest on the charge of colluding in an attempted murder.

Gelli and Ortolani, although temporarily out of action because of the uncovering of the P2 Lodge, were constantly demanding money for influencing people who might help in Calvi's appeal, which was his only chance of avoiding three or four years in jail.

July 1982 looked like being a very bad month for Calvi. The loans had to be repaid to the Banca Andino, the Vatican letters of patronage were going to run out (and Marcinkus was not going to be persuaded to write any more) and it was the month when his appeal was to be heard. The pressures building up on him were immense. Rosone later said that Calvi's biggest fear, which was almost reaching the level of insanity in spite of his cool exterior, was going back to prison.

On 4 June, he received another letter from the Bank of Italy. It said that they wanted the letter to be read out to the members of the board of the bank and that they wanted to see the minutes of that meeting to confirm that their demand had been met. They also stated that they wanted to know the exact details of a $1.4 billion loan made by the Banca Ambrosiano to its subsidiaries in Peru, Nicaragua and the Bahamas.

The board meeting was held on 7 June and Calvi, however unwillingly, read out the letter. This time, instead of backing him, the board asked for answers. He refused and on a motion of no confidence he was ousted from the presidency by ten votes to four.

His son, Carlo, was already in New York, doing a degree in economics, so he sent his wife there. He did everything he could to persuade his daughter Anna to join the rest of the family in New York, but she refused because she wanted to finish her studies in Milan.

Calvi then fled to a city where he had no contacts and which he hardly knew: London.

25

DEATH OF GOD'S BANKER

On 29 April 2005, Flavio Carboni, Silvano Vittor and Manuella Kleinszig were charged with murdering Roberto Calvi 23 years earlier. Along with them, two jailed mafiosi were also charged, Pippo Calo, who was by then serving a life sentence for planting a train bomb in 1984 that killed fifteen people, and Ernesto Diotavelli, who was implicated in the shooting of Roberto Rosone.

The trial started in October 2005 in a fortified courtroom next to a jail on the outskirts of Rome. The chief prosecutor, Luca Tescaroli, claimed that four of the five accused – Carboni, Vittor, Kleinszig and Calo – had lured Calvi to London so that he could be handed over to his assassins. But evidence that could have linked them to the actual murder was not strong enough and in June 2007 they were acquitted and released.

The Italian and British police cooperated in the preparation for trial but, as always, strange things happen in Italy. In May 2004, the City of London coroner, Paul Matthews, while in Rome working with the Italian police, was staying at the four star Abitart Hotel. On one occasion when he left his room for what he described as only a few minutes, someone used a pass card to enter and steal his laptop, which held details of the investigation. After this, even though he suspected that he was under surveillance, he went alone to Termini station to get the train to Fiumicino airport, but his briefcase, containing hard copy of the files, was snatched.

Calvi was found hanging from scaffolding under Blackfriars Bridge in London on 18 June 1982 at 7.30 a.m. He was first noticed by an employee of the *Daily Express* who was walking to work. The body was hung with a noose around the neck and a yard-long length of rope attached to the scaffold by two half hitch knots; his feet and trouser bottoms were trailing in the water. He wore a lightweight grey suit and in the pockets were $15,000 of mixed currency, two Patek Philippe watches, four pairs of spectacles and a passport in the name of Gian Roberto Calvini, the alias he had used to escape from Italy.

It was a bizarre scene made all the more curious by the Masonic symbolism that was either real or faked. The pockets of his suit contained four pieces of brick and concrete and a fifth piece had been pushed down the front of his trousers. In total they weighed about 12 pounds. Death by hanging is the penalty promised in some Masonic initiations for betraying the secrets of the lodge; the rocks in the pockets represent the bricks of the Masons, with the semicircular arch of the bridge representing the compass. Further examples of Masonic symbolism might be found in the fact that his feet were 'washing' in the water, the members of P2 wore black cassocks and Blackfriars Bridge is near lodge number 3722.

Or was it all coincidence together with wild and imaginative speculation?

The story of how he got there is much contested. There is testimony from his family stating that he made frequent phone calls to them and also from his companions about his last day. When pieced together, it goes as follows.

On the evening he was voted out at the bank, Calvi had supper with Sardinian property developer Flavio Carboni, a Freemason whom he had taken on as yet another protector. They had met in 1981, when Calvi lent him five billion lire for a development in

Sardinia. Carboni had an enormous network of important friends. Rosone later described Carboni as a 'person who makes you afraid just by looking at you'. By this time Calvi had descended into the depths of fantasy and the more dubious his associates, the more power he seemed to ascribe to them.

On 10 June, he went to Rome and told his driver to pick him up at 6.30 a.m. But when the driver arrived, he wasn't there. Evidently, Carboni had taken him to a friend's house in disguise after which they had flown to Venice, where he was met by Ernesto Diotavelli, a criminal from Rome and the employer of the gunman shot while trying to kill Rosone.

He gave Calvi a false passport in the name of Calvini and after a motorboat ride to Trieste, he was driven to Klagenfurt in Austria to stay with the family of Carboni's girlfriend, Manuella Kleinszig. The next day they drove to Innsbruck, staying at the Hotel Europa-Tyrol. Later in the day Carboni flew alone to Zurich to meet again with Diotavelli. Meanwhile Calvi was taken by Manuella and her sister to the Austrian border town of Bregenz, where they met Carboni and a Swiss 'fixer', Hans Kunz, who had Reginald Mulligan fly him and the man who was to be his minder, Silvano Vittor, to London.

In London, their accommodation had been arranged by the law firm Wood, Nash and Winters, but it was awful. The company had been asked to find discreet accommodation for two executives of Fiat who wanted to remain anonymous, so they had booked an apartment in a dull block of flats called Chelsea Cloisters on Sloane Avenue, where there were 748 flats on nine floors occupied in the main by students. The poor quality of accommodation was something quite new for Calvi – it consisted of a bedroom, a bathroom and a sitting room/kitchenette, measuring ten by sixteen feet – and he felt uncomfortable from the start.

They arrived on the evening of 15 June. The next day Carboni and his girlfriend arrived in London, booking in at the London Hilton rather than sharing accommodation in Chelsea Cloisters. They all met in the evening, but Calvi, accompanied by his minder Vittor, would not go into the hotel for fear of being recognised; instead, they walked and talked in the dusk in Hyde Park, and although we do not know what they talked about one of the subjects was getting alternative accommodation to Chelsea Cloisters.

Calvi, however, had to settle for another night in his drab surroundings. He phoned his wife in New York and asked her to persuade their daughter Anna to leave Europe for America as soon as possible. He also told her that he was close to a new deal that would make things better. 'A crazy marvellous thing is about to explode which could even help me in my appeal,' he said. 'It could solve everything.' However, his last words to her were 'I don't trust the people I'm with any more.'

All his movements from 10 to 16 June are well documented mainly because of the various phone calls he made to his family. It is unlikely that he was being held against his will or that he made 'hostage-style' calls, as his family would certainly have suspected that something was wrong.

We know almost nothing that can be corroborated about the events of 17 June, the day of his death, other than that he left or was taken from the apartment some time in the evening without witnesses. Carboni claims that he spent the day with Alma, William and Odette Morris, his English friends, going round estate agents looking for alternative accommodation.

That same day, in Milan, Roberto Rosone had persuaded the board to dissolve the Banca Ambrosiano and call in the Bank of Italy. While he was fielding telephone calls from the press, there was a commotion. Calvi's long-time secretary, 55-year-old Graziella Teresa Corrocher, had thrown herself out of a window to her death, leaving a note denouncing Calvi. 'He should be twice-damned for the damage he did to the group and to all of us who were at one time proud of it.'

Within a few hours, her boss would also be dead, but while we know what happened to Graziella we will now never know how Calvi came to be hanging from a bridge in London 12 hours later.

There were two inquests into Calvi's death. The first was presided over by David Paul. He kept the jury hearing evidence for more than nine hours, summed up for an hour and then asked the jury to be quick about their verdict, giving them incorrect instructions about the application of an open verdict. They voted by a majority for suicide, but it was no surprise that the verdict was overturned on appeal and a second inquest ordered. The main witness at the first inquest was the famous forensic pathologist Dr Keith Simpson. These were the days of eminence-based rather than evidence-based medicine, when a famous medical expert's opinion would invariably be believed. Simpson said that death had occurred around 2 a.m. and the cause was asphyxia due to hanging. He did not opine as to the probability of either murder or suicide, but from the way he presented his evidence it seemed that he favoured suicide. He testified there was no evidence of drugs or alcohol in the body, but he was not asked whether he had tested for other drugs.

The second inquest lasted two weeks, and this time Simpson admitted that a number of drugs could have been used to immobilise Calvi prior to his being hanged.

What was certain was that it would have been virtually impossible for Calvi himself to have reached that point on the scaffold, carrying 12 pounds of bricks, and to arrange his own hanging. Also, he could have saved himself all the discomfort by staying in Chelsea Cloisters and swallowing the hundreds of barbiturate tablets that were in his luggage. He would not have had to travel four miles from the apartment, and, indeed, no taxi could be traced that had carried a fare to Blackfriars at that time of night. The second jury not surprisingly returned an open verdict.

Carboni went into hiding after Calvi's death and later failed to give a convincing explanation as to why he and Manuella had felt it necessary to go from Heathrow, where they spent the night, to Gatwick, in order to get a plane to Edinburgh, when in those days there was an hourly shuttle service from Heathrow. He said he panicked when he heard Calvi was dead and wanted to get as far from London as possible. After spending a night in the George Hotel, they were flown back to Zurich by private plane. This story was part of a written statement submitted to the second inquest by Carboni, written by himself, not under oath. The George Hotel could not find any records.

After the initial confusion caused by the negligent first inquest, the probability that Calvi was murdered became far more believable than the alternative explanation of suicide. The cynical Italians have an elegant way of circumventing this conundrum by using the word *suicidare*, which means that someone was 'suicided'.

Much of the evidence for murder rests on the virtual impossibility of his having hanged himself at the point where he was found. In the unlikely event that he planned his death this way, it would mean that he left enough barbiturates in his luggage in the apartment to kill several people, that he made his way on foot to a bridge four miles from where he was staying and that en route he visited a building site a block away to collect twelve pounds of bricks and stones, which he put in his pockets and down his trouser front. Having arrived at the bridge, he then had to climb over a parapet to a scaffold walkway, climb down a ladder to the level of some other temporary scaffolding, jump over a three-foot gap and crawl eight feet along the bars in order to secure the rope, tie it around his neck and jump.

A more feasible explanation would be that he was dead before he was hung, and the only thing that prevented this conclusion was that Dr Simpson could find no other cause for death than hanging. He did not, however, test for traces of insulin, opiate or ricin, which would have been the most likely poisons used.

Calvi obviously went willingly to London, because he was in constant touch with his family and expressed no doubt about his companions until shortly before his death. It is quite credible that he was making one last attempt to find someone to either buy or refinance his bank. When that failed, his 'minders' murdered him. Had it been otherwise, he would have been shot in Milan or Rome and his body buried in the wilderness or dissolved in acid. In 1991, one of the more credible Mafia informers, Marino Mannoia, testified that in his opinion Calvi was silenced by the Mafia not only because he had lost a great deal of money, but because he had been caught, was about to go to prison and would certainly have talked. His crimes of financial fraud, illegal political donations and involvement with the attempted murder of Rosone would certainly have kept him in jail, and after that he was going to have to answer for P2 membership and also details of Vatican involvement.

We have seen the importance of symbolism in Mafia murders, but in this case Calvi was not murdered with the usual paraphernalia of a financial killing (bank notes stuffed in the mouth or the rectum); instead, he was surrounded by heavy Masonic symbolism. So much so, in fact, that the symbolism rather than the murder became the story.

The Italian government put together a group of banks to bail out the Banca Ambrosiano, but the exercise would be limited to the Italian bank and have nothing to do with the Banca del Gottardo or any of the other Lichtenstein, Argentinian, Nicaraguan or Peruvian outlets. The reason that they excluded everything outside Italy was that most of it was illegal: if the Vatican had become involved, however innocently, it was their problem to sort out, not the Bank of Italy's.

Relations between the Italian government and the Vatican were at an all-time low. Prime Minister Spadolini, the Minister of Justice and the president of the Bank of Italy, put pressure on the Vatican to give a businesslike explanation rather than a 'we've been duped' story. After many denials and an internal 'Three Wise Men' investigation, the Vatican admitted ownership of two of the shell companies, which, in turn, controlled another eight. But having admitted this, they continued to refuse to accept responsibility for any of the debts. Their argument was that Calvi must have made them owners without their knowledge. As a result of the impasse, a commission was established, made up of representatives of both the Bank of Italy and the Vatican, and the outcome was that the Vatican made a partial payment with no admission of any liability.

Carboni, having fled from Britain, was apprehended on 30 July 1982 in Lugano, while driving a Volkswagen, accompanied by Manuella. In April 1983, he and Manuella, together with Diotavelli, were charged with the murder of Calvi but were not brought to trial because of lack of evidence.

Before Carboni was captured, one of his aides, after being arrested, led the police to three sites containing important documents – in Carboni's office in Rome, a Volkswagen car and a field near the Yugoslavian border, where they had been buried. Among these documents were fourteen cassette tapes holding eight hours of conversations between Carboni and Calvi. One might wonder why a 'friend' was having conversations wired up to a tape recorder!

Although Calvi's luggage was left in the apartment in Chelsea Cloisters, his black briefcase, which he never allowed out of his sight, was missing. It turned up again, however, on Italian TV on 1 April 1986, along with Vittor and Carboni, both vouching for its authenticity. But what had been in it originally?

In May 1988, while investigating a heroin smuggler, Judge Mario Almerighi found some letters attempting to blackmail the Secretary of State of the Vatican, Cardinal Agostino Casaroli. The drug dealer was offering to sell Casaroli documents, which he claimed to have bought from Carboni, for a million dollars. It transpired that these were documents that had been delivered to a 'bishop within the Vatican' who had given him cheques drawn on the IOR. When Almerighi traced these cheques, it became apparent that Carboni had received at least $2 million of Vatican money.

Vatican officials insisted that whoever 'the bishop' was – and they refused to admit that it might have been Marcinkus – he had paid for these documents without official approval.

Sindona had indicated that P2 funds were scattered among numbered Swiss accounts. When Carboni was arrested the police found many of these numbers and asked the Swiss to freeze accounts belonging to 'dubious' South Americans. With their resolve steadied, and in view of the world clamour about the death of Calvi, P2 and Sindona, all of which happened within a few years, the Swiss banks decided to cooperate.

This is why when Gelli entered the Union Bank of Switzerland on Monday, 13 September 1982 in order to withdraw his $100 million, he was arrested, even though he had changed his appearance by dying his hair, growing facial hair and dispensing with his glasses in favour of contact lenses. He was charged with espionage, terrorism, conspiracies to overthrow the Italian government, extortion and fraudulent bankruptcy.

Whatever else, it seems that the following facts are true. The Vatican Bank was a fully consenting partner in the creation of ghost companies, it was fully aware of what Calvi was involving it in, and by issuing letters of patronage it enabled Calvi to mislead Ambrosiano shareholders about the true financial situation of the bank, while also misleading the Bank of Italy. It helped to carry out a 'cover-up'.

In July 1983, 15 new Cardinals were appointed. The name that was missing was that of Marcinkus, who by virtue of his position as virtual mayor of the Vatican should have been on the list automatically. His omission signalled the end of his Vatican career. He retired to Sun City, Arizona, where he devoted himself to golf (handicap six) and refused ever to speak again about 'Italian' affairs. He died peacefully on 20 February 2006 at the age of 84, by which time most of the mafiosi who had made the money that caused his downfall were in jail.

PART 3

THE FALL

26

THE MAFIA CIVIL WAR

Although nowadays, with decent roads, Corleone is less than two hours from Palermo, in the nineteenth century it was so far away that the local aristocrats would move to the capital for the winter and leave their estates in the hands of the *gabellotti*, who would eventually come to own them. In the days before motorised transport, Corleone was in the middle of nowhere and so, in isolation, it became a Mafia town. Like other mafiosi, the Corleonesi were treated badly by the Fascists and so, after the war, when the Mafia was identified as anti-Fascist, they found favour with the Americans. What else could the Americans do other than admire an anti-Fascist town with a society led by the local doctor?

Just as there are clusters of disease patterns in various parts of the world, Corleone must have the largest cluster of psychopathy per head of population in Europe. For such a small place to have created such a history of violence over the last hundred years, the people have to be 'different'. Certainly Luciano Leggio and Toto Riina filled the bill.

Born in Corleone in 1930, Riina prospered in the post-war black market, working from within the Navarra family. One evening in 1949, he lost his temper during a harmless game of bowls (*boccia*) and, displaying the aberrant behaviour of a psychopath, beat his opponent to death. He was sentenced to ten years in jail, of which he served six.

On his release he worked for Leggio, helping him to wipe out the Navarra clan (chapter 19), but in 1963, in the post-Ciaculli-bomb crackdown, he was remanded along with his boss in the Ucciardone prison in Palermo, and after the Bari trial was acquitted.

While Leggio went north, Riina returned to Corleone, where he was re-arrested as a result of his conviction after the Bari trial, but was only sentenced to internal exile in the Northern province of Emilia-Romagna. From there, it was easy to abscond and he spent the next 24 years on the run, Sicilian-style – which means he was able to lead a normal life at home provided he was surrounded by 'friends'. He married a schoolteacher, Ninetta Bagarella, whose father was a prominent mafioso, and they had four children.

Riina can be credited with two very important achievements between 1970 and 1975. First, he restored the finances of the Corleonesi, which had suffered during the time that he and Leggio were on remand, and the method he chose was kidnap for ransom.

Second, he succeeded in widening the contacts of the Corleonese family. He made alliances with other Mafia groups outside Palermo, in places such as Trapani and Agrigento, and he stepped outside the accepted bounds of traditional Mafia policy by making links with the Neopolitan Camorra, who, like all other groups, had never been trusted by the Sicilian Mafia.

Although physically short, his stature did not seem to limit his bravado and he continually tried to provoke a quarrel with Bontade, Badalamenti and Inzerillo, the main leaders of the Palermo Mafia. In 1972, he had kidnapped the son of Count Cassina, but in 1975 he went one better and kidnapped one of Bontade's relatives, Luigi Corleo, a man in his early 80s, who was the father-in-law of Nino Salvo, one half of the government's tax-collecting authority in Sicily, the other half being his cousin Ignazio. This was a breach of Mafia law, but it went unpunished.

Kidnapping old people carries added risks: medical conditions can deteriorate during captivity, requiring doctors to provide medication. If they can't be found, the victim may well die, leaving the kidnapper with a much more serious problem. This is what must have happened with Luigi Corleo, because after the first ransom demands, nothing more was heard and the body was never seen again. While failure to return a body grossly enhances an insult in terms of Sicilian culture, in this case it was probably unintentional.

Bontade, however, did not rise to the bait. There was no attempt at retaliation, which, in Sicilian terms, was strange. What he did do in an attempt to stem the violence that he saw as inevitable was to invite Tomasso Buscetta back to Sicily to act as a peacemaker – or this is what Buscetta claimed. Like many of Buscetta's claims, it might be looked on as just another story that he spun to impress on his captors his importance within the Mafia.

Buscetta claimed that he did not attempt to broker peace because it was clear to him at that stage that the Corleonesi were set to take over the whole of the Sicilian Mafia, if not by persuasion then by force. He saw only trouble if he remained in Sicily and so he once again walked away, returning to his comfortable, opulent life in Brazil.

The insults continued. In April 1978, a Mafia *capo*, Giuseppe Di Cristina, arranged to meet a *carabinieri* officer and explained to him that if the Corleonesi were not stopped then he and many others would be murdered. He told the *carabinieri* about Leggio and his past, and also the names of his henchmen. A few weeks later Di Cristina was shot in his car in a suburb of Palermo controlled by Inzerillo.

This was another insult because Mafia killings on someone else's territory, not agreed on by the Commission, were forbidden, but just as Bontade had not reacted to the kidnappings on his territory, so Inzerillo refused to be drawn on this episode.

Since they and most of their families are now dead, we will never know the reason for this apparently supine response because the message that Riina was sending was very clear. He wanted not only to control the Commission and the Mafia in Sicily but also a much larger share of the drug profits and a bigger say in the American operation. Bontade and Inzerillo were not withholding anything from him, but it was *their* business, *their* contacts in America and *their* relatives. However, the Corleonesi saw it as Mafia business that should have been made open and equal to all, even though the key to the arrangement was the blood relatives of the Bontades, Inzerillos and the rest of the Palermo/Castellammare families.

Riina's failure to realise how impractical it would be for him to take over this particular operation was just another example of his psychopathic personality. He didn't realise that taking on the world's police and drug enforcement agencies required more than thuggery; in that way, he was more Camorra than Mafia.

When Buscetta returned to Brazil (if indeed he had ever left), the Palermo families decided to resurrect the Commission, allowing them to at least meet Riina in a safe environment to talk. They knew that the previous Commission had been a failure because there was no one on it with any decision-making power, so this time they kept it small, with just the main players meeting. The first new Commission consisted of Stefano Bontade, Toto Riina and the man who ran the airport, Gaetano Badalamenti.

In 1978, for some reason that has never come to light, Badalamenti, who at that time was head of the Commission, was not only deposed from his position but also expelled from the Mafia, which meant that he could be shot on sight. But again, for some unknown reason, no attempts were made on his life and, instead, he continued to work, but from South America rather than Sicily, using his contacts and relatives in the Midwest of the United States.

His place on the Commission was taken by the very respectable and civilised Michele Greco. He was a good leader and a pillar of society, and persuaded Riina and Bontade to keep the peace at least between 1978 and 1981, a situation that Riina found very difficult.

It perhaps seems strange that the head of a big family in Palermo did not attempt to kill off a 'country cousin' who was not only causing him grief at that time but also looked like a long-term threat. The reason was almost certainly manpower.

Bontade had a big family of almost 200 men, along with the other smaller Palermo families, but during the early '70s, when Riina was restoring the family fortunes of the Corleonesi, he had created a huge extended family numbering over a thousand, including some Camorra groups. He was in league not only with Agrigento in the south, Trapani in the west and Catania in the east but also had allies in Palermo, having infiltrated the Porta Nova family once run by the La Barbera brothers. Bontade and Inzerillo both knew that if there was a fight, there would only be one winner.

Riina was not a one-man band. He had two lieutenants who were every bit as psychopathic as himself: Giovanni Brusca and the man who managed to evade capture until 2006, Bernardo Provenzano.

Brusca, in terms of psychopathy, was a Riina clone; it was probably appropriate that his actual godfather was also Riina.

The zenith of Brusca's killing career came when he pushed the button on the remote control that blew up the magistrate Giovanni Falcone and his entourage – but that was years later.

Bernardo Provenzano was born in Corleone in 1933. He was an enforcer first for Navarra and then for Leggio, acquiring the nickname 'The Tractor' on the basis that he left nothing alive in his path. In spite of this, he always kept a low profile and, although a killer, he always behaved moderately. Not for him the slaughters carried out by Riina or the use of missile launchers, which had everyone wary of Brusca before his arrest; he epitomised the spirit of moderation and conciliation that was the *marque* of the old Mafia. Leggio once said of him: 'Binu has the brain of a chicken but shoots like an angel.'

He disappeared into the countryside after Navarra's death and was on the run for 40 years until his recent capture. Over the years, rumours of his death kept surfacing, but in 1992, when his common-law wife returned to Palermo from the countryside to open a laundry, she had two children.

The real 'war' started in March 1981 and lasted three years. On one side were the Corleonesi led by Riina, Brusca and Provenzano, with the 'General' (Leggio) conducting strategy from a jail cell. On the other side were the Palermo families led by Bontade and Inzerillo, who controlled the drug trade and who were by this time billionaires.

Although the Corleonesi were not as rich as the Palermo families, since they lacked the American connection, they had secured the right to import China White from South-East Asia to Sicily and they also controlled the port of Catania, where much of the heroin landed. The Inzerillo and Bontade connections were far away – America, Brazil, Venezuela and Montreal – and they were not going to be of much use in the shooting war that was about to erupt on the streets of Palermo.

The catalyst seems to have been an episode in February when Riina caught Inzerillo and Bontade 'skimming'. A certain amount of skimming would be expected in a business such as narcotics, and it was always difficult to prove. As long as it did not become too gross, most operators had the sense to live with it. What Bontade had been doing, however, was saying that whole cargos for New York were being refused on account of poor quality and that some 'poor quality' heroin from unknown provenance had been taken as proof. By the time Riina confronted Inzerillo and Bontade, the sum involved had risen to $10 million.

Realising what was about to happen, Bontade and Inzerillo planned to kill Riina. Unfortunately for them, this plan got back to Leggio. He advised Riina to call for a meeting of the Commission in March and order Inzerillo to bring the $10 million with him and to hand it over with the promise of peace and a new start.

However, no one of importance from Riina's side turned up for the meeting, and it was a non-event; it was, however, a clear message. Bontade and Inzerillo must have realised that their time had come, but they had been in charge for so long that they could not have imagined even in their worst dreams what was about to happen.

A month later, on 2 April, Stefano Bontade had his head blown off by a Kalashnikov fired into his car. There were five lorry-loads of flowers sent to the church, but only his family actually attended the funeral. He was 43 years of age, but had lived a 'full life'.

Inzerillo thought he was safe because he still owed the Corleonesi $10 million and doubted that they would attempt to kill him while a debt of this size was outstanding. He was wrong.

Thirty-nine days later, on 11 May, he was killed in the same way with the same gun. The Inzerillo family were so sure that the missing $10 million was the reason for Salvatore's murder that, in an effort to keep the peace and prevent anyone else in the family from being killed, especially his 16-year-old son, they sent his brother, Santo, to a 'peace' meeting with the money in cash. Both he and his bodyguard were strangled – and Riina took the money.

Then the killing spree began in earnest. Over the next three years, twenty-one Inzerillos were murdered, including Salvatore's sixteen-year-old son, who had his right arm removed with a chainsaw prior to being strangled. Cutting off his right arm was symbolic, indicating that the sons and nephews would not be able to avenge the father's death. Of the Bontade clan, 120 members were assassinated and the survivors either fled or changed sides. They could not even find safety in jail – one of them was stabbed thirty times in the exercise yard of the Ucciardone prison.

The violence was not confined to Sicily. Pietro Inzerillo was found in the boot of a Gambino Cadillac in New York, his body in a plastic bag, his hands tied and five one-dollar bills stuffed in his mouth and one in his rectum – a Mafia symbol of greed that has been punished.

The enigmatic Badalamenti clan, whose chief had not only been expelled from the Commission but also the Mafia, lost only seven men. And the Corleonesi suffered no casualties at all because no one fought back. The lucky victims were shot; many others endured a death that would be regarded as a war crime had it occurred during a legitimate war.

The reason that we know this is because a stupid young thug called Vincenzo Singara went to the police terrified that he was about to be killed. He was a low-level burglar who, while employed by the Mafia, had done a job for himself in a suburb of Palermo that he later found out was under the protection of his masters. He was petrified not that he would be shot or strangled, because that would have been expected, but that he would suffer one of the deaths with which he routinely assisted in what became known as the Death Chamber of Piazza Sant'Erasmo. His specific fear, which had made him hysterical at the police station, was that he would be put to death by being put slowly, head first, into a vat of concentrated sulphuric acid.

Piazza Sant'Erasmo is a derelict square near the old Palermo port which sensible people avoid even during daylight hours. There are places like this in every major city: areas full of discarded trucks and cars, some burnt-out and some rusty, discarded corrugated-iron sheets, empty tins of chemicals, and filth. They have a sense of menace and other-worldliness that keep people who don't have to be there away.

On one side of the space, there was a cement hut that comprised one room with a small window, with a table and chairs and an assortment of tools of the type which would be expected in a chamber of sado-masochism. There was also the six-foot-deep lead drum full of steaming sulphuric acid in which Vincenzo Singara feared he would end. It was run by Palermo allies of the Corleonesi, the Corso dei Mille family, led by Filippo Marchese, who, Singara said, would sniff cocaine and masturbate as he watched the tortures.

Victims were brought there for a slow death and perhaps for interrogation at the table. Death was by garrotting, with a man on either end of the rope, a manoeuvre that would almost certainly crush the larynx, causing an obstruction of the airway. The lucky ones were shot in the head: death by sulphuric acid would take several minutes, the bodies having totally dissolved in 15 or 20 minutes.

The bodies were then dumped at sea, chopped up into pieces and stuffed into a car boot for transportation to a ravine, or fed to pigs after mutilation and dissection.

Although he told his stories to the police, Singara's basic Mafia training had taught him to feign madness. At his initiation he would have been told that if he was ever caught, 'You will get yourself into a lunatic asylum or die trying.' So he attempted to persuade the police that what he had said was all nonsense and that he was really mad. He was not a young man of any great ability because he failed at that as well.

What occurred was a massacre rather than a war. Previous Mafia disagreements or vendettas had been fought out by men of honour and part of that 'honour' was your attempt at retribution for what had been done to you or yours. But there was no response. Never before in the history of the Mafia had anything like this happened. The scale of the massacre, which went on for three years, was such that it acquired the title the Mattanza, which is the name given to the traditional slaughter of tuna fish. In Sicily, the fishermen tow their catch into a bay, circle their boats, lift the netted fish to the surface and club them to death with spikes. By the time they have finished, the sea has turned red.

The General was commanding the campaign from a prison cell, albeit a luxurious one. Leggio was freer than he had been on the outside for many years. He was ageing and unwell most of the time. He wore a back brace for his ever-increasing spinal scoliosis and he probably also had trouble with his joints, eyes and urinary system. He could order outside events from jail as effectively as he could from his home in Corleone; he claimed to be able to have the same powers as the governor of the jail. When he appeared at the Maxi Trials and faced Buscetta, he said, 'I've been a great power in prison for years; I'm a myth.'

The slaughter of one gang by another worried few because it

did not spill into the public domain and hardly any of the locals were harmed. Although reading about the assassinations, seeing bodies photographed spilling out of cars and heads blown off with Kalashnikovs and people just vanishing, makes Palermo sound like a war zone, it never seemed to bother the citizens who did not live in the ghettos. I asked a young doctor who had graduated from Palermo medical school in 1991, and who had lived through the whole period, what his impressions were. He seemed puzzled at the question because none of the violence affected ordinary people. He said that the closest he had come to the troubles was being friendly with a girl in his year from the Bontade clan, but even she did not seem to react. I persisted, saying that what he was saying seemed so strange because of all the sensational stuff I had read. He wasn't moved and said that although the newspapers carried photographs of murders every day, they occurred in parts of Palermo that right-thinking people would not enter.

It was a disappointing interview, but perhaps it does add a truer perspective to the sensationalism that accompanies the descriptions of those years.

While it was one thing to murder other criminals, it was quite another to assassinate officials of the State. So while the Corleonesi carried on killing and threatening politicians with open arrogance, the government had to be seen to respond. They knew that this placed the government in a difficult position, but instead of keeping things quiet, they upped the ante.

27

THE MAGISTRATES

In April 1982, they shot one of their first major figures, a Communist politician. The Mafia had been shooting Communist politicians ever since Salvatore Giuliano's time, so why was this one any different?

Pio La Torre, the Communist Party leader in Sicily, was murdered not just because he was a Communist – that phase was coming to an end and in a few years the Berlin Wall would fall – but because he was promoting a law that would be extremely damaging to the Mafia. La Torre was proposing that individuals could be prosecuted for having been 'associated with the Mafia', but there was a sting in the tail: conviction would be accompanied by sequestration of assets.

Mafia prosecutions were rare because almost every crime required witnesses to give evidence and in Sicily that was not what people did if they wanted to stay alive. Pio La Torre's law, however, did not require witnesses. A further danger for mafiosi was that the process would be open to abuse by police intent on targeting individuals. But, as always in Italy, what you see is not what you get.

Pio La Torre had two agendas running simultaneously. One was his attempts to get an anti-Mafia law through parliament, but the second had more international significance. NATO wanted cruise missiles in Comiso, Sicily, as an important cog in Reagan's anti-Russia policy, and Pio La Torre was attempting to stop this. There are strong rumours that the primary reason for his death was the latter rather than the former and that the real killers of La Torre were the CIA rather than the Mafia. But the Mafia got the blame.

The reaction to the killing made headlines not only in Sicily, where it could be conveniently forgotten, but all over Italy. There was a public outcry for government action because to the public it was obvious that things in Sicily were getting out of control. The government of Christian Democrats under Prime Minister Giulio Andreotti therefore made a high-profile appointment. The man they chose could not have been more suitable.

By 1982, Carlo Alberto Dalla Chiesa was an Italian hero. Having been credited with the destruction of the Red Brigades, he had entered Italian folklore as one of the few military heroes since Garibaldi.

He knew Sicily well because one of his first postings had been to Corleone, at a time when the Leggio clan were trying to eliminate the Navarras. Although as a young officer in Corleone he had arrested both Leggio and Riina, he had known that there was little point in trying to abolish crime because there would have been no political support. This time, he thought, it would be different. But he was wrong.

He had been given enormous political support when he had fought the Red Brigades and, while welcoming this, he had not realised that the support was down to the fact that the politicians were frightened at a personal level: both their lives and their jobs were at stake. By the time he realised that things were going to be different in Sicily, it was too late.

He had not understood that if he succeeded in destroying the Mafia, those same politicians would once again be at risk because the rump of a beaten Mafia might be moved to extract vengeance on them both personally and electorally. In fact, for the politicians it was just the same as the Red Brigade days – only this time the threat to their lives and jobs would occur only if Dalla Chiesa won. If he failed, they would be safe. And when he realised this, he knew he would die in Sicily.

Before he had left for Sicily, Dalla Chiesa, a member of the Christian Democrat Party, had a meeting with Giulio Andreotti to discuss the posting. Instead of feeling confident of assured political support, Dalla Chiesa left the meeting feeling apprehensive.

His son Nando, a sociology professor and a left-wing student activist in the '60s, later wrote that his father had said to him that when he had told Andreotti what he knew about Sicily, including information about the Salvo cousins, Salvo Lima and the Bontades, Andreotti went 'white in the face'.

He arrived as Prefect of Sicily on 1 May 1982 and his first duty was to attend the funeral of Pio La Torre. There he witnessed the young leftists demonstrating against the Mafia, indicating that they knew the government had been complicit in the murder of their leader.

His worst fears then became true. Although he was cheered in public, he felt snubbed by the politicians, not even being able to arrange a meeting with the leader of the Christian Democrats in Sicily before he was murdered. In his last weeks, he ran around like a headless chicken, knowing that he was going to be killed but not sure when or how. He realised that he had been placed in Sicily as a symbol for the corrupt politicians and he felt that he was on his own with absolutely no political support. He wrote to his wife at the time: 'The powerful man is killed when this fatal combination is brought about; he has become too dangerous but can be killed because he's isolated.'

The end came 126 days after he had arrived on the island.

On 3 September 1982, he arranged a secret meeting with Ralph Jones, the American Consul in Palermo. He told him of his concern about the Cabinet in Rome, the members of which had failed to keep their promises, his concern about the behaviour of the local politicians and, above all, his impotence in the face of what he saw as the Christian Democrats' flagrant association with the Mafia. He asked Jones to get the United

States to intervene, even though he knew that he was asking him to break with protocol.

He then went back to his office, where he was met by his wife, a former Red Cross nurse half his age, who had come to Sicily against his wishes and who was going to drive him home in her small Fiat. They had only recently married. They were overtaken by two motorcycles and four men in a BMW and, on Via Carini, killed with the same Kalashnikov that had been used to kill Bontade and Inzerillo.

This time the public reaction was even fiercer. Rome had no alternative other than to set up another Anti-Mafia Commission. And true to form, Italian-style, Pio La Torre's law was passed. Without this law, which introduced the word 'Mafia' into the Italian penal code for the first time, a Prime Minister would never have come to trial, Falcone could never have had so many Mafia *capi* convicted at the Maxi Trials and the backbone of the Mafia would never have been broken. Once the details were put together, the law could be applied.

There had been killings of law officers before Dalla Chiesa arrived. In 1979, the head of police, Boris Giuliano, was shot four times in the back while having his morning cappuccino in a bar, but the significance of his murder was not realised till much later.

In the previous chapter, I described the murder of the potential informer Giuseppe Di Cristina, but on his death his pockets were found to contain a Pandora's box of information. As well as a $6,000 cheque from Salvatore Inzerillo and two currency-exchange records for $24,000, he had the private telephone numbers of the richest men in Sicily – the tax collectors Nino and Ignazio Salvo.

Apparently at the same time, the head of police, Boris Giuliano, along with his American colleagues in the DEA, whom he had met when he had attended the FBI Academy in Virginia, was getting very close to uncovering the Sicilian-American heroin connection.

Within two days, Giuliano had made two important discoveries. The first was a suitcase found in Palermo airport as unclaimed baggage, containing half a million dollars in small bills from New York, and the second was finding four kilos of heroin in a Palermo house with evidence that the drug had actually been produced in Sicily. Working on this information with his colleagues in the DEA, he was getting too close to uncovering the link between the Sicilians and the Americans in the heroin trade. But within seven days of the finds, he was also dead.

Cesare Terranova was the judge who had crossed swords in a very big way with Leggio after the Ciaculli bomb arrests and the Bari trial. When he was sent to Palermo as a judge, he survived only two days.

So many important people were killed during this period that the victims acquired the description 'excellent cadavers', a title used by Alexander Stille in his detailed account of the time. The final death was of Police Captain Emanuele Basile, who had taken over the drug investigations from Boris Giuliano. He sent out 55 warrants for the arrest of members of the Bontade and Inzerillo families and was then shot.

During his 126 days in Palermo, Dalla Chiesa failed to meet another two young magistrates who were working in the anti-Mafia pool and who would be the ones to finally bring down the second Mafia: Giovanni Falcone and Paolo Borsellino, both of whom were 'good and pure and honest', just like Eliot Ness in another place at another time.

The names of the Sicilian 'Untouchables' will live on for a hundred years in Sicily. Almost every town has a street, a school, a college or a building named after them. Palermo airport is now called Falcone-Borsellino, having been changed from Punta Raisa, a name that was associated with drug smuggling. Although Sicily has been civilised for 1,000 years longer than Britain, it has had no heroes; no generals, politicians or athletes that people could give as examples of excellence to their children. Apart from the composer Vincenzo Bellini and the writers Leonardo Sciascia and Pirandello, there are no artists of repute. For 2,000 years, it has sat under the rule of invaders who did not encourage the rise of any local talent. But now they have two heroes who were born and bred in Sicily and who began the destruction of the Mafia.

It took eight years to get the accused into court and then another five years of waiting for the interminable cycle of appeals to get them into jail. As was said at the time, eight years to dig the hole and get the bodies in the coffins and another five years to close the lids and bury them. But when the coffins were finally buried, the two brave magistrates also went to their deaths, murdered by the creature from the grave. Unfortunately it was only after their deaths that they, along with many of their colleagues who had died during the anti-Mafia struggles, became heroes.

Both Falcone and Borsellino were born into middle-class families in the La Kalsa area of Palermo, at that time lower-middle class. It now hosts the headquarters of Mother Teresa's mission to the poor in Palermo since she considered the island to be as deserving as any country in the Third World.

The men were born respectively in 1939 and 1940 and both had damage to their homes in the bombing of Palermo in 1943. Falcone's father was a chemist working for the state and Borsellino's family owned a pharmacy. They went to the same schools, where they were educated alongside children from known Mafia families, something Borsellino admitted had made him jealous. Both studied law at Palermo University, but there their political paths separated.

Falcone favoured communism while Borsellino joined a neo-fascist student movement. In the tradition of the time, Borsellino would be addressed as *camerata* and Falcone as *compagno,* indicating where their sympathies lay. They would have also spent time in different bars and cafés because there were communist bars and right-wing bars. The Second World War took a long time to go away!

There are two types of magistrates in Italy: those who investigate and prepare a case (the investigative magistrates) and those who argue a prepared case in court (the prosecuting magistrates). Both Falcone and Borsellino became investigative magistrates, but while Falcone was posted to Monreale in the west, Borsellino went to Agrigento in the south. Both are major Mafia centres, but they could live with this essentially normal part of Sicilian life because they had both been brought up with it.

What the two men were going to police was not Mafia customs such as *pizzu* but state law and order. They were part of the professional middle class and so neither they nor their families had ever been asked for *pizzu* from local Palermo Mafia. In those post-war years that saw the transition of the first Mafia into the second, they would not have been exposed to any more violence than in a present-day English city.

Borsellino was transferred back to Palermo in 1970 and worked in the investigative office of the magistrature. Falcone moved on to Trapani, where his marriage to his first wife fell apart. It did so in the way that every Italian man dreads – he was cuckolded for his boss. He therefore welcomed a transfer to Palermo in 1978 to work in the bankruptcy section and this is where he developed the financial expertise that was to serve him well in the future.

In America at that time, the public debates were about civil rights, Vietnam and Cuba, but in Italy people were arguing about divorce, abortion and terrorism from the Red Brigades, often conveniently 'framed' for acts of terrorism by the CIA, who were still running their own anti-communist agenda.

The Mafia were working quietly at their new business of drug-refining and distribution, having relegated the basic functions of extortion, abuse of public-works contracts and protection to a lower level. The Commission was functioning well and there was a peace, however uneasy, between the families that had existed since the Ciaculli bomb in 1963.

Cassara, the head of the investigative magistrates, and thus the boss of both Borsellino and Falcone, wrote a report in July 1982, the so-called Greco+161 report, which demonstrated that the police knew almost everything that was going on in regard to the Sicilian involvement with drug supply and distribution in the United States. He proposed the arrest of the Ciaculli Grecos and 161 others, among whom were the Salvo cousins. During this investigation, the police made the alarming discovery that there was a Mafia in Catania on the east coast, previously considered to be a Mafia-free zone.

By now the multiple killings of state officials were beginning to embarrass an already frightened cohort of politicians in Rome and an uproar of protest was simmering in the press, urging that the Sicilian question be tackled firmly. As a result the government firmed up the funding for the anti-Mafia pool. There would now be ten judges and none would ever work on his own again: if one was killed, he would be replaced and the work would continue.

Falcone was moved from the bankruptcy section to work with Borsellino in the investigative office. His first assignment was to investigate Rosario Spatola, a cousin not only of Salvatore Inzerillo but also of John Gambino, a family boss in New York. Falcone quickly found that the Spatola Construction Company was merely a front for Palermo–New York drug smuggling and Spatola was arrested.

Italy is still one of the least computer literate countries in Europe, and at that time there were no computers, never mind a network, in the magistrature or the police service. Falcone sorted through tens of thousands of currency exchange records from every bank in Sicily for the previous five years by hand. With the information he uncovered, he was able to jail the rest of the Spatola family. This resulted in his being in so much danger that he was given bodyguards with whom he was to live and eventually die.

In the process of this investigation, he had worked with the Milan magistrates on various serious crimes in the past and they found him different from any other Southerners that they had previously encountered. He wasn't *meridionale* – a word that describes the typical fun-loving, superficial Southerner. He had the characteristics of a Northerner: painstaking routine, thoroughness, scientific and logical application of data. Most importantly, he was apparently not on the payroll of the Mafia.

His approach also brought him friendship with and cooperation from the FBI in New York, where he frequently visited.

His hard work brought success and he obtained seventy-four convictions, mainly because he had used two newer techniques. First he realised that no case was watertight if it depended on witnesses who could be silenced, and secondly he framed the charges so that it did not require a civil jury that could be tampered with. He had the cases heard before only three judges and he kept to the financial and travel records, relying solely on facts that had to be challenged specifically – an impossible task for even the most articulate Mafia lawyer.

His work and convictions confirmed that Sicily, and not France, was now the main conduit for drugs being smuggled to America and that criminals in both countries were working in harmony.

Meanwhile, Borsellino had been prosecuting those suspected of killing Police Captain Basile. He was not only horrified but also very frightened when, on appeal, Judge Carlo Aiello declared a mistrial. This meant that three killers were on the loose with Borsellino in their sights. His chief, Rocco Chinnici, therefore took him off all Mafia cases, but, in the lunacy of the time, this was no guarantee of safety.

In July 1983, three things happened. Chinnici and Falcone issued 14 warrants for the murder of Dalla Chiesa. Falcone went to Thailand to interview a drug courier and while he was away, Chinnici was blown up by a car bomb in Palermo.

The vacancy left by Chinnici as chief prosecutor was eventually filled by a 63-year-old man from Florence, Antonino Caponetto, who had no background in Mafia cases. It was initially suggested that this was a ploy on the part of the Christian Democrats to slow down what was becoming a threatening exercise that was getting too close for comfort.

If it was a political manoeuvre, then it backfired because it marked a new beginning for Falcone and Borsellino. This surprised them both because they thought that their stars were in the descendent. For the last year of his life, Chinnici had started to mistrust and dislike both of them. They were at this stage too young to have even thought about applying for a job that was not only politically controlled but part of a gerontocratic ladder.

The office in Palermo still did not have a computer, the last request from Chinnici having been turned down by the Minister of the Interior, but Antonino Caponetto changed the office policy and, in advance of computer networks, demanded that all the anti-Mafia magistrates shared information and dedicated themselves solely to Mafia cases. The four main investigators were Falcone, Borsellino, Giuseppe Di Lello and Leonardo Guarnotta. They were to work in concert with the prosecutor's office, which would similarly have a pool of magistrates who would plead the cases in court.

In 1984, Bettino Craxi was elected as Italy's first Socialist Prime Minister, and his new Minister for Justice took an interest in what was going on in Palermo, ordering the modernisation of the office and the systems. They got computers that could deal with the mass of financial information, together with help from the Treasury Police. For the first time, Palermo had the tools necessary to fight the war against the Mafia.

But it was not until June that year that Falcone found the key that was to unlock the secrets of the Mafia.

28

THE BREAKTHROUGH

Every Sicilian sent to work in the pizza/drug trade went to live in Little Sicily in Brooklyn, the natural homing point for them in New York. Knickerbocker Avenue is now a Hispanic area, but in the 1960s it was like a suburb of Palermo. Immigrants cluster together to speak the same language, to eat the same food, to understand one another, but most of all for protection. There would always be someone available who might 'fix' things if they went wrong. The rather sad story of Salvatore Catalano illustrates the problem that arises when an immigrant group does not integrate into its host country.

Catalano was one of the mafiosi who fled in the aftermath of the Ciaculli bomb. Initially, he opened a small newspaper shop on Knickerbocker Avenue, but after getting involved in the pizza/drug parlours he quickly rose to be in charge of the local rackets. At the time, the head of the Bonanno family in New York was Carmine Galante, who had been one of the representatives of the Bonanno family at the Palermo meeting in 1957 when the idea had been discussed of having Sicilian boys with no police records, the so-called zips, come into New York and push drugs from the outlets. Galante was assassinated in 1979 by a group of imported zips.

Catalano led the killers and then took his place as the local captain, but unfortunately the succession was neither seamless nor successful. Catalano had omitted to add the ability to speak any English to his American education and so he was forced to retire from the position after two years.

Some immigrants came into America on forged passports, some under their own steam and cunning, but most entered through organised illegal immigration via Montreal, being helped by the branch of the Bonannos there: the Rizzutos. In those years, it was easy to slip into the USA: with the mere 100 customs and immigration officials who were employed at that time, it was quite impossible for America to secure the 1,200-mile Canada–USA border.

The pizza trade was perfect cover for importing drugs because they could be hidden among the other Italian imports that were needed for pizza – mozzarella, mushrooms, oil, anchovies and salami – and the popularity of the outlets in America at that time was immense. No one noticed anything odd about the growth of pizzerias across the country because the public loved the product and it had that important ingredient for success: newness. Most Americans still firmly believe that pizza was invented by them and, at the time, it was even introduced to Britain as Italian Welsh rarebit!

The 1960s were also the days of civil rights and so freedom was the watchword. One of the New York dons, therefore, took advantage of the anti-Italian public feeling generated by the McClellan Commission and started the Italian-American Civil Rights League, which would protest about discrimination if a young Italian got into trouble. It developed into a formidable electoral weapon, but whereas the civil rights movement was real and necessary, the Italian-American Civil Rights League was bogus.

In Chapter 18, we followed Tomasso Buscetta into New York and the pizza/drug trade, and his subsequent deportation to Brazil, where, under cover of an insurance agency, he started up again, this time with one of his sons and the father and brother of his new wife. The whole family were arrested with Buscetta in 1972 and it is claimed that they were all tortured by the Brazilian police. A US customs official present at the time said electric shocks were applied to Buscetta's genitals, anus, teeth and ears. Some of his nails were torn out and he was hung from a beam in the sun with a hood over his head. He said that he didn't talk, but he did, and when he did so it was to protect his son, who, as a result of the information he gave, was allowed to stay in America.

Buscetta himself was sent back to Italy, where he was imprisoned to serve out the 14 years that he had received *in absentia* after the 1969 Bari trial. We do not know his working relationship with the Palermo Mafia while in Brazil, but it would have been inconceivable that he was acting in isolation. Had he been a nuisance to the Mafia and suspected of intruding in their business, he would never have survived his decade in the Ucciardone prison in Palermo. On the contrary, he had a very comfortable time: all his meals were brought in from neighbouring restaurants and other prisoners supplied him with room service. He lacked for nothing, wearing designer clothes rather than prison uniform. Since he had been a model prisoner, he was transferred in 1980 to serve the last three years of his sentence in an open prison near Turin, but one day he simply walked out. Prior to his transfer, there had evidently been a queue of prisoners visiting his cell to pay respects.

He went back to live an open life in Palermo under the protection of the Mafia but the longer he stayed, the less he liked it. He could see what was brewing and knew that his side, the Bontades and Inzerillos, were going to lose if a shooting war with the Corleone clan started. Buscetta could read the writing on the wall: one of his best decisions was to get out of the country because, as one of the head Palermo mafiosi, he would certainly have been assassinated in the slaughter that was to follow. As it was, he survived, but most of his family were killed.

When he decided to leave Palermo, he used his two other identities, Thomas Roberto Felice and Roberto Escobar, to return to Rio de Janeiro. The man who eventually became the innocent cause of his downfall, thus turning him into an informer, was Gaetano Badalamenti, who had been a *capo* in Palermo and had originally developed the airport as a drug conduit.

Badalamenti was born in Cinisi, just outside Palermo, in 1923. He initially fought with the Italian Army but after 1943 returned to live as a mafioso in Palermo, eventually becoming the *capo* of a family. There was a small interruption in 1947 when he had to flee from a charge of murder and he went to work for relatives in Michigan, but three years later he was deported from America and managed to live freely again in the Palermo area, buying a lemon farm. The choice of site for this farm was fortuitous because it was exactly where the new airport was to be built, Punta Raisa.

He became influential in the growth and activity of the airport and arranged that the workers at the airport all came from his home town of Cinisi; he therefore came to boss a key territory in the Mafia world, the new airport being the natural site for drug transportation. For the next 20 years, controlling the entire workforce, Badalamenti was able to make sure that packages and luggage could be collected, hidden from customs and forwarded to the 'correct' people.

How or why he survived the Corleonesi slaughter of the other Palermo families is unknown, but he left Palermo undamaged late in 1981 and went to Brazil, from where he conducted a narcotics business through relatives in small American Midwest towns. Thousands of hours of conversations from these years were taped by the FBI and used in the Pizza Connection Trial, after which he was sentenced to 45 years in jail along with 22 others of the Bonanno family. However, before that he had managed to wreck Buscetta's life.

When he arrived in Rio in 1981, he tried to persuade Buscetta to return to Palermo to lead the fight against the Corleonesi, but, knowing what he did about the upcoming war, Buscetta refused. When word got out that the meeting had taken place, the Corleonesi, not surprisingly, suspected a plot and started to slaughter Buscetta's family. A month later, his Brazilian brother-in-law, Homero Guimaraes, disappeared. Two weeks later, his two sons, Antonio and Benedetto, vanished in Palermo. Three months after that his son-in-law was murdered in his Palermo pizzeria.

And three days later his brother, Vincenzo, and his nephew were shot in their Palermo glass factory.

Badalamenti was also punished because during this period a dozen of his relatives were shot; however, he did not keep a low profile like Buscetta and retaliated by sending two hit men from Miami to shoot a Corleonesi ally, Pino Greco, in Palermo. Unfortunately, they failed and six weeks after returning to Miami both gunmen were found in the boot of a car, having been shot. The tragedy of this for Buscetta was that one of those men had once worked for him and so, to the Corleonesi, it appeared that it was Buscetta and not Badalamenti who had sent the men to Palermo.

Buscetta knew he was in great danger, so fled to his 65,000-acre *fazenda* in the Amazon delta. Since he planned to stay undercover in Brazil, he left his wife, Cristina, in the flat in Rio. She was, of course, under surveillance and eventually was seen loading six suitcases into her Chevrolet Chevette. She was followed to the fazenda and, in October 1983, she and her husband were arrested by the Brazilian police. They also uncovered a firm called Major Key, whose assets had grown from $6,000 to $1 million in a year and were paying bills for both Buscetta and Badalamenti.

The Brazilians kept Buscetta in jail for nine months while discussions went on between themselves, the Americans and the Italians, the objective being to decide who had a greater right to try and imprison him. The Brazilians wanted him for drug offences because they had identified him as the head of the cocaine and heroin ring that existed between South America, Europe and the USA; the Americans wanted him for his connection with the distribution of drugs from pizza parlours; and the Italians were claiming him as an escaped prisoner.

The Brazilians had to drop out of the auction when it became apparent that they had acted too quickly and had not collected enough evidence that could be presented successfully at trial. His wife Cristina begged the Americans to take him because she claimed that he would be murdered within hours of setting foot in an Italian jail, a view shared by Buscetta, but the Americans were concerned about the amount of evidence that they had and were not sanguine about a conviction against a skilled defence lawyer. So it boiled down to which country was most certain to gain a conviction and hand down the longest sentence.

To Buscetta's dismay, the Italians won.

When he heard this, Buscetta attempted suicide with strychnine, and when he was resuscitated he claimed that he had attempted to kill himself because he knew that not only would he be killed but he would also be powerless to save all of his remaining relatives, including his wife, from the same fate.

When he had recovered, he told the investigators that he would like to cooperate with them in exchange for protection.

In June 1984, Giovanni Falcone flew to Brazil more in the hope than the belief that this very prominent mafioso would do as he had claimed because no man of his rank and importance had ever talked to the police before. He was asking himself: why should this guy be any different from the others? What has he to gain by becoming an informer?

He had been told that Buscetta's motive was neither revenge nor self-preservation: he wanted to save what remained of his family in Brazil from being slaughtered in the same way as his sons and brothers. This, however, was in direct contradiction to what he had said after his suicide bid – that his relatives would only be safe when he was dead!

Why he decided to talk to the police both in America and Palermo still remains a mystery. It was either in the hope of a lesser sentence or out of hatred for what the Mafia had become, but he claimed that it was the latter. He played up his old-fashioned Mafia credentials, telling people how he had been brought into the Mafia in the early post-war years when it was still a system of honour and a self-help socially aware group. He surprised Falcone by admitting that he was willing to talk about the Mafia and to help the magistrates to bring down what he considered had become a mutation of the Mafia that he had known. In this way, he confirmed what many Sicilians had told me about the second Mafia: that it was a criminal rather than a social organisation. He further surprised the authorities by saying that he would only talk to Falcone because a chemistry and mutual admiration had started to grow between the two men. Much of what he told Falcone was make-believe and from the transcripts of his evidence it became clear that Buscetta regarded himself as a form of Mafia 'royalty'.

He told Falcone that there were two levels of Mafia activity. The first was the drug trade and, to a lesser extent, collecting *pizzu*, backed up by local violence in the construction and other industries. The second was maintaining contact with politicians who were by now their servants. He said that he would talk about the first level of activity, but not the second.

He kept talking in measured quantities for several years, but he obviously didn't have the insight to see that it was not honourable to carry out extortion or ruin lives with the supply of drugs. He played his interrogators for two years with drops of information which not only suggested that the American Mob and the Sicilian Mafia were two different things but also that the Sicilian Mafia had become an integral part of the Christian Democrat electoral machine.

One can understand why Berlusconi later decided that this could never happen again and that an informer should give all his information in six months, as the temptation to embroider further theories or fanciful pieces of information in the light of events in order to delay punishment could be and was too readily abused. There is little doubt that at least some of what Buscetta told Falcone was imaginative and opportunistic, but without him first the Pizza Connection Trial in New York and then the Palermo Maxi Trials would not have seen so many stunning convictions.

What Buscetta told was initially unbelievable. No one had realised the way in which mafiosi thought and behaved. People had little idea of the values that had been transferred from the first to the second Mafia and once Falcone understood the way of thinking the problem became much clearer. He was able to re-open lines of investigation that had previously ended up in blind alleys because he could now imagine what a mafioso would think and do, an essential piece of missing knowledge.

By the end of September 1984, the four anti-Mafia magistrates had almost completed the work that would allow them to make hundreds of arrests. But as they were nearing a conclusion, their case nearly fell apart when they heard that a widely read weekly magazine, *Panorama*, was about to run a story revealing Buscetta's cooperation. They therefore moved quickly and, in dawn raids on 30 September, rounded up 366 Mafia suspects and jailed them.

Before any trials could begin in Palermo, however, Buscetta had to be in New York to testify in the Pizza Connection case – a phrase no doubt modelled on the French Connection. It took place in Manhattan between 24 October 1985 and 2 March 1987 and concerned the $1.6 billion worth of narcotics brought into the USA between 1975 and 1984. The prosecution was led by Rudolph Giuliani, later to shine as New York mayor at the time of the Twin Towers attack, and the trial was the springboard for his political career.

His job had been made easier by the introduction of two new laws, namely the RICO law, which made any association with rackets, plus two indictable offences, a basis for conviction, and the witness-protection programme, which gave important witnesses a new identity and protection should they testify.

Because of the importance of the trial the prosecution took a year to present their cases against the 22 accused Americans and Sicilians and by the end of the trial the costs had risen to an astronomical $50 million. But the sum was small considering that the trial was the first to reveal the connection between the Sicilians and the Americans; it was the first time that there seemed to be a real possibility of putting Mafia bosses in jail for long periods of time and also of denting the Mafia involvement in drug dealing.

The trial took place just before the Palermo Maxi Trials, although there was some overlap. Success in neither would have been achieved had it not been for Buscetta and another former mafioso, Salvatore Contorno, who both testified in each trial and were successfully protected from assassination.

Buscetta's action had sown seeds of doubt in the minds of others who were under threat from the Corleonesi. One such man was Salvatore Contorno, who was languishing in a Tuscan jail when he was approached as a likely informer by the police. Before he would break *omerta*, he demanded to see Buscetta to verify for himself that the code had already been broken by a high-ranking man. When he met him, he fell to his knees and had his hair ruffled by Buscetta, who said, 'Cosa Nostra is finished now. You can talk.'

As a result of his testimony, another 127 mafiosi were arrested, and the Corleonesi assassinated 35 of Contorno's relatives in response. All that this achieved, however, was to persuade others who were in fear of their and their families lives that the only way to save themselves was to ensure that the Corleonesi were jailed for a very long time.

Although it would be another eight years before Buscetta would talk about the politicians, he did tell Falcone enough for him to arrest Vito Ciancimino and the Salvo cousins in November 1984.

Although it put the Mafia out of the narcotics trade in New York, unfortunately the hole was quickly filled by Hispanics and Colombians and the trade, if anything, increased.

With the success in the Pizza Trial in New York, the stage was set for the biggest criminal trials in the history of Italy: the Maxi Trials. Although the Mafia were annoyed at the confrontation – the trial, the fact that evidence from informers was being accepted and that Falcone was arrogant enough to believe that he could get them into jail – they did not expect that the result of this trial would be any different from those of the '60s. Even if guilty verdicts were announced, there were two further stages of appeal in which the convictions could be overturned.

For the Maxi Trials, a special courtroom was built near the Ucciardone prison in Palermo under the direction of the lawyer Liliana Ferraro, who had initiated the improvements in the magistrate's office in Palermo on the orders of Craxi. The bunker hall is the size of a small sports stadium and inside there is a single massive courtroom with 30 huge steel cages round the periphery with a capacity for over 600 defendants. On the green carpet in the middle stood a dozen large tables for the lawyers and witnesses. A public gallery with a capacity of over 1,000 overlooks the well of the court, which in turn is screened from any possible violence from the gallery by bulletproof glass. The bunker was built with slabs of reinforced concrete that could resist moderately heavy gunfire, but to get near the walls it would have been necessary to penetrate a barbed-wire defence, blow up a tank and take on 3,000 armed soldiers.

Not surprisingly, none of the Criminal Court judges in Palermo were willing to take the case, so Alfonso Giordano, a judge from the Civil Courts, was transferred to the Maxi Trials. A small man with a high voice, he seemed at first not to have the gravitas to sit on such a case, but he did a brilliant job.

He had two judges flanking him when the trial opened on 16 February 1986, but it looked like turning into a circus because of the behaviour of the defendants. Giordano, however, showed many of the skills of the judge who, some 20 years later, was to preside over the trial of Michael Jackson in California, letting everyone have their say, and eventually everything calmed down.

The drama heightened at the beginning of April 1985, when Tomasso Buscetta returned from the Pizza Connection Trial in New York. He gave evidence for a week and even impressed the Sicilian author Leonardo Sciascia, who was otherwise very critical of the whole episode, especially Falcone's role; he thought Falcone was a poseur.

Buscetta had confrontations (allowable in an Italian court, where accused and accuser sit side by side in front of the judge) with Pippo Calo and then the redoubtable Luciano Leggio, who had been brought to court from his jail cell. He was followed by Contorno, who brought a credibility that surpassed Buscetta's testimony. There were over a thousand other witnesses.

Nino Salvo died of a brain tumour in a hospital in Switzerland during the trial, but his cousin Ignazio was alive to give evidence. He made a point that we shall return to in the chapters on the third Mafia when he said, 'I am one of the many businessmen who, in order to survive, has had to come to terms with the enemies of society.'

On 16 December 1986, the verdict of the court was pronounced by Judge Alfonso Giordano. Of the accused, 114 were released due to insufficient evidence, but 344 were found guilty and sentenced to a total of 2,665 years in jail. Surprisingly, in view of their invaluable contributions, Buscetta was given three years and Contorno six, but they did not actually spend time in prison.

29

REVENGE

The magistrate Paolo Borsellino, along with his family (three children, a divorced wife, a sister and a mother), had always been more aware and more afraid of personal danger than his colleague Giovanni Falcone. Although brought up and educated in the same way, Borsellino was the typical fun-loving, family-oriented Italian man. He was an extrovert, with as much interest in sport and recreation as in his work, and he exuded warmth and happiness in a typical Italian way.

Falcone, on the other hand, was an introvert who found solace in hard work, especially after his first wife had left him *cornutu*. He didn't make new friends easily and was happiest working long hours and listening to classical music. His work had become his life after his marriage break-up, but things picked up again when he met appeals judge Francesca Morvillo. During the trial, they married in a quiet ceremony attended only by a few friends.

After the trial Borsellino felt that a chapter of his life had been completed and wanted to step out from under Falcone's shadow. He applied successfully for the post of chief prosecutor of Marsala, a town about two hours' drive from Palermo, best remembered as the British wine-making centre where Garibaldi landed.

The magistrates' boss, Antonino Caponetto, by now sixty-eight, had been living as a virtual prisoner under guard day and night for four years in Palermo and not surprisingly he wanted to go back to his family in Florence. He wanted Falcone to succeed him because he was so familiar with the evidence and he needed someone with that knowledge to lead in the two Maxi Trials that were still to be heard.

At this time, Falcone was 48, but his rank was still fairly low. His position vis-à-vis his opposite number in New York, Rudy Giuliani, illustrates very well the frustration of young and middle-aged Italians even today when they see that they would have been promoted in any other country, but not at home if your father didn't own the business. Starting at the same time as Falcone, Giuliani had been made a US attorney in his mid-30s and was now number three in the Justice Department. But in Italy seniority and *raccomandazione* ruled!

Falcone's main opponent for Caponetto's job was Antonio Meli, a 68-year-old appellate court judge from central Sicily, and in January 1988, as expected, Meli was appointed. The decision split the Italian judiciary and later Borsellino commented that 'Giovanni Falcone began to die on 19 January 1988'. Falcone himself began to feel as Dalla Chiesa had before he was killed: isolated and vulnerable.

When Meli took over the efficient unit that Caponetto had set up, instead of continuing with the anti-Mafia pools, he distributed cases to magistrates on an apparently random basis. He did not seem familiar with the names of the dangerous players in town nor did he subscribe to the view that crime fell into the pattern of Mafia activity. Meli rarely discussed cases with Falcone, and if Falcone asked for evidence discovered in other cases to see how it fitted into his anti-Mafia work, he was often denied access.

This troubled state of affairs continued for six months and, in July 1988, Borsellino spoke out publicly against what he saw as the dismantling of the anti-Mafia pool. As one experienced in the machinations of politicians, he also had the courage to wonder aloud if those in higher places wanted it so. Again the judiciary was split pro- and anti-Falcone. While Borsellino had some support, there were those who were spreading the story that his outburst had been orchestrated and scripted by Falcone, yet this was the opposite of the truth: confrontation and conspiracy was not Falcone's style. At the end of July, Falcone had had enough and decided to resign, but he was talked out of it, the compromise being that Domenico Sica, a Roman magistrate, would become the new High Commissioner with much increased power.

This show of disunity encouraged the Mafia. The killings in Sicily went on. Salvatore Contorno (now being hidden in America, even though he had been sentenced to imprisonment) lost his 30th relative and Stefano Bontade's brother, Giovanni, was killed, together with his wife, as he opened a door to a stranger.

After spending two months in Palermo, Domenico Sica told the government that it had effectively lost control of the southern half of Italy. Towns such as Naples, Catania and Reggio Calabria had replaced Palermo as the murder capitals of Italy and the Neapolitan Camorra and the 'Ndrangheta were becoming more powerful. Serious crime had gone up by 50 per cent while the number of people arrested fell by the same amount.

The situation worsened when Italy's highest court sided with Meli and agreed that instead of all the expertise being concentrated in Palermo, the anti-Mafia fight should be spread throughout 12 offices in Sicily. In his disagreements with Meli, Falcone was always looking for a compromise, but his remaining two colleagues in the anti-Mafia pool, Giuseppe Di Lello and Giacomo Conte, realising what was going on, always dissuaded him, encouraging confrontation. It was a stalemate and finally, in January 1989, Meli fired them all from the pool.

Falcone, who had apparently been resistant to a fear of death, was visibly shaken when one afternoon in mid-June 1989, while he was taking some Swiss friends to his rented seaside house in Addaura, a security guard discovered a bomb in an Adidas sports bag left near the rocks where they were swimming. So few people knew of his plans that he realised not only was he becoming isolated but also that there were higher forces at work.

Falcone had by now been promoted to deputy chief prosecutor, which meant working in an office with 20 other magistrates, most of whom supported Meli. He was bruised enough to be considering a move from Palermo and so he put forward his candidacy for a position on the Consiglio Superiore della Magistratura, the body that shapes judicial policy in Rome. He continued to resist the usual Italian method of getting elected to anything – parties, dinners, hospitality, 'pressing the flesh', doing deals and exploring trade-offs – and instead lectured at judicial seminars on his beliefs that Italy should have an equivalent of the FBI and a central criminal database. Not surprisingly, he didn't get the job.

Andreotti then appointed Antonio Gava, a Neopolitan suspected of close association with the Camorra, as Minister of Justice. When the inevitable row erupted, he replaced him with another Neopolitan, Vincenzo Scotti, but this was also opposed. Finally, Claudio Martelli, a Socialist, was appointed.

Martelli's first action was to invite Falcone to Rome in order to work for him as director of Penal Affairs. This was a surprising move because when Bettino Craxi (his *padrone*) had been under attack in Milan, Martelli had led the campaign *against* the judges in 1987. He had also followed the party line in criticising Leoluca Orlando, the anti-Mafia mayor of Palermo, whose resignation Craxi had forced.

For his part, Falcone had had enough of the internal politics of his home town and watched with sadness as others seemed to be taking apart six years of his work. But he was Sicilian and 'understood' what was afoot.

Just before he arrived in Rome in March 1991, the Court of Cassation, under the direction of Judge Corrado Carnevale, had released all but a handful of those sentenced in the Maxi Trials. There was a complex system of appeal whereby prisoners were freed pending their second or final appeal, which meant potentially 20,000 Mafia prisoners could be released. But Martelli put a stop to this with a decree that allowed the most dangerous ones to be re-arrested and put back in jail, including the *capi*.

Falcone's wish for an Italian equivalent of the FBI was resisted by many of his colleagues because they knew how corrupt the country had become and how an organisation like that could quickly become a tool of government. If that happened, then it would leave no other avenue for independent investigation, such as the magistrates.

Martelli, however, did not follow that line and embraced Falcone's concept wholeheartedly, concentrating investigation of organised crime in 26 cities and taking 2,000 officers from all of the forces to work solely on organised crime. He also created an anti-Mafia pool of 20 magistrates in Rome who would coordinate action against organised crime.

Over the following two years Martelli had a very rough political ride because of his associations with the Banca Ambrosiano and Craxi, and his political survival was largely due to his anti-Mafia work. It was by that time very difficult to remove anyone from an anti-Mafia campaign because of the questions that would be asked about 'who was going to benefit' from the removal.

The verdict for the final appeal of the convicted mafiosi from the Maxi Trials was given on 31 January 1992 and it upheld the original verdicts. The loss of this final appeal meant that the top men of the Mafia would spend the rest of their lives in jail. It created astonishment and intense anger in the Mafia and Falcone's death sentence was passed.

While he was serving in Rome, Falcone and his young wife used to enjoy returning for the weekend to Palermo, where they still owned a flat. On Saturday, 23 May 1992, they left Ciampino airport in Rome on the 16.40 plane for Palermo. An hour later they landed at Punta Raisa, where three cars were awaiting them together with bodyguards. Unusually, Falcone chose to drive the bulletproof white Fiat Corona, while the bodyguards, three in each car, drove one in front and one behind.

About halfway to Palermo there is a motorway exit to the small town of Carpaci and soon it would feature in every newspaper around the world. It became the site of Falcone's death.

When the lead car, with three *carabinieri* in it, passed a marker set by the Mafia on the side of the motorway (an old refrigerator), there was a huge explosion that destroyed the first and second cars, literally blowing up the motorway. The first vehicle ended up in an olive grove 150 metres away and Falcone's car fell into the huge hole; he and his wife died a few hours later.

I asked one of my Sicilian friends to show me how it was done. We drove along the motorway and took a left near Carpaci to go up some minor roads, which got narrower and narrower until we finally went down a lane where the high bushes scraped along both sides of the car. At this point we were about 20 feet below the surface of the motorway and above us cars zipped past. Above and behind us were lightly wooded hills between 300 and 400 feet high.

My friend showed me how the Mafia men drilled a tunnel about two feet in circumference under the motorway then passed a drainpipe down it. There was an incline from where we were standing to the point at the middle of the right-hand lane of the motorway where the explosives were laid. When a skateboard with thirteen small barrels, each containing about ten kilos of explosive, was placed in the drainpipe, it ran down to the middle of the right-hand side of the motorway.

Sitting up the hill were Giovanni Brusca and Pietro Aglieri. Brusca had the detonator in his hand and when the first car passed the refrigerator he pressed the switch.

Falcone's murder was, as far as the people of Palermo were concerned, a killing too far. Forty thousand people attended the funeral at Palermo Cathedral. The widow of one of the murdered bodyguards, Rosaria Schifani, spoke tearfully from the altar during the televised service. It was thus seen and heard all over Italy and it resonated with millions. Through her tears, she said, 'To the men of the Mafia – who are here in this church, too – I want to say something. Become Christian again. I ask you, for Palermo, a city you've turned into a city of blood.'

The *carabinieri* would not allow dignitaries near the coffins, which they quietly surrounded as the mass ended. Rosaria was among them. 'Men of the Mafia,' she said, 'I will forgive you, but you will also have to get down on your knees.'

As a result of these outbursts, two things happened. The first was the Sheets Campaign, which was started by a group of young feminists but spread throughout Palermo. People hung white sheets out of their windows with anti-Mafia slogans written on them. The second was that Giovanni Brusca achieved an even higher status within the Mafia. He was given the name 'Lo Scannacristiani', the man who kills Christians.

At the time of the assassination, Paolo Borsellino was back in Palermo in Falcone's old job as deputy chief prosecutor. They had started working together again, Falcone in Rome and Borsellino in Palermo, and they had been sketching out plans for the future. Falcone's murder was thus a life-changing event for Borsellino. He had reached the emergency room just before Falcone died. Ironically, the doctor who attempted to save Falcone, Professor Andrea Vassalo, was later convicted of Mafia association and sentenced to five years.

Since he had left Palermo, Borsellino had enjoyed life more than ever. He had achieved hero status and young, keen prosecutors from all over Italy wanted to work with him in Marsala, a typical Sicilian town where life takes place behind closed doors and no one goes out on the street after eight in the evening. When he arrived there, he was the only one on the staff, living in a one-roomed flat above the police station, but in a very short time all eight positions had been filled and he had built up a cohesive happy group of young magistrates.

Within a few months, he had culled the local Mafia, which had carried out a killing in broad daylight and had expected to get away with it. He applied the methods of the anti-Mafia pool in Palermo and worked closely with the magistrates in Agrigento and Messina, where smaller versions of the Maxi Trials were held. But he knew what was going on in Palermo. Cases that he had tried to share ended up back on his desk; he knew that what he and Falcone had built up since 1980 was being dismantled piece by piece. He did what he could to help his former colleague, but their paths diverged and they drifted apart, especially since Falcone had felt embarrassed by the public posturing of Borsellino when he had tried to help him.

While in Marsala, Borsellino had been approached by a number of important *pentiti*. Another of the Spatola clan, also called Rosario but not related to the Palermo developer, told him all about the Mafia in south-west Sicily, about its drug trade and the Masonic lodge in Trapani frequented by local politicians, businessmen and mafiosi.

His other informers were two women. Piera Aiello's husband, Nicola Atria, had been murdered in 1984, possibly because he could have avenged the death of his father, Vito Atria. Rita Atria, Piera's sister-in-law, was also a very nervous *pentita*. They were both from families where the men had been mafiosi for generations and from them Borsellino discovered that the local mayor and president of the bank also had close connections with the Mafia. Rita's mother, who had lost a husband and a son, denounced the two women as *una infama* (a disgrace) and they were thrown out of the family group. Borsellino was their emotional support; they called him Uncle Paolo and he had them moved to a safehouse in Rome.

When Falcone was murdered, Borsellino was publicly endowed with all Falcone's fame and more. A small political party put forward a motion that he be made President of the Republic; the Minister of the Interior, Vincenzo Scotti, wanted him to be the new 'super-prosecutor'.

It was a time of mass exodus from the Mafia ranks and three further informers, who were hidden in Rome and Germany, were giving Borsellino priceless up-to-date information. He was fretting about not having committed all the information that was in his head to paper and was working on that during a weekend visit with his wife and children to their seaside house in Villagrazia di Carini, a 30-minute drive from Palermo. Like any good Italian son, he went to see his *mamma* every Sunday, and so, late in the afternoon of 19 July 1992, he went to his mother's apartment in Palermo.

The terrible Sicilian heat was beginning to wane as he and his bodyguards arrived at his mother's house in Via D'Amelio just after five and parked their three cars outside. When he rang the bell on the gate, there was an explosion that could be heard all over Palermo. The first four floors of the building were gutted, even though they were 30 feet away from the bomb. Borsellino's wife refused a State funeral, and when politicians tried to approach the coffin, they were prevented from doing so by police who formed a phalanx against them while the crowd shouted 'Jackals', 'Assassins' and 'Resign'. In Rome, Rita Atria jumped to her death from her safehouse, writing in her suicide note: 'There is no one left to protect me.'

Rita was buried in Partanna, her home town. Three months later, her mother, who had lost a husband, a son and now her daughter, went to the cemetery one night and defaced her daughter's tombstone with a hammer.

The mood in Sicily and Italy changed. The actions of Toto Riina and his men were more than the nation could stomach. The searchlight was on the politicians and the truth of the last 40 years started to emerge.

30

THE POLITICIANS

Silvio Berlusconi serves as the 80th Prime Minister of Italy since the country was created in 1860. Prior to the end of the Second World War, there had been forty-one Prime Ministers with an average tenure of two years, and from 1945 to 2009 there have been thirty-nine serving an average of 1.6 years. Comparative figures from Great Britain are twenty-six before 1945 and thirteen since 1945.

Politics is a career that benefits the member of parliament and their extended family, and in order to maintain his or her position he or she must always focus on re-election. In such an environment, excesses are to be expected, but in Italy they have reached a level that makes that country's politicians even less respected than those of Great Britain.

There is no doubt that efforts to subdue the Mafia would have been more effective in the 1970s and '80s had political parties not benefitted from financial support from dubious sources. The Mafia electoral machine was behind the old Christian Democrat party from the time that they joined forces in the post-war fight against communism, and what might have begun as a political strategy ended up with many politicians being controlled by the Mafia.

A common saying in Italy used to be 'Corrupt politicians do not go to jail, mafiosi don't talk and you couldn't have a government without Giulio Andreotti' – but by the time Berlusconi first came to power in 1994, corrupt politicians were in jail, mafiosi were talking and Andreotti was awaiting trial for two very serious charges: Mafia association and accessory to murder.

Andreotti was Prime Minister on seven occasions, held every other major political office and was involved in writing the Constitution of the Italian Republic after the war. In an article published in the *New Yorker* magazine a few years after Andreotti resigned for the final time, Alexander Stille told the story of a farmer in Andreotti's constituency who was dying, saying to his family, 'Don't sell the land and vote for Andreotti.'

Although he was very popular throughout Italy, both for his amusing one-liners and his dignity, Margaret Thatcher saw him differently. She wrote, 'Andreotti seemed to have a positive aversion to principle and seemed convinced that a man of principle was doomed to be a figure of fun.'

His association with Sicily came about because of his friendship with the man who was to act as his alter ego on the island from 1968, Salvo Lima. Lima had begun his political career as mayor of Palermo and then served in the regional assembly prior to becoming a deputy in Rome in 1968. From there he went on to become a member of the European Parliament but seldom attended what was then an embryonic organisation, because his main job was to look after Andreotti's affairs in Rome and Sicily. For the next twenty-five years, he was always at Andreotti's side and was the campaign manager when Andreotti became Prime Minister in 1972 for the first of his seven terms.

Andreotti was the pillar around whom the United States built their anti-Communist strategy, and there is no doubt that had the Cold War continued, he would never have gone on trial for any misdemeanours. Some of his supporters in the Christian Democrat Party were what might be described as a 'rum' lot and a number have faced corruption and Mafia-association charges. Andreotti's attitude to this, however, was pragmatic, saying, 'Trees need manure in order to grow.' His downfall was slow, and since 1992, instead of becoming president of the republic, he has lived with the twin worries of Mafia death threats and the possibility of a long jail sentence.

The Mafia were relying on him to arrange that Judge Carnevale, a man well known for quashing the sentences of mafiosi, chaired the Court of Cassation that would hopefully reverse the sentences delivered at the Maxi Trials, but this was vetoed by the Ministry of Justice. On 31 January 1992, the sentences were confirmed, which was disastrous for the Mafia, who blamed Zio Giullio (Uncle Giullio, as he had come to be called in Mafia circles), and he in turn well knew what the response would be, having seen how the Mafia functioned from close quarters over a 20-year period.

The first victim was Andreotti's friend Salvo Lima. On 12 March 1992, ten days after Andreotti resigned, Lima was preparing to leave his seaside home at Mondello on the outskirts of Palermo when he was shot by a team of gunmen. Not only was this a clear message to Andreotti that his days with Mafia support were over but that he or any of his family could be next. He knew that the message also signalled the dissolution of the pact between the Mafia and the Christian Democrats made in the dark post-war days when Don Calogero and Salvatore Giuliano ruled. For all that time, Andreotti had been the intermediary between the two sides.

During his trials, which bridged the millennium, many ugly issues surfaced, such as the events preceding the murder of the conqueror of the Red Brigades, General Della Chiesa. A pattern of denial was adopted by Andreotti. He denied ever having met Della Chiesa or ever talking to him about the Mafia. He denied ever meeting or knowing the Salvo cousins, the tax collectors, even though the court was shown a photograph taken by the Sicilian photographer Lentitzia Battaglia. Some of the *pentiti* also gave evidence of his Mafia association. Both Baldassare Di Maggio, who had proved his reliability by being the informant who caused Riina to be captured, and Marino Mannoia gave evidence confirming that not only had Andreotti met Toto Riina, but that he had kissed him on both cheeks. The extraordinary lengths that Andreotti went to in order to save Sindona and his banks in 1974 were also resurrected and seen in quite a different light from the 'Saviour of the Lira' days. The fact that he also had face-to-face meetings with Stefano Bontade, Gaetano Badalamenti and Michele Greco came out into the public domain. This meeting, it was claimed, dated from the time in the early 1980s when there was a plan to kill the Christian Democrat President of the Sicilian region, Piersanti Mattarella, an event that Andreotti had tried but failed to prevent. After the killing, it was said that he met with the dons only to be told by Bontade that the Mafia were beyond his influence.

He was cleared of Mafia association at his first trial, but the prosecution appealed. At the Court of Appeal, chaired by Judge Salvatore Scaduti, the judgment did not overturn the original verdict and, in journalist Giullio Ambrosetti's words, 'could have been written by Protagoras and Gorgias', the two great Sophist philosophers of ancient Greece who managed to say one thing and its opposite simultaneously. In the judge's opinion, it was likely that Andreotti had contact with the Mafia until 1980 but thereafter he had encouraged the anti-Mafia commissions and fought for their defeat. In 2000, when the judgment was written, any wrongdoing prior to 1980 would have been time-barred. Italy was, therefore, told that Andreotti had 'made himself available to the mafiosi' albeit in an 'authentic, stable and friendly way' – but not for the last 20 years!

The second charge was more serious and involved the murder in March 1979 of journalist Michele Pecorelli. We do not know why he was initially linked with Pecorelli's killing, but it is supposed that Pecorelli was either blackmailing Andreotti or he had a shocking story that Andreotti wanted stopped. We know that he was about to print a story that would have embarrassed Licio Gelli, but we do not know what, if anything, he held over Andreotti.

Pecorelli was murdered by the mafioso Magliana, who pled

guilty to the killing but claimed that it had been ordered by Andreotti's legal adviser, Claudio Vitalone, a baseless allegation that was never confirmed.

In September 1999, Andreotti was acquitted of being involved in the murder, but again the prosecution appealed and this time succeeded in the second Court of Appeal. In 2002, this court sentenced him to 24 years' imprisonment. This was more symbolic than punitive, because in Italy no one over the age of 75 ever goes to jail. The verdict, however, left him a convicted felon and an accessory to murder, so his lawyers appealed to the Court of Cassation, which annulled the second-degree sentence without recourse.

Andreotti is now 88 years of age and sits in the Upper Chamber as a Life Senator. Since it is unlikely that he will produce an autobiography, a lot of Italian history will die with him.

The year 1992 was a seminal one for Italian politics. Not only were the Mafia sentences upheld, thus starting a Mafia War against the State, but government itself disintegrated – not because of a Mafia-related event, but instead because of sheer open corruption. It began in a comparatively innocuous way when the owner of a dry-cleaning company, Luca Magni, fell out with the director of a retirement home, Mario Chiesa.

Mario Chiesa, a socialist politician in Milan, was the social director of a council that ran a retirement home called the Pio Albergo Trivulzio, and he had got his job because of his links with the top man of Milanese politics, Bettino Craxi.

An important bonus of Chiesa's job was to receive kickbacks from every favour that he delivered, every contract he awarded and every job that he created, even for someone's relative. As a local politician, he 'controlled' 7,000 votes, and this gave him a small measure of political power. Not only were his residents a source of reliable votes, but he also had powers over cleaners, suppliers and contractors who were minded to do his bidding when it came to voting time. He had the reputation of being an arrogant bully who had lost sight of what was going on in the morass of corruption in which he lived.

Chiesa lived in a luxury apartment in central Milan, mixed with the best people in the best clubs and attended the best parties but refused to share his wealth with his estranged wife, who, as any woman scorned might do, contacted the authorities. When Luca Magni also complained, their suspicions were already high.

Luca Magni lived in Milan, owned a small cleaning firm and realised that the reality of business life was to pay kickbacks for any job he got, and he was comfortable with that arrangement because it was 'the way things were done'. What really annoyed him in this instance, however, was the way he was treated by Chiesa. Instead of exchanging the usual pleasantries of social intercourse over a cup of coffee, Chiesa never looked up from his paperwork and ordered Magni to leave the envelope on the sideboard. Magni was so cross that he did the unthinkable: he complained to an investigative magistrate, a man later destined for greatness and who today leads one of the small left-wing parties, Antonio Di Pietro.

Di Pietro had been appointed as a magistrate in Milan the year before and was totally familiar with the way Milan local government functioned. It is always difficult to get a conviction because a complaint has to be followed up with cooperation from the magistrates and the police, and a court appearance and the subsequent publicity that goes with it make it unlikely that the complainant will ever work again in Milan. Magni knew this, but he was a very angry man.

He decided to cooperate fully with Di Pietro, and the next time he met Chiesa he wore a microphone hidden in a ballpoint pen and carried a small camera concealed in a black brief case. When the recoding was transcribed, Di Pietro had indisputable evidence of Magni being asked for a kickback in cash, and a warrant was issued for Chiesa's arrest. He must have received some warning of what was about to happen, because when the police arrived with the warrant, he was found in the office lavatory trying to flush seven million lire down the toilet!

On 17 February 1992, Chiesa was remanded in custody in one of the less comfortable Milanese prisons, the San Vittore. He expected that his former friend and supporter Craxi, would, in view of the votes he could deliver and for past favours rendered, arrange to get him acquitted or at least for his trial be put into terminal delay. Instead, he saw Craxi on television, with a tear in his eye, bemoaning the fact that while he had devoted his whole life to wiping corruption out of politics, here he was being let down by a man who he had formerly trusted turning out to be a black sheep.

Chiesa was so incensed at being 'dumped' that he decided to talk, and his evidence changed the whole Italian political system. His story was so explosive that the Ministry of Justice had to set up a special team of investigators.

The team was well constructed in order to deflect the inevitable complaint of bias that would follow any possible convictions. Under the leadership of the chief prosecutor of Milan, Francesco Borrelli (who was later in charge of the 2006 inquiry into football corruption), Gerardo D'Ambrosio (late of the Calvi investigation), Gherardo Colombo, Pier Camillo Davigo and Antonio Di Pietro were a meld of rich and poor backgrounds, North and South origins, and right- and left-wing political views.

By October 1993, due to the publicity attendant on Chiesa's confessions and many others, more than 1,000 people were under investigation, 500 were in preventive detention and 200 had gone on trial. Among the thousand under investigation, there were almost 400 members of the two parliaments, which represented almost 30 per cent of the entire elected political Establishment.

The investigative magistrates asked for, and were granted, the lifting of parliamentary immunity, and those under investigation were informed by the serving of a document created to guarantee people's rights, known as a Notice of Guarantee. Among those receiving these notices were former Prime Minister Criaxi;

Gianni De Michelis, the Foreign Minister; Claudio Martelli, the Minister of Justice; and the entire Christian Democrat leadership in Naples.

Among those eventually convicted of corruption were Paolo Pillitteri, the mayor of Milan and Craxi's brother-in-law; Severino Citaristi, the Secretary of the Christian Democrats; and Salvatore Ligresti, Milan's leading building magnate.

Craxi at first maintained a public silence but then started using a defence that to outsiders says a lot about the depths to which Italian politics had sunk. He basically said that this was the way that Italy has been running for the last 50 years, that everyone was 'at it' and that no business could have been done if one had not acquiesced with the rules.

The glue that had held the Italian political system together for over 40 years was anti-communism. When the Berlin Wall came down in 1989 and the communist regimes of the East collapsed the loser was the Italian political system. The old attitude of corrupt Italians being better than communists disappeared, and Italy was left to look after itself and become more concerned about competing with the rest of Europe. The threat of Soviet tanks had been replaced by Japanese and German cars. Instead of appreciating this, politicians had merely upped their demand for bribes, leading the president of the republic, Francesco Cossiga, to lose his patience and dignity by phoning TV and radio shows, making strange rambling speeches, threatening to either resign or dissolve parliament, and finally going on TV threatening to take a pick-axe to the political system.

The Milan affair acquired the name 'Tangentopoli', which means 'Bribesville', because someone sprayed the word in graffiti on an entrance sign to the city. The subsequent campaign to eradicate corruption from politics was called *mani puliti*, or 'clean hands'.

What shook the country was that this had been uncovered in the North. Had it happened in the South, people would have merely shrugged their shoulders and complained about 'corrupt Southerners', but as it became obvious that Milan had become a cesspit of corruption, it was equally obvious that big changes had to take place all over Italy.

While everyone knew that to get things done in Italy 'brown envelopes' oiled the system, it was the sheer scale of corruption uncovered in Milan that shook the nation. It was well known that all public contracts involved kickbacks, but what was not really appreciated was that public-works schemes had frequently been ordered not for the public good or need but for the creation of a pool of government money that could then be distributed around politicians and their friends. All the North had done was to copy what had become the norm in Sicily for the previous 50 years

The affair triggered a much closer look at politics and politicians. While it was well recognised that some politicians had close links with the Mafia and that through them the Mafia had a say in the political process, what surprised people now was that mafiosi were seeking election as politicians in their own right. In the 1992 regional elections in Italy, 400 candidates were removed from the various party lists because they had previous criminal records. And with the normally docile Italian public incensed and ashamed at what had been uncovered, the Mafia could not have chosen a worse time to challenge the State directly.

31

WAR ON THE STATE

Immediately after the Maxi Trials, Riina had started to put pressure on his contacts to have the sentences squashed. Before killing Salvo Lima, he had issued death threats to the family, and Andreotti was under duress to have Judge Carnevale not only preside over the Court of Cassation, but to overturn the verdicts. There are uncorroborated statements from informers that he also turned the searchlight on Berlusconi well before the latter entered politics.

In 1990, Riina had moved his family into a villa in a private estate in Palermo that was approached by a long drive through trees. His wife, Ninetta, lived a rather closed life because she could not leave the villa in case she was spotted, thus leading the police to her husband. Their two sons and two daughters, however, went to school under assumed names.

Riina attempted to derail the court hearing by having one of the judges murdered in his holiday home in Calabria in August 1991, but the government merely appointed a new prosecutor. When the sentences from the Maxi Trials were confirmed in January 1992, Riina was incandescent with rage. He was not used to losing any battle. For more than a decade, he had ruled the Mafia with a mixture of force and fear, wiping out almost all of his opponents and creating a new drug alliance with the Colombian Orlando Vargas that had spread all over Europe. Worse than that, however, was what he saw as an insult to what he called 'the Cause', his mistaken belief that the Mafia of which he was head was the same as the first 'good' Mafia that had helped the poor and that had upheld the values of village life.

He also faced the problem of how to maintain the basic Mafia tenet that if a 'friend' went to jail, his family would be looked after and their standard of living preserved. The financial strain of supporting almost 400 families was going to prove problematic when the income generated by the hundreds now in jail had disappeared.

It had been a massive misjudgement on the part of the Corleonesi to allow raw emotions to triumph over the previously held pragmatism that had kept the older Mafia safe under the horizon. Although many politicians might be beholden to some mafiosi for funding, no central government could ignore what was now happening in Sicily. Riina's task of providing for the prisoners' families was made far more difficult by the arrival of 7,000 troops on the island, which freed up police for investigative work. Laws were also passed to make Mafia investigations easier. Police were now allowed to adopt the tactics used against Cosa Nostra in America, such as telephone tapping, bugging, sting operations and gang infiltration. But most significantly of all, Falcone's dearest wish was posthumously granted – the setting up of an Italian equivalent of the FBI, namely the DIA.

Riina then started a terror campaign. His philosophy was that to make a peace you first have to have a war so that you can negotiate from a position of strength. He gave up on politicians on the payroll. Not only had they failed him, but they were all under scrutiny and could not function as before in derailing any anti-Mafia legislation. Part of the lunacy that flowed from this was his attempt to create a new political party that would divide Italy into three independent regions – the North, the Central provinces and the South – where the Mafia, Camorra and 'Ndrangheta would rule, thus replicating the former Kingdom of the Two Sicilys.

After Riina had Lima assassinated in March 1992, he killed Ignazio Salvo, who had been part of the Maxi Trials, in his garden as he was seeing dinner guests out. He also had several other Mafia bosses killed because they disagreed with his intended terror campaign, and this had the effect of causing another cascade of informants.

No one was safe from Riina's rage (remember that he once shot an opponent dead over a game of bowls), and fear of assassination was the primary moving force in making mafiosi decide to cooperate and break *omerta*. By January 1993, a year after the sentences were confirmed, there were 270 informers who would be given new identities and placements under the witness-protection scheme. Their information created evidence for more arrests, which in turn caused some of those arrested to turn state's evidence and produce even more arrests. Riina's response to this was to increase his own personal security and put out an order that all informers and their families (including all children over the age of six) should be killed.

His nemesis turned out to be a shepherd's son, Baldassare Di Maggio, who started life as an apprentice motor mechanic. After doing some small jobs for the Mafia, he passed his test by killing an innocent truck driver and was initiated when he was 26. Because of the number of mafiosi going to jail, he quickly rose to the rank of local boss and carried out orders from above, including murders, dissolving bodies in acid, arms procurement and bombings. When Giovanni Brusca (the man who was to press the detonator to blow up Falcone) came out of jail in 1991, Di Maggio had to step down. Having grown accustomed to power and feeling he was doing a good job, he became dissatisfied with his lower rank and became involved with a young woman. Although the Corleonesi had been slaughtering people for more than a decade, they still retained old Catholic Mafia morals, and one did not leave one's wife and kids for another woman; affairs were OK but scandal wasn't. Realising this, he ran off to Canada with his paramour and augmented the scandal by fathering a child with her. They became homesick and returned shortly after to be rebuked by Riina.

Di Maggio realised that he would be killed sooner or later, so he became an informer. He led the police to Riina's address in Palermo, and on 15 January 1993 they followed Riina's car and pulled him out at a set of traffic lights. Riina was evidently terrified when he was dragged into one of the other cars and restrained, but he calmed down when he realised he wasn't the victim of a Mafia kidnap and was in the hands of the police instead.

Having been on the run for 23 and a half years, at his trial he insisted on describing himself as a poor building worker who only knew of the Mafia from television. He received a life sentence. The falseness of his claim of poverty was exposed over the next two years, with the police tracing £160 million to him. His total worth was estimated at £1.3 billion.

The day after Riina was sentenced in November 1993, his mentor, Leggio, died aged 68 in a Sardinian prison. His body was brought back to a very different Corleone. The mayor refused to allow a public funeral, and the private service was carried out by his cousin, Father Girolamo Leggio. Leggio is buried in an unmarked grave in a cemetery that holds dozens of his victims. Shortly afterwards, the town elected an anti-Mafia mayor, who renamed the main piazza, Piazza Falcone Borsellino!

Riina owned a magnificent 30-roomed villa on the outskirts of Corleone that was confiscated in 1992. After a civil suit filed by mayor Cipriani against the family, it was signed over to the province and converted into an agricultural college. L'Istituto Professionale di Stato per L'Agricoltura must be one of the best-appointed technical colleges in the world. It is on three floors, has an underground car park, central air conditioning, an elevator, and black and red marble floors – all left by Riina.

Riina's capture and imprisonment threw the Mafia into confusion because there was no clear successor. It was, however, going to be one of two Corleonesi.

Riina's brother-in-law, Calogero Bagarella, thought that the policy of waging war to negotiate a peace was correct, and he wished to continue it, not only within Sicily, but also on the mainland, in the hope that public opinion would force the new parties that had formed after the debacle of *Tangentopoli* to calm things down.

The demands that were being made by the Corleonesi all related to the conditions of imprisonment suffered by their colleagues and relatives. When a mafioso had gone to jail previously, he had been treated well. Now, however, they were being held in new maximum-security prisons well away from Sicily under harsh regimes, often in isolation, and their assets were being sequestered.

Reviews of the verdicts, abolition of the witness-protection scheme, a reform of the law that allowed assets to be sequestrated and new measures that would allow those in jail to serve their sentences under house arrest or in hospitals were all being demanded. That it nearly worked is shown by the fact that Carabiniere Colonel Mario Mori went to the former Palermo mayor and fixer, Ciancimino, now living outside Sicily, and asked if he would act as an intermediary between the police and Riina, offering him and his acolytes an easy time in jail if they gave themselves up. Ciancimino evidently threw up his hands in horror at the idea of approaching Riina with any such idea, saying that the likely outcome would be his own death!

Bagarella was challenged for the leadership by Bernardo Provenzano, who had been Riina's friend since boyhood and who wanted the Mafia to lie low for a decade and then to 'reawaken'. He thought that all the violence since Falcone's assassination had achieved nothing other than unheard of police activity, involvement of the military and great difficulty in carrying out core 'business' in extortion, drug dealing and construction.

Among Bagarella's early ideas were to leave HIV-infected syringes on Italian beaches, to blow up the leaning tower of Pisa and to destroy some Roman monuments. This campaign started at around 1 a.m. on the night of 27 May 1993. A car bomb went off in a side street adjoining the Uffizi gallery in Florence, bringing down the Torre del Pulci and crushing the guard and his family, starting a fire in an adjacent house and injuring 35 people. There was serious damage to two paintings by Caravaggio and blast damage to 173 others. Forty-two busts and sixteen statues were damaged, and the famous discus thrower was decapitated.

In July, a bomb in Milan killed five people and other bombs went off outside the Pope's church in Rome, the Basilica of St John and the Church of San Giorgio al Velabro.

A few days later, Bagarella sent a letter to several newspapers:

> All that has happened is only the beginning. After these latest bombs, we inform the nation that the next ones will only explode during the day and in public places, because they will be exclusively aimed at taking human lives
>
> P.S. We guarantee there will be hundreds of them.

Bagarella then did what Salvatore Giuliano did half a century before and resurrected the concept of Sicily becoming the 51st state of the United States. Harry Truman did not respond to Giuliano's letter, and Bagarella's emissary to sound this out with the Gambino family was similarly sent packing.

Riina's eldest boy, Giovanni, was taken under Bagarella's wing in an attempt to use family ties in the struggle for the leadership. On 19 January 1995, he invited Giovanni along to witness a murder, but Giovanni became an enthusiastic participant. Two days later, Bagarella was arrested, as was Giovanni.

The final advocate of violence was Giovanni Brusca, the man who killed Falcone and who became known as 'Scannocristiani'. He came from an old Mafia family; his grandfather had been part of Salvatore Giuliano's gang in the 1940s. His father was obviously a mafioso, and Giovanni paid his first visit to a jail when he was five to visit him. He was a badly behaved youth and would not attend school. His father gave him jobs such as taking food and clothes to the fugitives who often hid near their home between Corleone and Palermo. He was initiated in 1976 at the age of 19, having passed his test of murdering someone unknown to him with flying colours. Riina presided over the ceremony.

His final arrest was in the spring of 1996. He had excellent personal security, but the police found what appeared to be his mobile-phone number and traced the signal to near Agrigento, where they made the arrest. Brusca quickly turned state's evidence, which is when he confessed to 'more than 100 murders but not more than 200'. His confessions are documented, and much of what we know about Riina comes from these.

These arrests left Bernardo Provenzano in charge – but he hadn't been seen for four decades.

32

PAX MAFIOSA

Bernardo Provenzano was the son of a peasant farmer in Corleone. His father used to go to the piazza each morning in the hope of being chosen by an overseer for a day's work. There was very little choice for a boy in Corleone, or any other Sicilian agrotown, in those days. Bernardo could follow his father in waiting every morning to see if an overseer would give him work, he could become a priest or he could try to get noticed by the Mafia. Bernardo chose the final of these options, in spite of his family doing everything they could to stop him. He was the same age as Riina, and both were identified as likely Mafia candidates by Licio Leggio, whom they idolised.

Provenzano served his apprenticeship as a killer in the war waged by Leggio against Dr Navarra's clan, a period (1943 to 1961) during which Corleone witnessed 52 murders and 22 attempted murders, with bodies being burned, dissolved in lime graves or being dissected into small parts and distributed as pig feed. It brought Corleone to the notice not only of the police, but also of the American Cosa Nostra families. A struggling writer, Mario Puzo, must have also registered the town on his radar because it became the now world-famous base for the *Godfather* movies that followed his successful book.

Provenzano excelled with a gun in this local war and was memorably complimented by Leggio on his lack of brain power, compensated for by superb marksmanship. Later, as Riina moved into 'business' in Palermo, Provenzano's nickname changed from 'the Tractor' (given because he mowed down everyone in his path) to 'the Accountant' because he looked after the financial side of the businesses. He had no particular expertise, but he was a good manager, relying on the help of other apparently straight accountants, bankers and financiers.

Much of Provenzano's story has come to light thanks to the confessions of the man who was his adviser for decades, Antonino Giuffre. He started life as a teacher in a technical school, was initiated into the Mafia in 1980 and finally rose to be head of the Caccamo family near Palermo. He said in his confessions that 'he was born and raised in Provenzano's hand'. Just as Provenzano had a Damascene moment and became very religious at the end of his life, so did Giuffre, and disgusted with the wrong that he was doing he turned state's evidence.

Provenzano, in the same way that old pre-war godfathers had done, dressed and acted like a peasant, a tactic that kept him under the police radar. He never married, but in the 1960s he started a long-term relationship with a shirt maker 12 years his junior, Saveria Palazzolo. She bore him two sons, Angelo and Paolo, had their births registered in Palermo and then disappeared. She returned to Corleone in 1992, and the two sons did not follow their father into the Mafia. Paolo taught languages in Germany, and Angelo passed all his school exams and tried several lines of legitimate businesses with varying degrees of success.

Being at one time a supporter of Dr Navarra, Provenzano always had sympathy with the philosophy of peaceful co-existence with the State – a *pax mafiosa*. After the Maxi Trials and the war on the State carried out by Riina and Bagarella, his view of low-profile activity held sway. He wanted the Mafia to lie low for up to a decade and to 'make no noise'. He thought that if there were no murders, no bombs and no overt illegal action, the police and military pressure would fade away.

He also ordered a step back from dealing with politicians, for a number of reasons. He realised that in view of what had happened in the 1990s, if a politician was found to have Mafia connections, then his or her effectiveness would immediately be neutralised. He also saw that the political landscape was changing as were the values of politicians, even though re-election remained top of the agenda. His predecessor, Bagarella, reportedly talked to the 'new men' about getting support for the changes they wanted for their jailed comrades.

According to Giuffre, Provenzano had attempted to negotiate with Berlusconi in the summer of 1993 when he was putting together his new party, Forza Italia. When Berlusconi spoke out against informers, saying they only wanted to benefit themselves, it was claimed by some people that he had responded to Mafia requests, but it was a reasonable statement that could have been interpreted quite differently. Again according to Giuffre, Dell'Utri, Berlusconi's right-hand man, promised Mangano (see chapter 33) that if Forza Italia was elected, it would pass a series of laws that satisfied Mafia demands. In other words, prison conditions would improve, there would be no asset sequestrations and informer testimony would not be allowed.

In the election of 2000, Forza Italia won every one of the sixty-one Sicilian seats. They also did well enough in the rest of Italy for the Sicilian triumph to be welcome but not decisive. Nevertheless, it was the first time that a single party had won all the seats in Sicily.

When the results of the 2006 election were announced on 10 April 2006, showing that Forza Italia had lost half the Sicilian seats, Provenzano was captured the next day. This was probably a coincidence, because the police, led by Renato Cortese, had been following his path for two years; however, it was grist to the mill for the conspiracy theorists.

Cortese was a Calabrian, born in 1964, and thus conversant enough with southern dialects to interpret material from telephone taps and bugging operations. He joined the police the same year in which Falcone was killed and was so moved by that event that he immediately volunteered for anti-Mafia work. He joined a 40-strong squad dedicated to hunting down bosses and became the head of the unit in 1998. He realised he was chasing a ghost: a man with no mobile phone, no mistresses and apparently no family. In fact, many rumours had it that Provenzano was dead, something often stated as being true by his lawyer.

Cortese based himself in Corleone – but surreptitiously, because every new face is recognised and noted immediately. He based his small team in a disused police station and set up bugging devices in the homes of Saveria Palazollo, Provenzano's brothers, Salvatore and Simone, and others suspected of being close to Provenzano. He also set up small surveillance cameras at many sites in the town, especially in front of Saveria's house.

Eventually, they intercepted a phone call from Saveria to a man called Giuseppe Lo Bue, saying that 'the underpants, shirts and socks were washed, ironed and ready for collection'. On April 5, they tracked the parcel to a shack on a small sheep farm owned by a shepherd with no police record, Giovanni Marino, who was well known in the area as a purveyor of good fresh ricotta, which he sold from his battered Fiat Panda. They kept the shack under surveillance 24 hours a day for a week but saw no signs of life.

The farm was on Monte Cavallo, above which is a hill with a large monument to Saint Bernard, the local patron saint, in which they set up an observation post because it overlooked the shack. Cortese also made a check on the amount of electricity used on the farm, which was minimal until November of 2005 when it rose significantly. This made it obvious that the shack was being used, although there continued to be no sign of life.

In the morning of 11 April, they saw Marino approach the shack, stand with his back to the door, stare up the hill at the St Bernard statue and turn momentarily as a hand grasping a bag was thrust through a chink in the door. Led by the pistol-toting Cortese, the police burst into the shack and captured Provenzano without a struggle.

He had last been seen in public in 1963, and the only identification the police had was an old photograph from which forensic specialists had tried to reconstruct what they imagined an ageing Provenzano would look like. Neither did anyone know what he sounded like because the only tape of his voice dated from a telephone tap in 1959 and even that had (not surprisingly) disappeared from the police safe in Agrigento.

The police expected a struggle or perhaps a shoot-out given Provenzano's reputation as a killer in his early life, but they got it wrong. What they found was a little man who looked not unlike a bespectacled Jeffrey Archer, wearing an open-neck checked shirt, a white scarf, a navy-coloured winter jacket and a pair of old jeans. When they broke in, they found that he was beginning to write a letter on his 30-year-old Brother AX410 electric golf-ball typewriter, which stood on the only table in the room and in front of the only chair. The house had three rooms, with a 1950s bathroom built on to the side. On the table next to the single bed was a picture of Padre Pio, a rosary and a Bible, open at the Gospel of Luke 6.43–5, with an underlined section that read:

> There is no such thing as a good tree producing bad fruit nor a bad tree producing good fruit . . . Good people produce good from the store of goodness within themselves, evil people produce evil from within them.

Provenzano ran Mafia affairs by letter. These were not long letters but notes, which Sicilians call *pizzini*, written on scraps of paper folded into tiny packets so that they can be swallowed or easily destroyed. A *pizzino* might just contain some numbers, an acronym or a message in code. Provenzano, for example, used numbers to indicate people's identities in a series that went up to almost 150.

From CCTV pictures taken in prisons, police had learned how mafiosi and their visitors got around the security systems, especially in the new Palermo Pagliarelli prison, where physical contact between prisoners and family is forbidden and listening devices are positioned so that conversations can be monitored. Relatives and friends use a strategy of multiple visits to circumvent limits on numbers. For example, three or four 'family' members will sign in and initially speak to one prisoner but after initial greetings, when a *pizzino* might be flashed in front of the glass partition before being swallowed, they will move on to another prisoner, changing seats every few minutes so that a *capo* can speak to several lieutenants as well as his official visitor.

Provenzano, however, living for weeks on end on his own, not seeing anybody and without moving from his hiding place, was also a prolific writer of long letters. We know this because many of them came into the hands of the police. The first batch came from an informer, Luigi Ilardo, in 1996, but when this act was discovered, he was murdered. The second batch came from Antonio Giuffre, formerly Provenzano's right-hand man, when he turned state's evidence in 2002. The police by that time had 75 letters, but these proved useless in offering an understanding of someone who had evaded capture for so long. They apparently could not believe what they were reading. They are the testimony of a man who has realised that what he has spent his life doing does not tie in with God's teaching nor his present philosophy.

When Provenzano became head of the Mafia, he evidently shied away from ordering the murder of any individual, telling the proponent of the idea that he must 'do as he thought fit'. He had obviously become deeply religious; most of the letters started with phrases such as 'Dearest friend, I got your news with much joy, and it comforts me that all my friends send me greetings and are well. Thanks to God I can say the same of myself . . .' The Lord was similarly invoked at the end of his letters, with phrases such as 'May the Lord bless and protect you' being common.

Unlike many mafiosi, he was not a womaniser, and in Saveria, whom he never married but who bore him two sons, he had a patient and loving partner. He obviously missed her and his sons, writing, 'Motors can stop, but not my heart, as it wished all my nearest and dearest the most affectionate greetings . . . Kiss the children for me . . .'

He was taken first to Palermo and then by helicopter to the maximum-security prison in Terni in Umbria. When arrested, he was not a well man. He was suffering from prostate cancer and was incontinent as a result of a radical prostatectomy in the La Licome clinic in Marseilles. The fact that he was able to come out of hiding, pay two visits to another country, have major surgery and return to Italy to continue hiding is a tribute to his personal security systems.

With his arrest, there were no more Corleonesi vying for the top position because they were virtually all now in jail. The position as head of the Mafia probably passed to the elderly Palermo boss, Salvatore Lo Piccolo, but he was arrested along with his sons two months after Provenzano. Being outside the Corleone clan, he had forged links with Sicilians in America who had fled during the slaughter in the 1980s. They were mainly Inzerillos, and they planned to return to Sicily to become the new masters, but the plan was wrecked with the arrest of 43 gang members.

Among those arrested was Nino Rotolo, a jailed mafioso who had persuaded the authorities that his blood pressure was so uncontrolled that he had to live at home for the duration of his sentence – the sort of thing Riina had wanted for those jailed at the time of the Maxi Trials. Rotolo was videoed vaulting a fence that separated his villa from a cabin in which he evidently met with other mafiosi; when a conference was under way, a football was placed outside the door. Inside, there were eight plastic chairs and anti-bugging devices, but these were trumped by police technology. Rotolo was number 24 in Provenzano's coded list of colleagues and vied with Lo Piccolo for the top spot. His right-hand men were Dr Antonio Cina, a neurologist, and a builder, Francesco Bonura.

In April 2008, Berlusconi's Forza Italia party, in coalition with Alleanza Nationale and La Liga (a federalist party), defeated the socialist coalition, and Berlusconi became Prime Minister for the third time. On the first occasion, Italy was still floundering in the wake of the massive political scandal in Milan that had seen the end of the Christian Democrats and the old socialist parties, and he got caught up in this. On the second occasion, he spent five years being hounded by magistrates who were intent on getting rid of him by digging up his past business demeanours. This time he knew what had to be done and top of his agenda was to show the world and Italy that the Sicilian Mafia were not going to call the tune as they had been doing for more than a hundred years. Without this political will, the Mafia were never going to be defeated, because it was their hold over the last generation of politicians and the important funding of political parties that protected them. A military operation was mounted called Perseus, involving 1,200 police officers, helicopters and anti-drug units; Perseus was the mythological Greek hero who beheaded Medusa.

Since the 2006 arrest of Provenzano, the Mafia had been in disarray and was being controlled by Riina, now in his mid-70s, from his jail cell. Provenzano was not taking part in the attempted reorganisation because he had settled into a monastic existence in his top-security jail in Umbria, where he was kept in isolation. Riina was attempting a restructuring of the organisation and a re-establishment of the Commission that would oversee all activity and prevent inter-family wars (which was ironic coming from Riina, who had almost destroyed the Mafia with his 'wars'). Thanks to a level of intelligence gathering that politicians of the time had denied Falcone and Borsellino, police knew that a meeting of the family leaders who would choose a new overall boss had been arranged in Palermo. Riina had decided that it should be the head of the Villagrazia family of Palermo, Benedetto Capizzi, but this was going to be opposed by the old Porta Nuova family (formerly Buscetta's) who were in favour of bringing back from America mafiosi who had fled from the Corleonesi slaughter 20 years previously. If this had happened, another Mafia war would have been inevitable, thus the urgency of operation Perseus.

The plan to bring back American 'refugees' was discovered at the beginning of 2008, when a joint operation between the FBI and the Italian equivalent, the DIA, rounded up 58 suspects in New York and 19 in Sicily. At the time, New York Attorney General Andrew Cuoma told a news conference, 'Organised crime still exists. We like to think it's a vestige of the past. It's not. It is as unrelenting as weeds that continue to sprout in the cracks in society.'

On 16 December 2008, in a pre-dawn swoop, police arrested 94 top mafiosi, many of whom had recently been let out of prison after serving long sentences. Hours after being arrested, one of the bosses, Gaetano Lo Presti (the head of the Porta Nuova family), was found hung in his cell.

One who evaded arrest was Matteo Messina Denaro, known in the popular press as the 'playboy godfather'. He was given a life sentence *in absentia* in 2002 for his part in the 1993 bombings in Rome, Milan and Florence and came from an old established Mafia family of Trapani in the west of Sicily. He became the regional boss after his father, the previous boss, was found murdered beside a river in 1998. The news weekly *L'Espresso* ran an article about him in 2001, describing him as filthy rich, a womaniser, a Porsche driver and addicted to video games. He has not been seen since 1993 and will now be 47. After a particularly gruesome double killing of another rival and his pregnant girlfriend, Denaro is reported to have said, 'I am fighting for something which cannot be understood. However, one day it will be understood that I was on the part of reason.'

And this is the bit of the Mafia that is most difficult to understand and which makes it so different from all other organisations, including the Camorra and 'Ndrangheta. So, as Italy moves into another period of government by Forza Italia, can we presume that they are different from previous generations of politicians?

33

BERLUSCONI AND THE MAFIA

Since entering politics in 1994, Berlusconi, his family, his companies and members of his staff have been involved in more than 60 criminal proceedings, which have in turn involved more than 100 lawyers. In 2005, *The Economist* published a table of the main cases he has had to face, though it acknowledged that he has never had a conviction upheld on appeal.

Few other western politicians would have survived what has been thrown at Berlusconi, but he is successful and popular, at least among more than half of the electorate. In 2006, the international neuropsychiatry journal *Cortex* published a case study by Dr Sara Mondini and Dr Carlo Semenza, describing a 66-year-old Italian housewife with advanced dementia. Her brain scan showed severe changes, she could not recognise any of her family and she could not tell an onion from an apple; what she could do, however, was recognise pictures of Berlusconi.

His story of rising from being a successful builder to TV tycoon and Prime Minister has been told so often that it does not need repeating here, but his links with the Mafia through Mangano have been well documented.

Berlusconi is not a mafioso but had he never been influenced by the Mafia he would probably have been the first politician since Garibaldi to ignore them. In Italy, Mafia association is a crime punishable by imprisonment, but although Berlusconi has been investigated for (although subsequently acquitted of) money laundering, tax evasion, bribery of judges and police, making illegal payments to political parties and false accounting, he has never been charged with Mafia association.

Marcello Dell'Utri is one of Berlusconi's closest friends; he even has a space reserved for him in the family tomb at Villa D'Arcore. Brought up in Palermo, he met Berlusconi at university. As well as being a devout Catholic, Dell'Utri is a world-renowned bibliophile and his libraries hold magnificent collections of books, letters and documents, including works by Thomas More and Erasmus.

Berlusconi's problem is that this man, his closest friend and the head of Pubitalia, the advertising arm of his empire, has been convicted of Mafia association. Although still an elected MP, he is in the process of appealing the nine-year jail sentence handed down in December 2004, but in turn, the prosecution are appealing that his sentence should be increased to eleven years. Being Italy, the appeal process was still underway in 2009.

It was easy for any Mafia informer to 'finger' Dell'Utri. *Pentiti* have given testimony that Dell'Utri was the man the Mafia dealt with when they wanted to contact Berlusconi – but when relying on evidence from informers, not all of the information is reliable and some will say what they hope the magistrates would like to hear in the hope of more favourable treatment.

Dell'Utri comes from Sicily and Berlusconi from Milan. Dell'Utri, by virtue of his own ability and association with Berlusconi, had by the 1970s become a very prominent citizen of Palermo and, as such, would have become a target for the Mafia. They would have wanted to have contact with a person of his standing, especially to test whether or not he was sufficiently 'malleable' to do business with them. It might have been possible for Dell'Utri to challenge his prosecutors on this point because he could quite easily have claimed that he had no idea that his contacts were mafiosi. But this in turn would not have been credible, because knowing who you are dealing with in Sicily is a fundamental skill that every Sicilian develops.

From Berlusconi's viewpoint, even far away Milan was not guaranteed to be a Mafia-free zone because in the 1960s and '70s the Christian Democrats had adopted Mussolini's tactic of 'internal exile' for some mafiosi, and by the early 1970s there were almost 400 Mafia exiles living in or near Milan. Neither deportation nor exile curtailed 'family business'; in fact, the legitimate presence of mafiosi facilitated it. In the '70s, there were 72 high-ransom kidnappings in Milan and, for the first time, extortion was applied to previously untouched Milan businesses. The legitimate placements of mafiosi in the North also put a number of their people in highly strategic positions for drug distribution.

When Berlusconi bought Villa D'Arcore estate (one of his homes), he persuaded Dell'Utri to leave Palermo and become site manager for the planned refurbishments. These were also the years of the Red Brigades kidnappings and so Berlusconi would have known that he and his young family were prime targets.

The best protection available at that time was undoubtedly Mafia based. Even in the north of Italy, to harm mafiosi or anyone under their protection would invite the certainty of a fatal reprisal. The story is told of a Milan businessman who was facing increasing demands from Milan criminal gangs and so decided to go to a convicted mafioso living in Milan to ask for his protection. As a result, the Milan criminal gang came back to him, asking forgiveness for their previously crass behaviour.

Dell'Utri brought in Vittorio Mangano, who Tommaso Buscetta claimed was a 'Man of Honour', to work for him and to stay at Villa D'Arcore. He was hired ostensibly to look after the stables – but in the 'horse country' of Lombardy, bringing such a person from Sicily was bizarre. However, protection was very necessary because as well as threats from the Red Brigades it appears that the Catania Mafia had threatened the Berlusconi family with kidnap and extortion. According to various Mafia informers, the Catania mob were 'warned off' by the Palermo families.

Mangano's most important role was not to look after the horses, but to protect Berlusconi's children, whom he drove to and from school every day. So how did Dell'Utri, one of the brightest and most successful men in Italy, get tied up with a man such as Mangano?

We know Dell'Utri's side of the story from the published trial proceedings that resulted in his prison sentence. His association with Mangano went back to the late '60s, when he coached an amateur Palermo football team, Bacigalupo. Vittorio Mangano is said to be the man who painted the field markings and occasionally acted as a linesman, but he must have had another occupation because he had captured the attention of the police sufficiently to have spent three periods in jail between 1967 and 1974.

Not unreasonably, therefore, knowing Magnano's track record, Dell'Utri probably thought that he would be the best person to handle security at the villa, so he made the job offer – but not directly. According to Mangano's testimony, a meeting had been arranged between himself, Dell'Utri and another man who owned a dry-cleaning business. He told Mangano that Dell'Utri was about to offer him an interesting job in the North, where a friend had recently bought a property. He expressed interest in the job and testified: 'I went by myself to the offices of Edilnord at Foro Bonaparte, Milan, and met Berlusconi and Dell'Utri.'

Mangano was hired and lived at Villa D'Arcore, where he was 'often visited by friends'. He was, in fact, probably using the vast estate as a sanctuary for 'friends' who might at that time have needed to disappear from police surveillance. This was corroborated by Dell'Utri, who testified that Mangano 'would sometimes introduce me to various people, saying that they were friends of his, never giving their names. You don't use names when you are meeting people with someone like Magnano.'

Unfortunately, in December 1974, some of these 'friends' attempted to kidnap one of Berlusconi's dinner guests. They failed because of a car crash in the grounds, but the police became involved and when questioned about this event in a later election campaign interview Berlusconi admitted to the episode and said that he had fired Mangano as soon as he found out that he might have been involved.

In an interview with a French journalist published in *L'Espresso* in 1992 just before he was assassinated, Paolo Borsellino, the anti-Mafia magistrate, said that Mangano was one of the bridges between the Mafia in Sicily and the organisation in northern Italy. He said: 'The Mafia had . . . an enormous amount of capital that needed an outlet . . . It's normal that the owners of these enormous sums of capital would look for instruments to employ this money, both to recycle it and to make money on their money.'

In their book *L'odore dei soldi*, Elio Veltri and Marco Travaglio tell the story of the bankruptcy of a financial group headed by Filippo Alberto Rapisarda. It went under amid evidence of fraud, money laundering and Mafia connections. Rapisarda admitted to prosecutors that he did not feel able to say 'no' to the Mafia and hired Marcello Dell'Utri to work for him because of his connections with the Mafia. He said that he was introduced to Dell'Utri by the same person who had been involved in the placement of Mangano at Villa D'Arcore: the dry cleaner.

Rapisarda testified to having had a meeting with two of the most senior *capi* in 1979 near the offices of Edilnord in Milan. They were Stefano Bontade and Mimmo Teresi, who evidently told him that they were about to meet Dell'Utri, who had proposed that they invest in a TV company that Berlusconi was creating.

There has always been rumour that the real business of the Rasini bank, where Berlusconi's father worked and which financed his first construction project, was to launder Mafia money. It was a bank with only one office, but in Italy at that time there were another hundred or so similar 'little' banks which, because of the lax banking laws, could well have been used to launder money from whatever source. But there is absolutely no proof that Berlusconi's father was involved in anything illegal and no one has ever levelled that accusation against the family.

In the 1980s, Giovanni Ruggeri and Mario Guarino, two investigative journalists, published a book entitled *Berlusconi: Inchiesta sul Signor TV*. They alleged that the principal investor and the real owner of the second development at Brugherio was an anonymous Lugano-based company represented by an Italian-Swiss lawyer called Renzo Rezzonico that rejoiced in the glorious Swiss title of Finanzierunggesellschaft für Residenzen. The same Renzo was also involved in the setting up of the company that funded Milan Due, Akteingesellschaft für Immobilien Anlagen in Residenzzentren. Great names and even greater secrecy!

The closest investigators ever came to unravelling this mystery was in 1998, when the Palermo magistrates found that large amounts of cash had entered Fininvest during the 1970s when Berlusconi was expanding his TV empire. In 1977, the capitalisation of Fininvest jumped by $30 million and no one has ever been able to discover the origin of this money.

At the Dell'Utri trial, the Bank of Italy investigator, Francesco Giuffrida, told the court about the Palino Company, which had a very short shelf-life – less than a year. It appears that this firm played a role in the lucrative deal to buy the rest of the Villa D'Arcore estate from Anna Maria Casati Stampa in 1979.

During this investigation, Giuffrida also discovered 22 other companies all called 'Holding Italiana', which were listed as hairdressing and beauty salons but unlike most such establishments they had received 94 billion lire (£30 million) of funding between 1979 and 1985. As well as being puzzled about the need for hairdressing companies to deal in this sort of money, Giuffrida could also find no trace of professional fees for any of the transactions!

Eventually, the investigators found 16 more Holding Italiana companies and on 16 June 1998 asked Berlusconi for administrative and accounting documents, but Berlusconi refused to cooperate. By the time they had enough evidence to proceed to court, Berlusconi had become Prime Minister and was immune from prosecution.

The investigators persisted, but Berlusconi showed great

reluctance to meet them, repeatedly breaking appointments. A meeting finally took place in the Chigi Palace, the Prime Minister's official residence, when he allotted them half an hour, refused to take an oath and refused to answer any questions.

La Repubblica reported this on 28 November 2002, saying: 'The Italian premier had the right to refuse to answer, but he also had the moral duty to clarify the issue since he was Prime Minister of a democratic nation.'

The statement of the prosecutors also reflected this. It said: 'There are many obscure areas in the birth of Fininvest and there were substantial financial flows for which it has not been possible to arrive in any way at the source of the money involved.'

By the time of Dell'Utri's final trial, Mangano had been arrested and sentenced to life imprisonment for double homicide, drug trafficking and Mafia association but was unable to give evidence at the Dell'Utri trial because he died in prison of lung cancer in 2000. At the time of his death, he had risen to be *capo* of the Porta Nuova family in Palermo, which at one time had been the family of Tomasso Buscetta, the super-informer.

During the Dell'Utri trial, one of the prosecution witnesses, Antonio Giuffre, a key aide to Bernardo Provenzano, alleged that several mafiosi had been in contact with Berlusconi's Fininvest company to negotiate terms for their support for the 1994 election campaign. He also confirmed that several mafiosi, among whom was Stefano Bontade, the *capo* assassinated by the Corleonesi, had visited Berlusconi in Milan many years before he entered politics in 1993, at a time when Mangano was stable manager.

Giuffre also told the police that the Mafia had chosen to support and get the votes for Forza Italia because they always chose the 'winning horse'. For their part, the Mafia were assured that in the event of a Forza Italia victory, jail conditions for imprisoned 'friends' would improve and the pressure on confiscation of assets would soften. In exchange, the Mafia agreed to abandon their war on the State and to keep a low profile so as not to embarrass their new political allies.

If this is true, it was a successful alliance because in 2001 Berlusconi won all 61 seats in Sicily, a feat never before accomplished, even at the height of Christian Democrat control.

Antonio Mormino was both a Forza Italia MP and also a lawyer who had defended many mafiosi, including Toto Riina, Leoluca Bagarella, the Madonia family and also Antonino Giuffre. According to the latter, he was elected in Sicily with Mafia support. When a number of MPs received letters from jailed mafiosi about their conditions, many sought police protection apart from one –Antonio Mormino. He said that he had made no agreements with the Mafia and so had nothing to fear.

He was at the time Deputy Minister of Justice and had some involvement in drafting a bill pardoning prisoners (a not infrequent Italian method of clearing the jails and displaying the great Italian virtue of *misericordia*, meaning mercy and forgiveness). The bill was meant to exclude Mafia imprisoned after the Maxi Trials, but as written it could have been interpreted as meaning that they too could have been released. It was a point picked up by the Communist opposition and Mormino was reported as acknowledging that it was a 'small mistake'.

It is worth stating at this point that Berlusconi has always denied conspiring with the Mafia, and Dell'Utri is currently appealing his conviction on Giuffre's evidence. Berlusconi has never been convicted of Mafia association and to date has been acquitted of all allegations of illegality in political dealings. His government, however, has been the subject of much unsubstantiated rumour about Mafia associations.

Berlusconi has been accused of attempting to bribe judges but his lawyer Cesare Previti was charged and convicted, receiving a six-year jail sentence. To any Briton or American, the concept of even thinking of bribing judges is beyond the pale, but the story of Judge Corrado Carnevale's alleged pro-Mafia bias suggests that Italy is different. Carnevale was one of the most senior judges in the country, sitting on the highest Court of Appeal, the

Court of Cassation. There are two appeals available to anyone convicted of a felony in Italy. The first Court of Appeal can look at the evidence presented in the first trial and can reassess the verdict. The final court, however, cannot carry out a retrial; it can only act on points of law brought forward by the appellants. In the 1970s, Carnevale became known as the 'sentence slayer' because of the frequency with which he reversed decisions of the lower courts, especially those involving Mafia. After the Maxi Trials, Andreotti would have arguably been saved from unfavourable Mafia attention if Carnevale had presided over the final appeals of the convicted mafiosi, but he didn't. Had that been the case, it is possible that the second Mafia would have still been active.

In 1999, Carnevale was charged with systematically seeking to acquit mafiosi on legal technicalities during his career in the Court of Cassation. In the first trial in Palermo, he was acquitted, but the prosecution appealed and he was found guilty and sentenced to six years' imprisonment for Mafia association. The verdict was given a cool reception in Rome and it astonished Carnevale, who had been so certain of a second acquittal that he had urged the court to give its verdict as soon as possible so as not to interfere with an application for promotion! His own Court of Cassation, however, quashed the sentence. After the verdict, Michele Vietti, Under-Secretary at the Justice Ministry, commented: 'Verdicts like the one on Carnevale do not help to increase the confidence of citizens in the institutions of Justice, which have never been at such a low level as today.' This, of course, suggests there is still suspicion in the highest places of his guilt, notwithstanding his acquittal. Such suspicions have not prejudiced Carnevale, however, who has now been returned to the Bench, aged 76.

34

SICILY TODAY

One of the most ghoulish sights in Palermo is that of the catacombs that lie under the Capuchin convent. More than 8,000 mummified corpses of the good and the great of the city from the sixteenth century to 1920 are displayed in what were once their best clothes. As you walk down the rows and rows of barons, bishops, doctors and lawyers, you can be sure that you are looking at some former mafiosi, who, in their grotesque poses, are still refusing to divulge their secrets.

One day in April 2004, I was sitting in the bleak piazza in which the convent is sited, reading my newspaper while the drug addicts took their afternoon siestas on the slabs outside, when I came across a small news item quoting a complaint from a member of a Mafia family near Agrigento. Diego Provenzani (no relation to Mafia *capo* Provenzano) had indicated that he did not appreciate that 'friends' wives had had to take cleaning jobs while their husbands were in jail. He went on to explain that such a thing detracted from the 'respect' that was due to the family of a 'friend'.

The mummies in the catacombs beneath my feet would also have understood and agreed with what he was saying, because to them someone at the top of any society, no matter how small, should not have to go out and wash stairs, clean houses or do someone else's ironing. To a Sicilian, this would equate to the very fabric of life being torn apart and should not happen, even in post-Falcone Sicily.

In Sicily, I use a driver – whom I shall call 'Salvatore' – who seems to know a lot of things that I presume ordinary drivers would not. I got him to drive me down to the small town that Provenzani was complaining about, Palma di Montechiaro, which lies about 20 kilometres east of Agrigento. No one from the tourist board has considered the possibility of marketing the town, even though it is close to some attractive beaches. The broken signpost that originally welcomed people to the town in five languages (two have been partially broken off) announces: 'Palma di Montechiaro, "Land of the Leopard"' (referring to Lampedusa's book and Visconti's film *The Leopard*). There are about 25,000 inhabitants, the impression you first get of the town is one of sadness and deprivation, the houses are colourless, the surrounding fields are covered in scrub and rock, and on the day of our visit even the sky was grey with a fine drizzle. In other words, it is a dump.

Provenzani was complaining that things had changed and that the outcome was unacceptable. The Mafia family was suffering, like all others, from the fallout of the Maxi Trials – many men in jail, less manpower to generate income, much of the former wealth confiscated or paid to lawyers, and what was left insufficient to provide the guarantee that every mafioso receives at his initiation, namely that if he goes to jail and doesn't talk, his family will be looked after and their standard of living preserved. Cleaning stairs is not part of the pact.

Pizzu was formerly only requested from people who ran businesses, but now not enough were earning sufficient money to pay up, there was a limit to the amount that could be demanded and there were not enough Mafia men to collect what was due. So, the rules had changed, and now everyone had to be approached. In Don Calogero's day, to have requested *pizzu* from the local doctor or lawyer would have merited the death sentence, but these professionals were now being targeted, not only in Palma di Montechiara, but in many other small towns.

In 2003, according to Carmelo Casabona, the police commissioner of Agrigento, there were 420 reported incidents of intimidation or damage in Palma di Montechiaro, which represented roughly one incident for every sixty people living in the town. This number of reports indicates that there is not as much fear of or support for the Mafia, because probably ten and certainly twenty years previously there would not have been a single complaint to the police.

To demonstrate the desperation of the local Mafia, the story of a local doctor is illustrative. The doctor, whom I shall not name, refused to pay money to provide for the comfort of his patients languishing in jail, and soon afterwards a fuse was found beside a gas cylinder on the doorstep of his seaside home.

Pensioners are another group that were formerly exempt from paying *pizzu*, but evidently no longer. One couple who live right in the middle of town heard their bell ring late one night. As the wife approached the door, she heard the crackle of flames and on opening it found it ablaze. They managed to put out the fire, but shortly afterwards received a phone call, which went as follows: 'It's the relatives of Mandarino . . . He only wanted a hundred euros . . . You said "No", so we made a little fire . . . Think we're joking?'

On the way back to Palermo, Salvatore and I chatted about present day Sicily and the apparent decline of the Mafia. I asked him what his opinion was. 'If Sicily was a plc, then it would be in receivership,' he said. 'The population is falling, no one wants to do business with us and because of the Mafia everything is more expensive here than on the mainland. Like lots of poor places in the world, those with get up and go got up and went, so the gene pool that remains is weak and the Mafia has had an uncomplaining client base. There's no investment, because if you do business in Sicily, you know you'll be screwed. You'll get dud goods, you'll not get paid or heavies will arrive on your doorstep in six months' time, demanding you make another order for things you neither want nor need.'

I disagreed with him about investment and cited the high-tech development in the Etna valley area and the container terminal at Gioia Tauro in Calabria. 'That all went to 'Ndrangheta, not us,' he said dismissively.

When Salvatore brought up the subject of 'Ndrangheta, I was not too surprised, because I had repeatedly met the same response in my researches – namely that the important people now came from Calabria and not Sicily.

The organisation's origins were contemporaneous with the Sicilian Mafia in the first half of the nineteenth century and took the same form of a mutual-aid society in a place where there was an absent State. It is centred in the village of San Luca in the Aspromonte mountain chain in the province of Reggio Calabria, the same place where, in 1862, Garibaldi was shot in the leg by the Piedmontese Army when he was leading a revolt against their occupation of the area.

It is likely that most of the males in San Luca are in 'Ndrangheta, and they meet more openly than the Mafia in their headquarters of the Sanctuary of Polsi. Power is centred on San Luca, and any new *cosca* must ask permission from the parent family to start up in business; there is no such 'centralisation' in Sicily. A new group is called a *locale*, and, similar to new outfits in the Mafia, they must pass a percentage of their profits upwards to the parent family in San Luca. The 'Ndrangheta relies far more than the Mafia on blood relations when recruiting so that in most instances it is difficult to unravel blood ties from 'Ndrangheta ties.

Like Arabia, Calabria is a male-oriented society, so a married couple must produce sons rather than daughters – the more sons, the more manpower in your *cosca*. An illustration of the importance of this comes from the vendetta between two families from the small town of Sidemo on the Greek side of Calabria, which started because of a dispute over the ownership of some guns. Between 1987 and 1991, thirty-four males from the two families were killed. In Berlin during the summer of 2007, six youths from a family working in Germany were shot after a birthday party as part of another vendetta.

Women have the same place in 'Ndrangheta society as they did in the old Mafia. Their role is to be perfect mothers, stay at home, produce sons, have no affairs, let their husbands have freedom and stay silent. But things are changing even in that society.

In Calabria in May 2004, a 25-year-old housewife informed on her husband and his friends, leading to 90 arrests. She said that she was tired of the vendettas and murders being planned around her kitchen table and that she wanted a new life for herself and her children. Her testimony led to the solving of eighteen murders, including one of an entire family – husband, wife and three sons aged seventeen, sixteen and five – whose bodies were dismembered and fed to pigs. She also told of a husband and wife being shot dead in front of their two autistic children. She and her four children were given new identities and relocated.

In Sicily in April 2005, a mother of three turned state's evidence after being arrested with her husband. She claimed that her reason for abandoning her Mafia life was that she was sickened by the violence. She knew that if her children remained in that environment, they would inevitably join their father and end up dead or in prison. She, like many other wives who have become informers, was tired of having her house act as a crime headquarters and weapons dump, with her laundry being used for the planning of murders because the house was probably bugged. As an example of what her life was like, she told of how her husband even expected *pizzu* from her father who owned a discotheque, but when a sacked bouncer burned it down in revenge for his dismissal, her husband gave her father a nice present – he had the bouncer killed!

The largest 'Ndrangheta family is the Piromalli cosca, which has more than 200 men operating in the Gioia Tauro area near the new container port that was established with EC money in 1994 and grew to be the biggest in the Mediterranean by 1998. It was an $86-million investment and moves more than two million containers per year. It is now completely controlled by the Piromalli family, since the majority of the workforce are 'Ndrangheta placements.

There are also suspected strong links with east European crime groups.

But 'Ndgrangheta did not escape the crackdown on organised crime and corruption in the 1990s. In January 1999, the Reggio Calabria court handed down 62 life sentences and another 141 sentences that amounted to more than 1,380 years of imprisonment. In the same year, in the Tirreno Maxi Trials in Palmi, 89 of the 99 defendants received life sentences. As importantly, properties worth more than $88 million and goods to the value of $24 million were appropriated, making the total assets seized since 1998 over $900 million.

I talked to Salvatore again after Provenzano was captured. He had never subscribed to the view that Provenzano was dead. I asked him why, because up until then no one had admitted to setting eyes on him since 1963. 'If he had died, the police would have created a set-up as they did with Salvatore Giuliani 60 years ago, claiming that their superb intelligence had uncovered his hiding place and that he had been shot whilst resisting arrest.'

When Provenzano was caught, Salvatore said, 'He was always going to be taken in. The only unknown was the timing. The only thing that surprises me is that he was taken alive, because he has the whole history of the Mafia at the end of his tongue, and a lot of politicians will be very worried'

One of the first things Berlusconi did when he came to power in 2000 was to resurrect the idea of building the biggest bridge in the world, which would run from Messina to the mainland, thus joining Sicily to Italy for the first time. To my surprise, the vast majority of Sicilians were in favour of this. It was, however, an unlikely dream – not because of the technology involved (Japanese engineers have solved all the potential problems), but because of the Mafia/'Ndgrangheta involvement.

Berlusconi initially appointed a Parma builder, Pietro Lunardi, as Minister for Infrastructure and Road Building, and after looking at the proposals for a few months, he said, 'One needs to get along with the Mafia and the 'Ndrangheta. Everyone should resolve problems of criminality as they see fit. The Mafia has always existed and always will.' Later, he was quoted as saying, 'We are forced to live with the Mafia, as well as other realities, like, for example, the 7,000 killed on the roads.'

No one was very surprised, therefore, when on 11 February 2005 the anti-Mafia group announced at a press conference that they had uncovered a plot by organised crime to control the selection of the building consortium. At the head was Vito Rizzuto, the *capo* of the Montreal Mafia family that had at one time been an offshoot of the New York Bonanno family.

Since the verdicts of the Maxi Trials were confirmed in 1992, there has been a gradual disablement of the Sicilian Mafia, and the present situation bears comparison to the 1930s when Mussolini sent Cesare Mori to Sicily to wipe out the Mafia and Freemasonry. The weapons of today are not imprisonment without trial plus or minus physical violence, but two changes in the legal process: the Mafia Association Law and the admission of evidence from informers who were then subsequently given new identities, which have enabled trials to be concluded and convictions obtained without reliance on witnesses or juries.

In 'business' terms, the loss of their influential role in the drug trade and the huge profits they made was disastrous because it was that income that oiled the wheels of Italian politics, enabling the Mafia to ensure their own protection. They had made the mistake latterly of relying too much on drug dealing, had not diversified enough and for too long they had been a one-product organization. Their predecessors made their money from building, persuading government to give their acolytes contracts for major works and the traditional *pizzu* from businesses. In America, the main activities of Cosa Nostra were labour racketeering, loan sharking, gambling and extortion, but Sicilian workers had never become sufficiently unionised for the Mafia to exert profitable control over the workforce and thus the cities as their American cousins were able to do.

The most profitable of the illegal markets today is the smuggling of humans for their exploitation in the sex industry and the 'black economy'. There has been a long-term antipathy to organised prostitution in Sicily and not enough industry or work for a thriving black economy dependent on illegal immigrants. Unable to diversify their personnel out of the drug industry and without the contacts or skills for arms dealing or people smuggling, they have had to fall back on local extortion and getting what they can from increasingly tightly controlled government disbursements to the South.

From the earliest days of rigging elections in Piedmontese-occupied Sicily, the Mafia realised that as well as offering 'protection' to local businesses it too required protection from the judiciary. They achieved this by having their people elected and 'friends' placed in strategic public positions. After the war, this requirement for protection spread wider and was provided initially by the Christian Democrat Party and latterly by the socialists prior to the *Tangentopoli* scandal in the 1990s. The basis of the cooperation was that some of the drug-industry profits were laundered into political party funds with some, no doubt, passing into the pockets of important politicians.

In chapter 11, we saw what Pisciotta, the cousin who killed Salvatore Giuliano and who was poisoned by strychnine in prison, said at his trial, 'We are a single body – bandits, police and the Mafia – like the Father, Son and Holy Ghost.' In the subsequent years, politicians took the place of the 'bandits'.

When Italian Party politics imploded in the 1990s and the Christian Democrat leader, Andreotti, retired, the Mafia tried to infiltrate and influence Forza Italia. At first they were optimistic, because of Berlusconi's earlier links with some mafiosi; however, because of his wider power and wealth, Berlusconi did not require a Mafia crutch, and gradually the protection of the past was removed, ending in the recent mass arrests that have followed on from the capture of Provenzano. With the new laws allowing bugging and tapping to be used in evidence, the witness-protection scheme and the admissibility of informer testimony, convictions have become possible, and mopping up the remaining Godfathers will be relatively easy. This century has seen the first government since Mussolini to have shown the will to wipe out the Mafia, because they are a blight on Sicilian investment, a block to the construction of a vitally important bridge and a stain that Berlusconi needs to wipe out. All that is needed to complete the culling is the will and strength of the ordinary Sicilian to resist paying *pizzu*. There are positive signs that this is happening, but that is perhaps going to be the last and most difficult step.

EPILOGUE

After a decade of studying the organisation known as the Mafia, I find myself in agreement with those Sicilians who told me, even before I started researching, that the criminals who ruled the roost for the second half of the twentieth century and who were glamorised in the *Godfather* films were not the Mafia and had nothing to do with the original organisation. They were people who had come from a Mafia background who were erroneously using the horse of tradition as a convenience to draw the cart of illegal profiteering. And yet this is 'denied' over and over again in informer testimony, with 'our cause' or something similar being continually referred to.

Certainly, the Mafia started out both with an aim and a 'cause', which was to supplement local governance abandoned by an absent State and to help the deserving poor. Just as a State would expect its citizens to pay taxes, so did the original Mafia ask for contributions from those it protected from rural anarchy. It was this role as a protector that allowed it to gain support from the ruling aristocrats and become a universally accepted way of life.

The Mafia started about 80 years after modern Freemasonry spread like wildfire throughout Europe; there are many similarities between the organisations. Fraternity and equality mean that both are open to people from all levels of society and once initiated all are equal. The most seminal moment in the development of the Mafia was the liberation of Sicily by Garibaldi, who was not only funded by Freemasons but rose soon after to become Italy's Grand Master.

But while Freemasonry grew to become an estimable world-wide movement, what went wrong with the Mafia? Basically, it was the acceptance of violence, at first in family feuds or vendettas about status, money or both, and later the enforcement of higher taxes (*pizzu*) that caused its downward spiral into outright criminality.

Italians love secret societies. The shock discovery of the P2 Lodge was matched only by the intense curiosity and titillation felt by the public that such a thing could exist. It is easy, therefore, to understand why Italy has more Grand Lodges than any other country in Europe, and the influence of their rather aberrant form of Freemasonry is as powerful in present-day Italy as it was in pre-war Britain.

Prior to the shooting wars of the 1980s, I think that many Italians, whether professionals or business people, would have welcomed an invitation to be initiated into the Mafia. When I sat on the General Medical Council, we were told that roughly 4 per cent of doctors could be expected to have problems with either competence or integrity. It would be from a group such as this that the Mafia would have imported its professional expertise – people who wanted something that they, like aspiring gangsters, lacked in their professional lives: respect.

'Respect' is defined in the OED as deferential regard or esteem, and it is the sort of emotion one might feel for a school teacher, a professional adviser or a sporting hero. But that is not what is meant by 'respect' in Mafia circles. I have seen this in a jail near to where I live in Italy. Along with a number of low-grade mafiosi, there is a *capo* from another area. He is short and has no aspect of menace about him, but in his presence the others freeze in a way that reminds me of the days when I was an attending surgeon to Sadaam Hussein and Dr Hastings Banda of Malawi. It is not the sort of fear that might be engendered by a monster such as Idi Amin; it is a fear accompanied by love and adulation.

So what now? Will the 2008 arrests allow another Provenzano to persuade the organisation to lie low for another decade so that it might one day rise again? Almost certainly not. The original criminal activities have been taken over by the Camorra, 'Ndrangheta and Eastern Europeans and will not be recoverable. At the same time, the new Italian government has demonstrated a determination not seen since the days of Mussolini to eliminate both the organisation and with it the embarrassments that it has caused to people in high places.

And what will happen then in law-abiding Sicilian society? Perhaps yet another Grand Lodge will emerge.

NOTES

1: Why the Mafia Developed

The definitive two-volume *History of Sicily* was written by the late Denis Mack Smith. The second volume, entitled *Modern Sicily (after 1713)*, was most useful in my research.

Much has been written about Garibaldi and the unification of Italy, but I have relied mainly on Trevelyan's *Garibaldi and the Making of Italy* (1920), Riall's *Sicily and the Unification of Italy* (1998) and, for light relief, *The Garibaldians in Sicily* (1861), a very readable but romanticised book by Alexandre Dumas.

Anton Blok wrote two very helpful articles in the journal *Comparative Studies in Society and History*, 'South Italian Agro Towns' (1969) and 'The Peasant and the Brigand' (1972). Much of what he wrote was brought together in his 1974 book *The Mafia of a Sicilian Village*.

Franchetti's famous report on the Mafia, a virtually unknown entity in 1876 when he wrote it, was reprinted in 1925 as *La Sicilia nel 1876*.

Two more modern books give helpful insights into the structure of Mafia families, Gambetta's *The Sicilian Mafia* (1993) and Paoli's *Mafia Brotherhoods* (2003).

2: What the Mafia Had to Offer

Evidence from the proceedings of Salvatore Contorno's interrogation.

The British vote-rigging scandal was reported on BBC News on 13 April 2005.

Other sources for this chapter include Gambetta, *The Sicilian Mafia* (1993); Blok, *The Mafia of a Sicilian Village* (1974); De Stefano and Oddo, *Storia della Sicilia dal 1860 al 1910* (1963); and Bloch, *Feudal Society* (1961).

3: An Offer Not to Be Refused

Vincent Cafaro's quote comes from Jacobs et al., *Busting the Mob* (1994).

Girolama Lo Verso's work on what he learned from Mafia defectors with psychological problems was published in *Psychoanalytic Psychology* in 2004.

A great deal is now available in scientific literature about the nature of psychopathy because of the advent of special types of MR imaging. I have used two articles in the main, both published in *Biological Psychiatry* (2004 and 2005), written by Raine et al. and Yang et al.

There have been many descriptions of the Mafia initiation ceremony, but I have relied on one of the best, from John Dickie's excellent *Cosa Nostra* (2004).

I was told of the story of Antonio Labate and checked it in his trial proceedings from 1984 at the court in Reggio Calabria.

4: Portrait of a Godfather

I became interested in Don Calogero on reading about him in John Dickie's *Cosa Nostra* (2004). I went to Villalba and talked to those who would talk to me. I was also helped by a GP who works in a nearby town but wishes to remain anonymous.

I do not know if Guiseppe Amico is still alive, but he was such an admirer of the don that I am sure he will not mind being named.

5: A Republic Within a Kingdom

The facts about the conditions in Sicily that led to emigration, the statistics of emigration and the politics of the early unified Italy come from Denis Mack Smith, *Modern Sicily (after 1713)*, published in 1968.

The effect of the abolition of feudalism was described in two articles from *Comparative Studies in Society and History*, both by Blok: 'South Italian Agro Towns' (1969) and 'The Peasant and the Brigand' (1972).

The life of the peasant is also well represented in the report written by Sidney Sonnino in 1879 entitled '*I contadini in Sicilia*', which includes an interview with the Baron Turrisi Colonna.

The latter's role was also expanded by one of his descendants, N. Turrisi Colonna, who wrote *Pubblica sicurezza in Sicilia nel 1864*, published in 1988.

The conditions behind the 1866 riots were described by Maurici in *La genesi storica della rivolta del 1866 in Palermo* (1916).

6: Exodus to L'America

There have been many descriptions both academic and non-academic on the subject of chain emigration, but the one I am most familiar with because it relates to British Italians is Dr Terri Colpi's *The Italian Factor* (1991).

The stories about the emigration to New Orleans are well known and many authors have written about the murder of David Hennessy and the subsequent lynchings. I have relied on Short, *Murder Inc* (2003); English, *Paddy Whacked* (2005); and Gambino, *Vendetta* (1977).

My information on the history of Tammany Hall comes from Allen, *The Tiger: The Rise and Fall of Tammany Hall* (1993).

Herbert Asbury wrote about nineteenth-century gangs in many American cities and I have referred to his book *The Gangs of New York* (1928). For further information on the Black Hand Gang, I referred to Pitkin, *The Black Hand: A Chapter in Ethnic Crime* (1977).

The story of Joe Petrosino has been written about by many writers, but perhaps the best I read was Petacco, *Joe Petrosino* (2001).

7: Mussolini and the Mafia

The most recent book about Il Duce, *Mussolini* (2005), was written by M. Clark, Professor Emeritus of Italian history in Edinburgh, and I have used it, as well as the other older texts.

Denis Mack Smith's successor as one of the premier Italian historians in the UK, Christopher Duggan, wrote *Fascism and the Mafia* (1989) and I found it a great help to understanding.

Pasquale Squittieri made a film about Cesare Mori in 1977 entitled *Prefetto di Ferro,* based on a book by Arrigo Petacco of the same title, published in 1975.

I also referred to Blinkhorn, *Mussolini and Fascist Italy* (1984).

8: Prohibition and Profits

I enjoyed the first book I read about the Prohibition years more than any I have read since. Allsop's *The Bootleggers* (1961) acts as the foundation of what I know about the period.

Kobler wrote two excellent books that have filled in gaps in my knowl-edge: *The Life and World of Al Capone* (1971) and *Ardent Spirits* (1973).

Background about Chicago came from Asbury's *Gem of the Prairie: An Informal History of the Chicago Underworld* (1940).

The story of Joe Valachi was first told by Peter Maas in *The Valachi Papers* (1968), which was later published in Britain as *The Canary That Sang* (1970).

Other books that I referred to were Nelli, *Italians in Chicago: A Study of Ethnic Mobility* (1970); Fried, *The Rise and Fall of the Jewish Gangster in America* (1980); and Reppetto, *American Mafia* (2004).

9: Crime Gets Organised

I referred to Reppetto, *American Mafia* (2004) and Raab, *Five Families* (2005) for details on the meetings between 1928 and 1931 that resulted in crime in America becoming organised.

I also referred to Short, *Murder Inc* (2003) and Downey, *Gangster City: The History of the New York Underworld 1900–1935* (2004).

10: Liberation, American-Style

For details about the preparation for the invasion of Sicily by the American Army and the part played by the Mafia and US Naval Intelligence, I referred to many popular books, but the most detailed is Campbell, *The Luciano Project: The Secret Wartime Collaboration of the Mafia and the US Navy* (1977).

For details of the interface between the Mafia and the American liberators, I found the most credible source to be Caruso, *Arrivano I nostri* (*Our Guys Have Come*), published in 2004.

The story of yellow handkerchiefs, low-flying aeroplanes and American tanks taking Don Calogero to Palermo came from Lewis, *The Honoured Society* (1964).

Although the story of Antonio Canepa is well documented, I referred to Gaja, *The Army of the Lupara* (1990).

11: Salvatore Giuliano

For the classic story of Salvatore Giuliano, I reminded myself of the details by reading Maxwell's *God Protect Me From My Friends* (1957) and its fictional equivalent, Puzo's *The Sicilian* (1984).

As well as reading Guiseppe Giuliano's privately published memoir, *My Brother Salvatore Giuliano* (2000), I interviewed him at his hotel, named after his uncle.

For details of the deaths of Giuliano and also Pisciotta, there is some detail that is of rather dubious provenance in the Anti-Mafia Commission Report on Mafia and Politics (1993).

Some of the background to the killing of Communist mayors in 1947 was gained from interviews with Nino Miraglia, the son of Accursio Miraglia, one of the mayors killed, and also a thesis written by Accursio's grandson, Francesco Miraglia, in 1999 entitled *'Movimento contadino nella Sicilia del Secondo Dopoguerra'* ('The Peasant Movement in the Post-War Years').

12: The Unholy Alliance

For a better understanding of the competing agendas of post-war Italy, I referred to Ginsborg, *A History of Contemporary Italy* (1990), but much of what I've written is from personal experiences and observations of the time.

Mangold wrote an excellent biography of James Angleton entitled *Cold War Warrior* (1991).

Williams, in his book *The Vatican Exposed* (2003), described the so-called rat-runs and the role of the Vatican in providing help to those seeking to leave the war arena.

The quote from Pope John Paul's 1993 speech in Agrigento was taken from *L'Osservatore Romano*, 10 May 1993.

The role of the Mafia in these years is described in Lodato, *Quindici anni di Mafia* (*Fifteen Years of the Mafia*), published in 1994.

13: The Mafia Comes to the City

In *Cosa Nostra* (2004), Dickie gave a very clear and accurate account of post-war Sicily. I had the opportunity of confirming much of the information during interviews with people I had been introduced to in Palermo, some of whom were professional men and some who were not, but none of whom wished to be identified.

The comment of Vittorio Nistico in *L'Ora* I took from Fentress, *Rebels and Mafiosi* (2000), because I could not get access to the primary source.

14: The American Cosa Nostra

The story of Chile Acuna came from English, *Paddy Whacked* (2005).

The details on Meyer Lansky came from his biography by Messick, *Lansky* (1971) and English, *The Havana Mob* (2007).

The episodes involving Dutch Schultz are set out at length in Sann, *Kill the Dutchman: The Story of Dutch Schultz*.

For further information about Jimmy Hoffa and the Mafia, I referred to Moldea, *The Hoffa Wars: Teamsters, Rebels, Politicians and the Mob* (1978).

15: How the Mafia Moved on to Drugs

There are a number of texts that purport to tell the story of Lucky Luciano, but none of them are reliable because Luciano was a secretive Sicilian, not given to public confession. Klerks's *Lucky Luciano: The Father of Organised Crime* (2005) is unreferenced and, while near the truth, is probably journalistic rather than academic.

Gosch and Hammer claimed that Luciano had confessed all to them before he died, but the veracity of this has been questioned; however, *The Last Testament of Lucky Luciano* has been widely quoted.

The remarkable American reporter Claire Sterling went into the dragon's den and interviewed Luciano, writing an article in 1957 for *The Reporter* entitled 'The Boys Who Did Bad'.

Luciano and drugs are mentioned in Kessler, *The Bureau: The Secret History of the FBI* (2002) and English, *The Havana Mob* (2007).

Finally, I make reference to the findings of the Kefauver Committee that Estes Kefauver put into book form in 1951 as *Crime in America.*

16: Lucky Luciano's Summit

Although Lucky Luciano's summit meeting in Palermo is described in almost every Mafia book, there are very few original references to the event that actually bear scrutiny. This is not surprising because it was meant to be a very secret event. Some evidence comes from the interrogation of Tomasso Buscetta by Falcone in 1984, but there is little else other than the descriptions in all other similar books.

I quote from Joe Bonanno's autobiography *A Man of Honour* (1983), but in my view this is unreliable.

Some of the statistics I refer to came from the Findings of the McClennan Committee, 4 March 1965.

My own visit and the background supplied by various interviews with Palermitani fill in the rest of the chapter.

17: How the French Connection Became Sicilian

The early history of cigarette smuggling and the Marseille outfit came from Panteleone, *Mafia e droge* (1966) and Claire Sterling's seminal work on the Mafia, *Octopus* (1990).

The Kintex connection was alluded to in a statement by J. Lawn on 7 July 1984 to the House of Representatives Foreign Affairs Committee.

As well as *Octopus*, Sterling also wrote about the Bulgarian connection in 1984 in *The Time of the Assassins.*

Information on Aruba comes from *Corriere della Sera*, 14 March 1993, and the reference to the Venezuelans arrested in Rome also from *Corriere della Sera*, 28 February 2005.

The early references to the Cuntrera–Caruana families come from Stajano, *Mafia: L'atto d'accusa dei giudici di Palermo* [*Mafia: Indictment by the Palermo Judiciary*] (1986). Later references to these families are from Sterling, *Octopus*, and Lamothe and Humphreys, *The Sixth Family* (2006).

Francesco Di Carlo's initial conviction was noted in the *Evening Standard*, 12 March 1987, and the conviction of Michelangelo Aiello in *Corriere della Sera* on 14 September 1988.

The arrest of the Cuntreras in Rome was shown on BBC's *Panorama* on 27 September 1992 and the stories about Alfonso Gagliano were on CBS News, 18 November 2004.

18: The First Cracks Appear

For facts about the Ciaculli bomb, which I either did not know or had been told about in interviews, I referred to Sterling, *Octopus* (1990). The background to the bomb was revealed by Tomasso Buscetta when he was interviewed by Falcone and details can be accessed in the documents 'Interrogation of Tomasso Buscetta' in Palermo.

I referred to a book about Buscetta by Biagi, *Il boss e solo* (1986) and also Pantaleone, *Mafia e droga* (1966).

A good source of material about the Camorra is Behan, *See Naples and Die: The Camorra and Organised Crime* (2002).

19: Corleone – The Mafia Heartland

The story of Dr Navarra was told by Dalla Chiesa in *Michele Navarra e la Mafia Corleonese* (1990) and the attempts to socialise land by Bernardino Verro are documented by Anselmo, *La terra promessa* (1989). The period is also well described in Sterling, *Octopus* (1990) and Dickie, *Cosa Nostra* (2004).

20: How the Mafia Laundered Money

The sources for this chapter came from my own knowledge of the way banks function in Italy and some secondary sources, namely Sterling, *Octopus* (1990) and *The Terror Network* (1981). A lot of information came from Di Fonzon, *St Peter's Banker* (1983) and Tosches, *Power on Earth* (1986).

There was a long review article on Michele Sindona in the *Sunday Times* on 27 January 1980, and another on the help that he got – or tried to get – from Licio Gelli in *La Stampa*, 3 October 1982. Much of what Sindona was accused of was in the warrant for his arrest, issued by the magistrate Giuliano Turone on 22 October 1982; listed among these alleged crimes were arranging his false kidnap, and threatening Giorgio Ambrosoli and Ciccio Cuccia.

The taped telephone conversation between the unknown caller and Ambrosoli was printed in *Corriere della Sera* on 20 May 1984.

21: Why the Vatican Needed a Bank

For the history of the Vatican from earliest times to the signing of the Lateran Treaty, I relied mainly on four sources: Williams, *The Vatican Exposed* (2003); J. Cornwell, *Hitler's Pope* (1999); Reese, *Inside the Vatican* (1996); and Malachi, *Rich Church, Poor Church* (1984).

The quote by Cardinal Spellman about Bernardino Nogara came from Yallop, *In God's Name* (1984).

Stories about Bishop Marcinkus abound. He was used as a model for Bishop Frantisek in Morris West's book *The Salamander* (1973) and useful information can also be found in Willan, *Puppetmasters: The Political Use of Terrorism in Italy* (1991).

22: The Death of a Pope

My sources for everything up until Pope John Paul I's death were Williams, *The Vatican Exposed* (2003); De Rosa, *Vicars of Christ* (1988); and Manhattan, *Murder in the Vatican* (1985).

The policy of the Catholic Church in the 1970s was set out by O'Brien and Shannon, *Renewing the Earth: Catholic Documents of Peace, Justice and Liberation* (1977).

The only description of the last day in the life of Pope John Paul I is in Yallop, *In God's Name* (1984). Unfortunately, Yallop does not list his sources and any descriptions of the Pope's death here merely mirror what he wrote unreferenced. As it stands, it is only speculation that the Pope was actually murdered – but it was possible.

23: Propaganda Massonica Due

The story of Roberto Calvi has been told in many articles, TV programmes and two major books to which I have referred. Cornwell, R., *God's Banker* (1983) is unfortunately not referenced, but Gurwin, *The Calvi Affair: Death of a Banker* (1983) is well researched and referenced. Two other books give a larger picture of the period and the other strange happenings: DiFonzon, *St Peter's Banker* (1983) and Piazzesi, *Gelli: La carriera di un eroe di questa Italia* (1983).

I have referred constantly to Sterling, *The Terror Network* (1981) and *Octopus* (1990).

Barberi et al. wrote about P2 and the aftermath of its discovery in *L'Italia della P2* (1981).

The information about the Pope choosing Michele Sindona to be financial advisor was in *La Stampa* on 25 July 1982.

Roberto Rosone's career was summarised in *Corriere della Sera* on 28 April 1982 and his shooting was reported in *La Repubblica* on 13 July 1982. On 26 July, the same paper wrote about Calvi's morbid fear of jail.

The texts of the letters from Marcinkus were printed in *The Observer* on 23 January 1983.

The loans to the Socialist Party, which were denied by Craxi, were shown to probably be true in an article in *L'Espresso* on 3 July 1983.

24: The Man Who Duped the Vatican

Much of the Calvi story has been recycled in the press of most European countries and everyone will know who is referred to when the words 'God's Banker' are mentioned. I referred to many articles, but in particular those featured in *La Stampa* on 30 December 1982 (for its description of Calvi's flight to England) and on 21 June 1982 (for the letter left by Calvi's secretary before she committed suicide) were informative. On 15 September 1982, *La Stampa* offered a good description of Calvi's attempted disguise. Much of this was also summarised in a BBC *Panorama* edition aired on 5 July 1982.

The Flavio Carboni tapes were quoted in *Panorama* magazine on 15 August 1982 and Silvano Vittor revealed his part in the death during his interrogation by Domenico Sica on 24 June 1982.

The first Coroner's Inquest of 23 July 1982 was read, as well as the second of 13–27 June 1983. The taped conversations between Calvi and Carboni were described in *L'Espresso* on 22 August 1982 and Carboni's arrest in Switzerland was described in *Corriere della Sera* on 1 August 1982.

There was a good article on the failure of the clerical career of Bishop Marcinkus as a result of the scandal in *The Guardian* of 6 January 1983.

Finally, many papers reported the trial of Carboni and the others in Rome in 2004 and useful references can be found in various editions of *The Independent* at that time, especially 10 May 2004 and 7 June 2007.

25: Death of God's Banker

My primary source for this material was the well-known Masonic historian Yasha Beresiner. Some of the information he gave me he had previously set down in a book, *Masonic Curiosities* (2000).

The reference to Garibaldi can be found in 'Transactions of the Quator Coronati Lodge of Research' under Garibaldi: Freemason (1989). The full list of members of P2 was published in Flamigni, *Trame atlantiche* (1996), and the parliamentary inquiry was authored by Tina Anselmi in *Commissione parliamentare d'inchiesta sulla Loggia massonica P2* (1984). This information was amplified by reference to Cecchi, *La Storia della P2* (1985) and Barbieri et al., *L'Italia della P2* (1981).

Very little has been written about Licio Gelli (which is not at all surprising) but an attempt was made by Piazzesi in *Gelli: La carriera di un eroe di questa Italia* (1983) – an ironic title if ever there was one. Gelli was interviewed by Constanzo in 1980, who reported his views in *Corriere della Sera* on 5 October 1990.

The information about Forlani locking up the P2 lists in his desk came from *L'Europea*, 1 June 1981.

Information on the background to Italy at the time was found in Ginsborg, *Italy and its Discontents* (2001).

26: The Mafia Civil War

The letters to the judges in the Bari trial are well documented, but I chose to refer to Poma and Perrone, *La Mafia: Nonni e nipoti* (1971).

The psychological background to the threats of Riina to the others becomes clear from the interrogations of Tomasso Buscetta.

When Giovanni Brusca describes how many men he has killed, I referred to Dickie, *Cosa Nostra* (2004), and similarly for the description of Provenzano by Luciano Leggio.

The facts about the Death Chamber at Piazza Sant'Erasmo came from the interrogation of Vincento Singona in Palermo in 1986.

The best description of Leggio versus Buscetta in the Maxi Trials is in Arlacchi, *Addio Cosa Nostra* (1994).

27: The Magistrates

For the Pio La Torre and Dalla Chiesa period, I relied heavily on Nando Dalla Chiesa, *Delitto Imperfetto* (1984) and Stajano, *Mafia: L'atto d'accusa dei giudici di Palermo* (1986).

Alberto Dalla Chiesa's meeting with the American Consul in Palermo was reported in the *Wall Street Journal* on 12 February 1985.

The assassinations of Boris Giuliano, Emanuele Basile and Cesare Terranova are best described in *Excellent Cadavers* (1995) by the well-known Italian-American writer Alexander Stille.

The life story of Giovanni Falcone was told by La Licata in the appropriately titled *Storia di Giovanni Falcone* (2002).

The Cassara report, known as Greco+161, was published on 13 July 1982 in Palermo.

Antonio Caponetto wrote about his experiences in Palermo in *I miei giorni a Palermo* (1992).

28: The Breakthrough

The outcome of Falcone's interrogation of Tomasso Buscetta, which took place between 16 July and 12 September 1984, can be accessed in Palermo. Excerpts have been used in many books about the Mafia since that time, especially those written by Claire Sterling, Alexander Stille and Emilio Biagi.

Evidence relating to the assets of Major Key was presented to the Drug Enforcement Agency by M. Ewell in December 1983.

The best descriptions of the events leading up to the so-called Pizza Connection Trial are in Alexander, *The Pizza Connection* (1988) and Lamothe and Humphreys, *The Sixth Family* (2006).

Leonardo Sciascia published his criticisms of the magistrates in *La Sicilia come metafore* (1979).

29: Revenge

In *I miei giorni a Palermo*, Antonio Caponetto's reminiscences of his time in Palermo, he quoted Paolo Borsellino's remark about Falcone's disappointment at Meli beating him for Caponetto's job.

Domenico Sica telling the government that it had lost control over the southern half of Italy was reported in *Corriere della Sera* on 2 December 1986.

Falcone's suspicion that Andreotti knew about the bomb on the beach from the start was stated in his book with Padovani, *Cose di Cosa Nostra* (1991).

Much of the information about Borsellino's time in Marsala comes from Lucenti, *Paolo Borsellino: Il valore di una vita* (1994).

I have referred to the newspaper *La Repubblica* for four events: Domenico Sica being politically damaged (28 July 1986); Martelli rearresting the mafiosi who were about to be released as a result of Carnevale's judgment (23 May 1991); Falcone's murder (24 May 1992); and Rita Atria's suicide (22 July 1992).

30: The Politicians

The tragic story of General Dalla Chiesa has been told many times, but for this chapter I relied on *Morte di un Generale* (1982) by P. Arlacchi. I referred to Alexander Stille's latest book, *The Sack of Rome*, for details of President Cossiga's behaviour and outbursts.

For information on Andreotti's background, I relied on M. Franco, *Andreotti visto da vicino* (1993); Alexander Stille, *Excellent Cadavers* (1996); L. Sciascia, *The Moro Affair* (1978); and Margaret Thatcher's reminiscences in *The Downing Street Years* (1993). For Andreotti's various trials, I referred to N. Tranfaglia, *La Sentenza Andreotti* (2001), court proceedings against Francesco Marino Mannoia (1986, Palermo) and *La Repubblica* of 2 October 2002.

31: War on the State

For background, I used contemporary newspapers, I conducted personal interviews with people in Palermo about their memories and I relied on the published testimony of informers, especially that of Giovanni Brusca: Lodato, *Ho ucciso Giovanni falcone: La confessione di Giovanni Brusca* (2006). The testimony of Salvatore Cancemi, *Deposizione al processo d'appello per la strage di Capaci* (1999), was also consulted. Saverio Lodato has published much else about this era, and I have used Rizzoli, *Trent'anni di Mafia* (2006), and a book he wrote with Marco Travaglio, the investigative journalist, *Intoccabili* (2005). I also consulted John Follain's *The Last Godfathers* (2008), which included much detail about the post-Maxi Trials years.

32: Pax Mafiosa

Much of the information about Provenzano comes from the testimony of his right-hand man, Nino Giuffre, and I have relied on his depositions of 2002, 2003 and 2006, entitled respectively *Deposizione al procedimento penale N124/97, etc.*, *Deposizione al processo di appello a carico di Salvatore Biondino* and finally *Deposizione al processo di assise a carico di Rizzo Rosolino* (Palermo, 2009).

The details of the mopping-up operations and later arrests were taken from contemporary newspaper reports.

33: Berlusconi and the Mafia

There is so much gossip and unsubstantiated rumour about Berlusconi's possible Mafia associations that I have tried to be totally objective and have stuck to facts that are in the public domain, most of which have emerged from the trial of his closest associate, Marcello Dell'Utri. The proceedings of this trial are in *L'Onore di Dell'Utri: I Legami del Berlusconiano Marcello Dell'Utri con Cosa Nostra, nella Richesta di Rinvio a giudizio per Concorso in Associazione Mafiosa* (Procura della Reppublica di Palermo 1997–2004).

The number of kidnappings in Milan was quoted from *Il Giornale* from 15 March 2002.

Travaglio is not one of Berlusconi's favourite people and there have been numerous challenges to the book he wrote with Veltri, *L'odore dei soldi* (2001), which states facts that are sensational and also challenged by Berlusconi and his supporters but which have never been disproved in court.

A similar book, again challenged by Berlusconi, was written by two investigative journalists, Giovanni Ruggeri and Mario

Guarino, entitled *Berlusconi: Inchiesta sul Signor TV* (1994), in which they suggested that Berlusconi's initial funding was from the Mafia.

Francesco Giuffrida, a Bank of Italy investigator, gave evidence at the Dell'Utri trial that implicated Berlusconi with the Mafia (6 February 2002).

The meeting between Giuffrida and Berlusconi at the Chigi palace was reported in *La Repubblica* on 6 and 28 November 2002.

Antonio Giuffre's evidence at the Dell'Utri trial, which I have referred to, was given on 6 February 2002.

The drafting incident involving Antonio Mormino was reported in *La Repubblica* on 18 January 2003. For the events involving Judge Carnevale, I have referred to *Corriere della Sera* of 30 June and 1 November 2001.

34: Sicily Today

In this chapter, I have referred to one of the many men (who might have been a 'man of honour') to whom I was introduced in Sicily. I have called him 'Salvatore', but that of course is not his real name; he has a wife and family and enjoys football!

The remarks of Nino Guiffre, that the Mafia would need time to recover, came from *Panorama*, 17 March 2005. What Ignazio de Francisi said at the conference was reported in *L'Independente* on 15 October 1996.

My journey to Palma di Montechiaro was stimulated by an article in *La Repubblica* published on 20 April 2004.

My information about the 'Ndrangheta comes from personal interviews amplified by information from Paoli, *Mafia Brotherhoods* (2003), and information gleaned from the court proceedings involving Pasquale Condella in 1999.

The story of Carmela Iuculano was garnered from *The Times* of 20 May 2005 and the Maria Foggia story was from *La Repubblica* of 2 June 2004.

The Bernardo Provenzano letters were published in *Panorama* magazine on 17 March 2005 and the details on the way information is transferred during prison visits came from a report in *The Times* on 20 May 2005.

SELECT BIBLIOGRAPHY

Books and Articles

Alexander, S. *The Pizza Connection: Lawyers, Money, Drugs, Mafia* (Weidenfeld, New York, 1988)

Allen, O. *The Tiger: The Rise and Fall of Tammany Hall* (Wesley, Massachusetts, 1993)

Allsop, K. *The Bootleggers: The Story of Chicago's Prohibition Era* (Arrow Books, London, 1961)

Alongi, G. *La Mafia nei suoi Fattori e nelle sue Manifestatione* (Fratelli Bocca, Torino, 1887)

Anselmo, N. *La terra promessa: Vita e morte di Bernardino Verro e del movimento contadino nel feudo* (Herbita, Palermo, 1989)

Arlacchi, P. *La Mafia imprenditrice* (Mulino, Bologna, 1983)

—*Morte di un Generale* (Rizzoli, Milan, 1982)

—*Addio Cosa Nostra: La vita di Tomasso Buscetta* (Rizzoli, Milan, 1994)

Asbury, H. *Gem of the Prairie: An Informal History of the Chicago Underworld* (Doubleday, New York, 1940)

—*The Gangs of New York* (Knopf, New York, 1928)

Balsamo, W. and G. Carpozi *Crime Incorporated: The Inside Story of the Mafia's First 100 Years* (Allen & Co., London, 1988)

Barbacetto, G. and M. Tarvaglio *Mani Pulite: La vera storia da Mario Chiesa e Silvio Berlusconi* (Editori Rivniti, Rome, 2002)

Barbieri, A. et al. *L'Italia della P2* (Mondadori, Milan, 1981)

Behan, T. *See Naples and Die: The Camorra and Organised Crime* (I.B. Tauris and Co., London and New York, 2002)

Beresiner, Y. *Masonic Curiosities and More* (ANZMRC, 2000)

Berlusconi, S. *Una storia Italiana* (Mondadori, Milan, 2001)

Biagi, E. *Il boss e solo* (Mondadori, Milan, 1986)

Blinkhorn, M. *Mussolini and Fascist Italy* (Routledge, London, 1984)

Bloch, M. *Feudal Society* (University of Chicago Press, 1961)

Blok, A. *The Mafia of a Sicilian Village, 1860–1960: A Study of Violent Peasant Entrepreneurs* (Waveland, Illinois, 1974)

—'South Italian Agro-Towns' in *Comparative Studies in Society and History* (11, 1969)

—'The Peasant and the Brigand' in *Comparative Studies in Society and History* (14, 1972)

Bonanno, J. *A Man of Honour: The Autobiography of a Godfather* (Simon and Schuster, New York, 1983)

Campbell, R. *The Luciano Project: The Secret Wartime Collaboration of the Mafia and the US Navy* (McGraw Hill, New York, 1977)

Caponetto, A. *I miei giorni a Palermo* (Garzanti, Milan, 1992)

Caruso, A. *Da cosa nasce cosa* (Longanesi, Milan, 2000)

—*Arrivano I nostri* (Longanesi, Milan, 2004)

Cecchi, A. *Storia della P2* (Rome, 1985)

Clark, M. *Mussolini* (Longman, London, 2005)

Collin, R. *The de Lorenzo Gambit: The Italian Coup Manqué of 1964* (Sage, London, 1976)

Colpi, T. *The Italian Factor: The Italian Community in Great Britain* (Mainstream, Edinburgh, 1991)

Cornwell, J. *Hitler's Pope* (Viking, New York, 1999)

Cornwell, R. *God's Banker* (Unwin, London, 1983)

Dalla Chiesa, C. *Michele Navarra e la Mafia Corleonese* (Palermo, 1990)

Dalla Chiesa, N. *Delitto Imperfetto* (Mondatori, Milan, 1984)

Davigo, P. *La Giubba del Re* (Pinardi, Bari, 1998)

Davis, J. *Mafia Kingfish: Carlos Marcello and the Assassination of JFK* (McGraw Hill, New York, 1989)

De Lutis, G. *Storia dei servizi segreti in Italia* (Rome, 1984)

De Rosa, P. *Vicars of Christ: The Dark Side of the Papacy* (Crown, New York, 1988)

D'Este, C. *Lo sbarco in Sicilia* (Mondadori, Milan, 1990)

De Stefano, F. and F. Oddo *Storia della Sicilia dal 1860 al 1910* (Laterza, Bari, 1963)

Dewey, T. *Twenty Against the Underworld* (Doubleday, NewYork, 1974)

Dickie, J. *Cosa Nostra* (Hodder, London, 2004)

DiFonzon, L. *St Peter's Banker* (Franklin Watts, New York, 1983)

Downey, P. *Gangster City: The History of the New York Underworld 1900–1935* (Barricade Books, New York, 2004)

Duggan, C. *Fascism and the Mafia* (Yale University Press, New Haven and London, 1989)

Dumas, A. *The Garibaldians in Sicily* (London, 1861)

Eisenberg, D. et al. *Meyer Lansky: Mogul of the Mob* (Paddington, New York, 1979)

English, T.J. *The Westies: Inside the Hell's Kitchen Irish Mob* (Putnam, New York, 1990)

— *Paddy Whacked: Untold Story of the Irish-American Gangster* (Regan Books, New York, 2005)

— *The Havana Mob: Gangsters, Gamblers, Showgirls and Revolutionaries in 1950s Cuba* (Mainstream, Edinburgh, 2007)

Exner, J. *My Story* (Grove Press, New York, 1977)

Falcone, G. and M. Padovani *Cose di Cosa Nostra* (Milan, 1991)

Fentress, J. *Rebels and Mafiosi: Death in a Sicilian Landscape* (Cornell University Press, 2000)

Flamigni, S. *Trame atlantiche: Storia della Loggia massonica segreta P2* (Kaos, Milan, 1996)

Follain, J. *The Last Godfathers* (Hodder & Stoughton, London, 2008)

Franchetti, L. *La Sicilia nel 1876* (Vallecchi, Florence, 1925)

Franco, M. *Andreotti visto da vicino* (Milan, 1993)

Fried, A. *The Rise and Fall of the Jewish Gangster in America* (Columbia University Press, New York, 1980)

Gaja, F. *The Army of the Lupara* (Maquis, Milan, 1990)

Gambetta, D. *The Sicilian Mafia: The Business of Private Protection* (Harvard University Press, 1993)

Gambino, R. *Vendetta: The True Story of the Largest Lynching in US History* (Doubleday, New York, 1977)

Ginsborg, P. *A History of Contemporary Italy* (Penguin, London, 1990)

— *Silvio Berlusconi* (Verso, London, 2004)

— *Italy and its Discontents* (Penguin Books, London, 2001)

Giuliano, G. *My Brother Salvatore Giuliano* (Arnone, Palermo, 2000)

Gomez, P. and M. Travaglio *La Repubblica delle Banane* (Rome, 2001)

Gosch, M. and R. Hammer *The Last Testament of Lucky Luciano* (Little Brown, Boston, 1974)

Gurwin, L. *The Calvi Affair: Death of a Banker* (Macmillan, London, 1983)

Jacobs, J. et al. *Busting the Mob: The United States v. Cosa Nostra* (NYU Press, 1994)

Kefauver, E. *Crime in America* (Doubleday, New York, 1951)

Kelly, R.J., K. Chin and R. Schatzberg *Handbook of Organised Crime in the United States* (Greenwood Press, 1994)

Kennedy, R.F. *The Enemy Within: The McClellan Committee Crusade Against Jimmy Hoffa and Corrupt Labor Unions* (Harper, New York, 1960)

Kessler, R. *The Bureau: The Secret History of the FBI* (St Martin's Press, New York, 2002)

Klerks, C. *Lucky Luciano: The Father of Organised Crime* (Altitude, Alberta, 2005)

Kobler, J. *The Life and World of Al Capone* (Putnam, New York, 1971)

— *Ardent Spirits: The Rise and Fall of Prohibition* (Putnam, New York, 1973)

La Licata, F. *Storia di Giovanni Falcone* (Milan, 2002)

La Sorte, M. 'Sicily and the Mafia: Mussolini Takes on the Mafia' on American Mafia.com (2004), feature article 267

Lamothe, L. and A. Humphreys *The Sixth Family: The Collapse of the New York Mafia and the Rise of Vito Rizzuto* (Wiley, John & Sons, Incorporated, New York, 2006)

Lane, D. *Berlusconi's Shadow* (Allen Lane, London, 2004)

Lewis, N. *The Honoured Society* (Eland, London, 1964)

Lo Verso, G. 'Psichiatria e pensiero mafioso' in *Psychoanalytic Psychology* (2004)

—'Lo Psichismo mafioso nell'indagine' in *Psicologica Clinica* (2004)

Lodato, S. *Quindici anni di Mafia* (Milan, 1994)

Lucenti, U. *Paolo Borsellino: Il valore di una vita* (Mondadori, Milan, 1994)

Maas, P. *The Valachi Papers* (Putnam, New York, 1968)

Mack Smith, D. *Modern Sicily (after 1713)*, vol. 2 of *History of Sicily* (Chatto and Windus, London, 1968)

Malachi, M. *Rich Church, Poor Church* (Putnam, New York, 1984)

Mangold, T. *Cold War Warrior: James Jesus Angleton* (Simon and Schuster, New York, 1991)

Manhattan, A. *Murder in the Vatican: American, Russian and Papal Plots* (Ozark Books, New York, 1985)

Maurici, A. *La genesi storica della rivolta del 1866 in Palermo* (Palermo, 1916)

Maxwell, G. *God Protect Me From My Friends* (Longmans Green, London, 1957)

Messick, H. *Lansky* (Putnam, New York, 1971)

Moldea, D. *The Hoffa Wars: Teamsters, Rebels, Politicians and the Mob* (Paddington, New York, 1978)

Nelli, H. *Italians in Chicago: A Study of Ethnic Mobility* (OUP, New York, 1970)

O'Brien, D. and T. Shannon *Renewing the Earth: Catholic Documents of Peace, Justice and Liberation* (Image Books, New York, 1977)

O'Connor, T. *The Boston Irish* (North East Univ. Press, Boston, 1995)

Pagani, P. *Forza Italia* (Novara, Boroli, 2003)

Pantaleone, M. *Mafia e droga* (Einaudi, Torino, 1966)

Paoli, L. *Mafia Brotherhoods* (Oxford University Press, New York, 2003)

Petacco, A. *Il Prefetto di ferro* (Milan, 1975)

—*Joe Petrosino* (Milan, 2001)

Piazzesi, G. *Gelli: La carriera di un eroe di questa Italia* (Garzanti, Milan, 1983)

Pitkin, T. *The Black Hand: A Chapter in Ethnic Crime* (Totowa, New Jersey, 1977)

Poli, E. *Forza Italia* (Bologna, 2001)

Poma, R. and E. Perrone *La Mafia: Nonni e nipoti* (Vallecchi, Florence, 1971)

Puzo, M. *The Godfather* (Putnam, New York, 1969)

—*The Sicilian* (Arrow, London, 1984)

Raab, S. *Five Families* (Robson Books, London, 2005)

Ragano, F. and Raab, S. *Mob Lawyer* (Scribner, New York, 1994)

Raine, A. et al. 'Hippocampal structural symmetry in unsuccessful psychopaths' in *Biological Psychiatry*, vol. 55, pp. 185–91 (2005)

Reese, T. *Inside the Vatican* (Harvard University Press, 1996)

Reppetto, T. *American Mafia: A History of Its Rise to Power* (Owl Books, New York, 2004)

Riall, L. *Sicily and the Unification of Italy* (OUP, Oxford, 1998)

Robb, P. *Midnight in Sicily* (Duffy and Snellgrove, New South Wales, 1996)

Ruggeri, G. *Berlusconi: Gli Affari del Presidente* (Kaos, Milan, 1994)

Ruggeri, G. and M. Guarino *Berlusconi: Inchiesta sul Signor TV* (Kaos, Milan, 1994)

Sann, P. *Kill the Dutchman: The Story of Dutch Shultz* (Arlington, New York, 1971)

Schwartz, T. *Joseph P. Kennedy: The Mogul, the Mob, the Statesman and the Making of an American Myth* (Wiley, New York, 2003)

Sciascia, L. *La Sicilia come metafora* (Adelfi, Milan, 1979)

—*The Moro Affair* (Granta Books, London, 2002)

Seale, P. and M. McConville *Philby: The Long Road to Moscow* (Penguin, London, 1978)

Short, M. *Murder Inc: The Story of Organised Crime* (Blake, London, 2003)

Sonnino, S. *I contadini in Sicilia*, vol. 2 of Sonnino and L. Franchetti *Inchiesta in Sicilia* (Vallecchi, Florence, 1974)

Stajano, C. *Mafia: L'atto d'accusa dei giudici di Palermo* (Riuniti, Rome, 1986)

Sterling, C. *The Terror Network* (Weidenfeld, London, 1981)

—*The Time of the Assassins* (Holt, New York, 1984)

—*Octopus* (Norton, New York, 1990)

Stille, A. *Excellent Cadavers* (Vintage, London, 1996)

—*The Sack of Rome* (Penguin Press, New York, 2006)

Summers, A. *Official and Confidential: The Secret Life of J. Edgar Hoover* (Putnam, New York, 1993)

Thatcher, M. *The Downing Street Years* (HarperCollins, London, 1993)

Tosches, N. *Power on Earth* (Arbor House, New York, 1986)

Tranfaglia, N. *La Sentenza Andreotti* (Cernusco, Milan, 2001)

Trevelyan, G. *Garibaldi and the Thousand* (Longmans Green, London, 1920)

Tuohy, J. 'Joe Kennedy and the Pantages Affair' in *Gambling Magazine* (1960)

Turrisi Colonna, N. *Pubblica sicurezza in Sicilia nel 1864* (Palermo, 1988)

Veltri, E. and M. Travaglio *L'odore dei soldi* (Riuniti, Rome, 2001)

West, M. *The Salamander* (Morrow, New York, 1973)

Willan, P. *Puppetmasters: The Political Use of Terrorism in Italy* (Putnam, New York, 1991)

Williams, P. *The Vatican Exposed* (Prometheus, New York, 2003)

Yallop, D. *In God's Name* (Bantam, New York, 1984)

Yang, Y. et al. 'The neuroanatomical basis of psychopathy: A review of brain imaging' in *Biological Psychiatry*, vol. 57, pp. 1103–8 (2005)

DOCUMENTS

Anti-Mafia Commission Report on Mafia and Politics, 6 April 1993

Cassara report (so-called Greco+161 report), 13 July 1982, Palermo

Commissione parlamentare d'inchiesta sulla Loggia massonica P2, Tina Anselmi, 1984

Coroner's inquest, 13–27 June 1983, London

Coroner's inquest, 23 July 1982, London

Court of Cassation, 23 November 1995

Court judgment, Milan court, Office of the Judge for Preliminary Investigations, 15 November 1999

Court judgment, Milan Court of Appeal, Fifth Criminal Section, 2001

Court proceedings against Francesco Marino Mannoia, 1986, Palermo

Estimate of US Bureau of Narcotics, McClellan Committee, 4 March 1965

Interrogation of Tomasso Buscetta by Judge Falcone, 16 July – 12 September 1984, Palermo

Interrogation of Salvatore Contorno, 1983, Palermo

Interrogation of Vincento Singona, 1986, Palermo

Miraglia, F. '*Movimento contadino nella Sicilia del second dopoguerra*' ('The Peasant Movement in the Post-War Years'), thesis (1999)

Proceedings of the Reggio Calabria court, 17 January 1994

Procura della Repubblica di Milano, N. 11749/97, testimony of Enrico Manca

Procura della Repubblicadi Palermo, Direzione Distrettuale Antimafia, *L'Onore di dell'Utri: I legami del Berlusconiano Marcllo Dell'Utri con Cosa Nostra, nella Richiesta di Rinvio a giudizio per concorso in Associazione*

'*Relazione sull'Indagine Riguardante casi di singoli Mafiosi*', Italian Parliamentary Anti-Mafia Commission, 2004

Report to DEA by M. Ewell et al., 15 December 1983

Statement of J. Lawn, head of DEA, to House of Representatives Foreign Affairs Committee, 7 June 1984

FILM

The following films were useful as background during my research: *Salvatore Giuliano* (1961) Director: Francisco Rosi; *The*

Godfather (parts 1, 2 and 3) Director: Francis Ford Coppola;
Prefetto di ferro (1977) Director: Pasquale Squitieri

MAGAZINES AND JOURNALS

The following magazines and journals were useful in my
research: *Biological Psychiatry, Comparative Studies in Society and
History, Cortex, L'Espresso, Land Economics, Newsweek, Panorama,
Psychoanalytic Psychology, Revista di Politica Economica, The
Economist, The Reporter,* 'Transactions of the Quator Coronati
Lodge of Research' (London, 102)

NEWSPAPERS

The following newspapers were useful in my research:
*Evening Standard, The Guardian, La Repubblica, L'Independente,
L'Osservator Romano, La Stampa, Il Giornale, New York Times, The
Scotsman, The Times, Wall Street Journal*